Toxic Couples: The Psych[Domestic Violence

Domestic violence is a major public health concern, affecting millions worldwide. It is underreported, often devastating, and sometimes ends in murder. In *Toxic Couples: The Psychology of Domestic Violence*, Anna Motz integrates psychological and criminological data with clinical illustrations and discussion of current high-profile cases. She examines the complex manifestations and multiple causes of intimate partner violence.

Motz disentangles the roles played by those involved and examines the addictive nature of these damaging partnerships. The book describes various forms of abuse, including physical, sexual and emotional, and analyses how intimate partner violence can escalate to murder. She explores important factors, including:

- the role of addiction;
- homelessness and vulnerability;
- the intergenerational transmission of abuse;
- sadomasochistic relationships;
- honour-based violence.

The book emphasizes the significance of female- as well as male-perpetrated violence and outlines the powerful impact on the children of abusive parents, extending the clinical awareness of professionals working with those affected.

Toxic Couples: The Psychology of Domestic Violence is ideal for clinicians working with the victims and perpetrators of intimate partner violence, for students of psychology, gender studies and social care courses, and for anyone interested in the psychological forces behind violence in relationships.

Anna Motz is a consultant clinical and forensic psychologist and psychotherapist with extensive experience of the assessment and treatment of victims and perpetrators of violence. She is a former president of the International Association for Forensic Psychotherapy, editor of *Managing Self-Harm: Psychological Perspectives* (Routledge, 2009) and author of *The Psychology of Female Violence: Crimes Against the Body* (Routledge, 2000, 2008).

'This book provides a scholarly and empathic analysis of what the author terms the "addictive force" of relationships in which destructive aggression and intimacy are interwoven. With great integrity, Anna Motz explores the role each partner can play when enmeshed in destructive forms of communication – "a kiss with a fist" – and how "the unthinkable" can in turn be acted out against one or more children whose parents have entered a state of malignant fusion. Detailed case discussions include headline cases of children who have evolved from helpless victim to powerful perpetrator in their re-enactment upon vulnerable peers of what they have witnessed but cannot process. Practitioners in the fields of criminal justice, forensic mental health, child protection and victim support will find this important book both illuminating and insightful.'

– Dr Celia Taylor, President, International Association for Forensic Psychotherapy and Clinical Head of Service, Millfields Unit, UK

'*Toxic Couples* is simultaneously dark and enlightening. It is essential reading for any clinician dealing with family conflicts since it courageously challenges the traditional view that women are always the victims of male violence. The acknowledgement that women can actively participate in domestic violence is accurately described and clinically proven. Reading this book will help to illuminate complex dynamics within violent partnerships, provide uneasy insights to all those involved in the assessment of domestic violence and prevent future failures in family court proceedings.'

– Dr Estela Welldon, Founder and Honorary Life President, International Association for Forensic Psychotherapy

Toxic Couples:
The Psychology of
Domestic Violence

Anna Motz

Routledge
Taylor & Francis Group

LONDON AND NEW YORK

First published 2014
by Routledge
27 Church Road, Hove, East Sussex, BN3 2FA

and by Routledge
711 Third Avenue, New York, NY 10017

Routledge is an imprint of the Taylor & Francis Group, an informa business

British Library Cataloguing in Publication Data
A catalogue record for this book is available from the British Library

Library of Congress Cataloging in Publication Data
Motz, Anna, 1964–
Toxic couples: the psychology of domestic violence / Anna Motz. – First Edition.
pages cm
1. Family violence – Psychological aspects.   2. Spousal abuse.   3. Mental health services.   I. Title.
HV6626.M68 2014
362.82'92019 – dc23
2013039317

ISBN: 978-0-415-58888-1 (hbk)
ISBN: 978-0-415-58889-8 (pbk)
ISBN: 978-1-315-81799-6 (ebk)

Typeset in Times New Roman
by RefineCatch Limited, Bungay, Suffolk

This book is lovingly dedicated to my remarkable uncles, Herbert and Stefan Edlis.

Contents

Foreword

Pink, the American singer-songwriter, recently released a song on her album *The Truth About Love* entitled 'True Love', which describes the intense mix of love and hate that can co-exist in intimate relationships. In this sense, the album title and the lyrics both reflect much of the material covered in *Toxic Couples*. Both convey, for instance, the often confusing continuum of emotions experienced in familial and romantic relationships (that is, from love and caring on one end, to violence, abuse and control, on the other) and how those emotions can ultimately lead to abuse and violence. Although it can often be difficult for outside observers to understand why a person would remain in a relationship coloured by psychological, emotional, financial, physical and/or sexual abuse, much less profess their love and desire for their tormentor, research demonstrates that these are not simple decisions. My own work in this area suggests that even highly volatile and violent relationships can often be punctuated by periods of calm and tenderness; most victims simply want the abuse to end while retaining the relationship (Nicholls, Hilterman and Tengstrom, 2010). Motz unravels these mysteries again and again for the reader through dozens of captivating case studies. She offers us insights rarely available to non-clinicians, revealing the process of malignant attachment and childhood adversity that is so often at the foundation of domestic violence and intimate partner abuse.

A particular strength of this book is the consideration given to diverse relationships and multiple forms of abuse and trauma. Coverage extends from neonaticide and infanticide, to familicide and honour-based violence. The exploration of the clinical cases depicts male and female perpetrated violence alike, as well as giving consideration to the issues of gender symmetry and mutuality in abusive romantic relationships. Importantly, Motz has actively avoided the commonly conveyed reductionist perspective that all domestic violence and intimate partner abuse reflects male patriarchy in isolation of the many other relevant risk factors that can influence one partner to inflict abuse and violence onto the other. She conveys respect and understanding for perpetrators and victims simultaneously, without dismissing the need for anyone who perpetrates violence to be held accountable. The author also rightly reflects on the importance of self-care, consultation and insight by therapists who work with these difficult clients and the trauma that can be experienced as an observer to the client's often extremely painful life history.

Motz reminds us of the importance of looking beyond an individual's current behaviours and the need to place a client's current circumstances and behaviours within the context of their personal history. In particular, the intergenerational transmission of violence occupies a central position in the book, as it should in any discussion of domestic violence, mental health, substance abuse, crime and violence. The Adverse Childhood Experiences (ACE) research conducted in the United States (http://www.cdc.gov/ace/) is one of the largest and most well-respected studies of traumatic stressors to date; the results illustrate many of the issues covered by Motz. First, the ACE findings demonstrated that adverse events experienced in childhood (e.g. neglect; physical and sexual abuse; witnessing intimate partner violence between one's parents; and other family dysfunction) are common. Nearly two-thirds of the more than 17,000 study participants reported at least one ACE, and more than one of five reported three or more ACE. Second, the study revealed that these adverse events can lead to social, emotional, and cognitive impairments and that those deficits and challenges have long-term implications for the individual's health and well-being. For instance, ACE can lead to an individual adopting risky behaviours (e.g. illicit drug use, alcohol abuse, early initiation of sexual activity) and exhibiting health-related problems (e.g. depression, chronic obstructive pulmonary disease, early and unintended pregnancies). Third, the study also illustrated that the more stress an individual is exposed to in childhood, the greater the health and social implications. It is important to note, however, that although adversity and trauma in childhood is common in the general population (e.g. one in three people have been physically abused), subsequent research revealed that populations who come into conflict with the law and who suffer from mental health problems carry a disproportionate burden of childhood adversity. For instance, a study of female American prisoners ($N = 491$; Messina and Grella, 2006) matched their design to the ACE study and found that whereas the community sample had amassed around 0–1 exposures to ACE (55.5%), 67.6% of prisoners reported exposure to two or more ACE; with one-third of the sample reporting exposure to five or more adverse childhood experiences. The evidence from the ACE study (reported in >50 publications) taken in combination with thousands of other studies which have been available since as early as the 1980s (http://pubpages.unh.edu/~mas2/) demonstrates the ubiquity of violence in the home and the associated public health burden.

Motz offers readers a richly interwoven tapestry of theory, research findings and clinical wisdom. This book is likely to appeal to the lay public as well as seasoned practitioners and novice clinical graduate students, alike. Although this is a 'heavy topic' and the case illustrations can certainly be heart wrenching, I was left with a feeling of hopefulness. Motz tackles some of the most difficult forensic mental health cases and does an exceptional job of peeling back the layers to reveal what underlies seemingly un-interpretable dysfunction. She exposes domestic violence for what it is: an urgent public health priority that is well within our grasps to alleviate. Eradicating child abuse, intimate partner violence and diverse forms of family dysfunction is a challenge that every reader can take a part in achieving – be it through getting mental health services to address our own needs, removing spanking from our 'parenting repertoire', or obtaining continuing education to ensure our clinical tool-box is sufficiently equipped to provide the care our clients need and deserve. As Motz concluded, we all have a responsibility to move domestic violence 'Out of the shadows'.

Tonia L. Nicholls, PhD

Associate Professor, Department of Psychiatry, University of British Columbia.

Senior Research Fellow, Forensic Psychiatric Services Commission, BC Mental Health & Addiction Services.

References

Messina, N. and Grella, C. (2006) Childhood trauma and women's health outcomes in a California prison population. *American Journal of Public Health*, 96(10): 1842–1848.

Nicholls, T. L., Hilterman, E. and Tengrstrom, A. (2010) *Decision-making in Abusive Relationships Interview* (*DIARI*), Consultation Version 1.0. Port Coquitlam, BC: Forensic Psychiatric Services Commission.

Acknowledgements

In writing this, I have tried to understand and make sense of some of the most traumatic situations I have encountered, often occurring between people who love one another. I have also been witness to remarkable examples of hope, resilience and the potential for recovery. Researching and writing this book has been an emotional, often disturbing, project. There are a few exceptional people who could both empathize with this and also retain the capacity for clear thinking; especially Jane Hammett and Sean Kelly, who read the book closely at various stages and made invaluable suggestions. I am most appreciative of their level of engagement and their astute insights. I owe thanks to Mark Coulter of Strength to Change, who is an inspirational and generous colleague. I am also deeply grateful to Tonia Nicholls, Arlene Vetere and Estela Welldon for their excellent research and willingness to share ideas and work.

I am indebted to Sheila Redfern, Sarah Shanahan, Kate Thompson and Nigel Warburton for reading various chapters and making thoughtful comments. I also thank Barbara Pizl and Vania Fernandes for their help with the research.

I am grateful to my close friends and colleagues Anne Aiyegbusi, Jo Burrell, Charlotte Couldrey, Elizabeth Grocutt, Sally Jones, Jason Jones, Gillian Kelly, David McMahon, Melissa Midgen, Jessica Yakeley, Phyllis Weiner and Elyse Weiner for their clinical wisdom, help and encouragement. I also owe thanks to Gary Bloom, Natasha Caswell, Ted Colman, Christian David, Melanie Edghill, Susan Edlis, Steven and Tina Gilmore, Claire Green, Chris Mawson, Gael Neeson and Marian Wassner, for their support and interest. Finally, I especially thank Hannah, Josh and Nigel Warburton for everything, as ever.

I appreciate the help of the Routledge editorial team, especially Joanne Forshaw, Susannah Frearson, Veronica Lyons and the anonymous readers who commented on the original proposal.

Finally, and most importantly, I thank the many men and women who shared their experiences with me, and who continue to work through the impact of their violent partnerships, in the hope that their children will have a different future. This book is inspired by that hope.

Extracts from a number of articles from *The Guardian* are reproduced here by permission. Parts of the clinical illustration in Chapter 5 first appeared in

Professional and Therapeutic Boundaries in Forensic Mental Health, edited by Anne Aiyegbusi and Gillian Kelly (2012) and reproduced here with permission of Jessica Kingsley Publishers.

1   Introduction

Kiss with a fist

I hate and I love. Wherefore would I do this, perhaps you ask?
I do not know. But I feel that it happens and I am tortured.
Odi et amo

Catullus 85

In this book, I describe the addictive force and power of violent relationships: those that are fuelled by passion, destructiveness, jealousy and a wish to control the other partner. I emphasize the ways in which both partners participate in these destructive relationships, while acknowledging the power differentials between individuals and throughout society that contribute to the development and maintenance of violent and abusive relationships.

Throughout this book, I use illustrative clinical material to demonstrate the situations I describe. All of these clinical illustrations have been carefully anonymized to preserve confidentiality without sacrificing essential aspects of the relationships that reveal the nature of the underlying dynamics. Where possible, I have obtained consent from those whose stories are told here.

I have drawn on my clinical experience over 24 years in forensic and adult mental health services, including evaluation and psychotherapy with men and women and extensive involvement in care proceedings assessments, many of which were for risk of child abuse and neglect in the context of domestic violence. I describe therapeutic work with victims and perpetrators of domestic violence – some of whom were both – and the particular challenges that arise in this treatment. I also refer to high-profile illustrative cases that have featured in the news, and are familiar to the general public.

This book refers to both violence and abuse, generally using the term 'domestic violence' to refer to intimate partner violence (IPV). I describe its impact on children and discuss fatal violence within the family. Domestic violence includes physical and sexual violence in different forms, but also psychological and verbal abuse, and financial and economic control. I prefer to use the term 'domestic violence' rather than 'intimate partner violence' to indicate the sense in which this violence has a systemic impact, and can reverberate throughout the family. However, I refer to 'intimate partner violence' where specific research has adopted this term. The title of this book refers to 'toxic couples' and I want to emphasize that it is not the individual partners who are 'toxic' but the relationship itself, with its entrenched destructive dynamics. The 'toxic couple' reflects the interaction of two disturbed individual attachment systems.

The particularly compelling nature of these relationships, and their development, with their roots in childhood, is the central problem I explore here, in order to identify the roles that both partners play in these toxic couplings. I describe the powerful forces that keep these relationships going, with reference to intrapsychic as well as social factors. In this introductory chapter, I outline the scale of the problem.

In this book, I discuss the specific mechanisms for the intergenerational transmission of violent relationships, as well as protective factors; the development of violent relationships; the issues faced by homeless women and men; forced marriages and systemic violence; domestic homicides and violence within high-risk groups, including those with a learning or physical disability. I discuss intimate partner violence within sadomasochistic relationships, and the role of addictions in toxic partnerships. Finally, I briefly describe treatment interventions, programmes and public policy developments that address this major public health problem.

This book is not a comprehensive overview of the field, but offers a psychological perspective on the development of domestic violence, and has a largely psychoanalytic orientation, informed by attachment theory, as well as offering other psychological models of understanding.

The field of domestic violence research is vast, and the variety of perspectives is diverse. There are culturally specific practices and difficulties, and I do not claim to have been able to address these in depth or to offer a comprehensive overview of the international perspective, although I draw on data from the United States, Canada, Australia and several European countries, as well as the United Kingdom. I describe underlying psychodynamics within violent partnerships that occur cross-culturally, but focus primarily on the United Kingdom and United States in relation to social norms, legislation and treatment perspectives within this text.

Kiss with a fist

Although we often think of violence as perpetrated by an individual, I suggest that within a toxic relationship it is the interaction of the two individuals that creates this destructive force, notwithstanding that one partner may be the principal enactor of the violence. Aggression and intimacy can be inextricably interwoven in these relationships, to the extent that the currency of communication is itself violent: a kiss with a fist. In this book, I explore this dangerous dance, revealing the conscious and unconscious dynamics of violence between partners, and its alarming complexity.

All kinds of couples can become enmeshed in destructive dynamics, with the potential for serious harm against one another and/or any children within the family. I argue that the role of both partners in the dangerous and compelling patterns of interacting that underpin violent relationships should be analysed, and their respective contributions disentangled. As with female violence generally, because females are not supposed to be violent, there is a danger that some aspects of toxic partnerships are literally unthinkable.

This book explores various manifestations of toxic relationships, and the symbiotic characteristics that define them. I explore why some couples are malignantly fused and turn as a force against one or more children and how, within such partnerships, each individual is destructively dependent on the other, unconsciously allied in a perverse bond. I discuss the complex and tragic cases of women who kill their violent partners and men who kill their abused partners.

In this book, I not only deal with sexual couples, but also address dangerous interactions between parents and children in the context of domestic and honour-based violence, exploring the dynamics of abuse and aggression within these relationships. The main focus of the book, however, is on violence between sexual partners.

In Chapter 2, I describe the destructive dynamics of violent relationships, and the difficulties for both partners of breaking away from them. Chapter 3 explores the impact of domestic violence on children and its intergenerational transmission, focusing on attachment theory and psychoanalytic approaches. In Chapter 4, I explore the roots of sadomasochism and their manifestation in violent relationships, looking at the spread of perversion through the whole family system. I then discuss couples who kill and domestic homicide in Chapter 5. I describe the particular vulnerability of homeless men and women in Chapter 6, focusing particularly on women, as they are most at risk of violence repetition. Chapter 7 deals with the sexual, emotional and physical violence often involved in forced marriages, citing these as paradigms of violent couplings. The subjugation of women in these situations is evident, but I also explore how such marriages can affect the males who are coerced into undertaking them. In Chapter 8, I explore the role of addictions and substances in violent partnerships, and their impact on the wider family system. Finally, in Chapter 9, I outline treatment approaches to working with domestic violence, and also discuss current policy and legislative measures in the United Kingdom, intended to address this central difficulty. Throughout, I present illustrative clinical material to bring to life the central concerns of this book.

The strength of violent relationships is often unintelligible to those who encounter them. Both psychoanalytic theory and attachment theory can illuminate how and why such toxic couplings continue to thrive, despite their destructive impact. In England and Wales, almost half of all women killed each year die at the hands of an intimate male partner or ex-partner (Women's Aid, 2001); the emotional and psychological consequences for partners and the children in their care may be severe and long term. Violence in intimate relationships is a central social concern, yet it is still poorly understood, and often ignored as a contributory factor in violence towards children. While it is undeniable that male-to-female violence is the most common form of severe intimate partner violence, the issues of same-sex violence and female-to-male abuse also require exploration and attention.

The cycle-of-violence model highlights the ways in which behaviour can be modelled and taught, passed down the generations. The assaults on the minds and the bodies of those who witness and experience parental violence leave deep scars that time alone cannot heal. For some children, one way of managing the pain of these experiences is to take on the characteristics of the aggressive parent, and to disown vulnerability, helplessness and humiliation. Within the violent partnership itself, though, there are more complex dynamics at play than simply the polarization of aggressor and victim; there are interdependent and sophisticated psychic arrangements.

Toxic partnerships can be understood in the context of Welldon's (2012) work on 'malignant bonding'; that is, the perverse, enmeshed relationships in which abuse and cruelty become the norm, and damage future generations. She describes how neither one nor the other can be considered solely perpetrator or victim: 'this (perverse bonding) can be initiated and even stimulated not only by the man but also by the woman in the couple. We are no longer talking of who is the victim or perpetrator within the couple.' She conceives of violent relationships as ways that partners attempt to overcome earlier trauma, through re-enacting experiences in which they were once helpless. As adults, they seem to be able to recreate these scenarios, but this time as the powerful ones, who can shape their own destinies, sometimes by inflicting pain on others, and sometimes by engineering situations in which they themselves are punished.

Freud's (1914) notion of the repetition compulsion and Melanie Klein's (1946) concept of projective identification are powerful psychic phenomena, repeatedly manifested by violent couples. The repetition compulsion refers to the repeated attempt to master a situation in early life, being drawn to repeat familiar patterns and relationships, despite their unsatisfactory or damaging consequences.

Through projective identification, unacceptable and unwanted aspects of one person are projected into the other, who is then treated badly by them, in an apparent attempt to annihilate these disavowed aspects of the self. Projection and projective identification are defences that keep these relationships alive, and serve important functions, which, while ultimately destructive, are temporarily enlivening and addictive. They are not necessarily available to the conscious mind.

Defining domestic violence

In this section, I outline the context of domestic or interpersonal violence, including the problems of reporting and detecting violence within intimate relationships. I offer the definition of domestic (interpersonal) violence adopted by London's Haringey Council, closely linked to the core definition provided by the UK government:

> Any incident of threatening behaviour, violence or abuse (psychological, physical, sexual, financial or emotional) between adults who are or have been intimate partners or family members, regardless of gender or sexuality.

This definition is also closely related to the United Nations (UN) Declaration on the Elimination of Violence against women, defining 'gender-based violence' in the following terms:

Any act of gender-based violence that results in, or is likely to result in, physical, sexual or psychological harm or suffering to women, including threats of such acts, coercion or arbitrary deprivation of liberty, whether occurring in public or in private life.

Physical violence in intimate relationships is a public health problem affecting hundreds of thousands of individuals and families worldwide (Black *et al.*, 2011). The prevalence and impact of physical intimate partner violence on female victims is well established. Data from the (2000) National Violence Against Women Survey (Tjaden and Thoennes, 2000) indicated that women sustained physical injuries in 42 per cent of IPV cases, received medical attention in 11 per cent of cases, and were hospitalized in 9 per cent of cases. In addition, 18 per cent of women surveyed, reported that they had lost time from work or suffered other economic hardship associated with victimization. Repeated physical assaults can also increase the risk of chronic diseases (e.g. chronic pain), neurological (e.g. fainting), cardiopulmonary (e.g. hypertension) and gastrointestinal symptoms (e.g. loss of appetite) (Coker *et al.*, 2002). Associations with adverse reproductive health outcomes, such as spontaneous abortion, haemorrhage, poor foetal growth and preterm labour and delivery, have also been identified (Janssen *et al.*, 2003). Importantly, these physical consequences can continue long after the abuse has ceased (Campbell, 2002). At its most severe, physical IPV can result in death (Campbell *et al.*, 2007).

The emotional impact of physical IPV on female victims has also been well documented. For example, a meta-analysis of 56 studies (Golding, 1999) found that the weighted mean prevalence of mental health problems among female victims of IPV was 48 per cent in studies of depression, 18 per cent in studies of suicidality, 64 per cent in 11 studies of post-traumatic stress disorder (PTSD), 19 per cent in ten studies of alcohol abuse, and 9 per cent in four studies of drug abuse. Below, I describe the context of domestic violence, including the problems of reporting and detecting violence within intimate relationships.

Domestic violence is known to be under-reported, but research carried out in the United Kingdom shows that:

- Domestic violence accounts for 14 per cent of all violent incidents.
- One in four women and one in six men will be a victim of domestic violence in their lifetime, with women at greater risk of repeat victimization and serious injury.
- In 2008/09, women were the victims in nearly eight out of ten incidents of domestic violence.
- One incident of domestic violence is reported to the police every minute.

Domestic violence currently claims the lives of around two women a week, and affects millions more people. This includes issues of concern to black and minority ethnic (BME) communities, such as so-called 'honour-based violence', female genital mutilation (FGM) and forced marriage.

Whatever form it takes, domestic violence is rarely a one-off incident, and should instead be seen as a pattern of abusive and controlling behaviour through which the abuser seeks power over his/her victim. Domestic violence occurs across society, regardless of age, gender, race, sexuality, wealth or geography. The figures indicate, however, that it consists mainly of violence by men against women. Children are also affected. Not only are many traumatized by what they witness, but there is also a strong connection between domestic violence, sexual violence and child abuse.

Interpersonal violence between intimate partners is a complex, primitive communication, whose meaning must be deciphered carefully for each individual case. With this in mind, it is still possible to identify certain characteristic patterns of interpersonal violence and factors that exacerbate the risk of serious harm or even death. It is also essential to highlight the communicative function of violence, which can be overlooked in the attempt to prevent or stop it (Mills, 2008).

The language used to describe violent partnerships has a brutality all of its own. People 'break away' from a violent relationship, or 'get caught in the trap'; abused women are typically described as 'broken' or 'battered', who have 'learned helplessness' and who are somehow without any agency or subjectivity. The metaphors resonate with battle imagery and connote breakage, explosion and fatal damage ('walking on eggshells') and weapons ('a hair-trigger response', 'explosive outbursts', 'revenge attacks') that further perpetuate a sense of warfare and action, rather than behaviour to be understood and managed. In some ways, this dramatic language simply mirrors the behaviour and feelings of violence and, in a sense, induces terror and prevents further thought. There is a destructive excitement in using this language, which careful, measured and dispassionate discussion can reduce; something I see as essential if effective work is to be done with victims and perpetrators.

Do victims of violence have any choices?

The degree of agency of victims of violence is seen as wholly constricted, as if they have no choice whatsoever – and, of course, it is true that their freedom is heavily curtailed. While it is undeniable that a situation of intimate terrorism is one in which fear is dominant and movement risky, to create this totally polarized view of those who are involved in violent relationships may, in fact, do more injury to them and to conceptualize them in ways that further restrict their choice and prevent the development of a sense of agency. It is essential to be as truthful as possible, without judgement, in making evaluations of each partner's role and their needs, both conscious and unconscious, within any relationship. Throughout this book, I will attempt to do this.

Gender asymmetry?

While some research proposes equivalent prevalence rates of male- and female-perpetrated violence (Mirrlees-Black, 1999; Morse, 1995), other research rejects the symmetry of men and women's experience of intimate partner violence, for the following reasons. First, the numeric extent of violence against women exceeds that of violence against men (Tjaden and Thoennes, 2000; Walby and Allen, 2004; Watson and Parsons, 2005). Second, the impact of the abuse is likely to be greater for women than men, both emotionally and injuriously (Walby and Allen, 2004; Watson and Parsons, 2005; Women's Aid and the Child and Women Abuse Studies Unit, London, 2001). Third, women are at far greater risk of serious and lethal abuse at the hands of their male partner than men are at risk from their female partner (Campbell, Sharps and Glass, 2001; Jaffe, Lemon and Poisson, 2003; Walby and Myhill, 2001; Krug *et al.*, 2002).

To some extent, violence follows patterns along lines of gender, in that women are far more likely to be hurt by male violence than men are by their female partners; but domestic violence doesn't only affect women who are hurt by men, but also men who are hurt by women, and same-sex partners who hurt one another. I will explore intimate same-sex violence alongside 'heterosexual violence' and look critically at some of the assumptions and myths that prevail here. I will discuss the debate in the field about the extent to which domestic violence is a function of male entitlement and societal patriarchal forces (Johnson, 1995) and the sense in which it can be considered a shared problem of injustice, inequity and poor communication across society, expressed within relationships where early relationships with significant others are reawakened and primitive anxieties evoked (Dutton and Nicholls, 2005; Bartholomew, Henderson and Dutton, 2001).

There is a fierce debate in the literature about whether greater gender symmetry exists than has previously been recognized. Some studies conclude that the rates of male and female aggression are much more equal than was previously suggested: 'It is important to recognise that intimate partner violence is no longer considered just as a situation involving a male perpetrator and a female victim, although women remain more likely to be injured by partner violence than men' (Whitaker *et al.*, 2007).

This finding has been disputed on the basis that it refers to the far less serious form of aggression of mutual couple violence, rather than intimate terrorism (Radford, 2008) and, by reference to the fact of the severity of injuries, in that the harm caused by injury is likely to be far less in female-to-male violence than vice versa. It is also suggested that these apparently equal distributions of violence across the genders do not take account of the impact of the respective acts of aggression on the health of victims.

There is some danger in seeing domestic violence as simply an expression of the male wish for power and control; this is both reductive and inaccurate. Some feminist analysis risks this when it is accepted unquestioningly, as Dutton and Nicholls (2005: 680) argue in their review of the literature: 'A case is made for a paradigm having developed among family violence activists and researchers that precludes the notion of female violence, trivializes injuries to males and maintains a monolithic view of a complex social problem.'

Johnson (2008), in contrast, states that the most severe forms of violence, those of intimate terrorism (or coercive violence), are committed by men against women and that rates of gender symmetry in violence perpetrators are found only in those cases of situational couple violence, where both men and women are violent, although to a lesser extent than in cases of intimate terrorism. He argues that wide variations in prevalence rates are an artefact of sampling methods such that women surveyed in shelters are likely to be victims of intimate terrorism, including psychological as well as physical abuse, whereas general samples reveal mutual violence occurring in couples. Desmarais *et al.* (2012a) demonstrate that the rates of physical intimate partner violence are equally distributed, based on studies that she and colleagues have surveyed, although she acknowledges that sampling bias may affect the reported rates. Johnson (2008) argues strongly for the need to classify perpetrators according to typology, and to deconstruct the unitary notion of violence perpetration.

It is evident that women are more likely to be victims of male violence than men are at risk of equivalent violence by women: men are generally physically stronger than women and capable of inflicting serious injury without weapons. In cases of 'intimate terrorism', men are more likely to be perpetrators than women. Likewise, most homicide/suicides are committed by men: 'Current rates of intimate partner homicide of females are approximately 4 to 5 times the rate for male victims. . . . The major risk factor for intimate partner homicide, no matter if a female or male partner is killed, is prior domestic violence' (Campbell *et al.*, 2007: 246). Nonetheless, in other forms of domestic violence, where both partners engage in conflict, the psychological consequences for both and for any children exposed to domestic abuse are significant. 'Bidirectional violence' refers to situations where couples routinely engage in mutual aggression, which tends to be less severe in terms of injury than in intimate terrorism. The aim of this violence is also different, in that total control over various domains is not the objective of either party, but conflict arises in relation to areas of stress including financial, social and emotional issues. Mental health issues and substance abuse may also be contributory factors.

In terms of the argument for gender symmetry, it has been suggested that in cases involving mutual violence (or, as Johnson (2008) calls it, 'situational couple violence'), as opposed to 'violent resistance' or 'intimate terrorism', the rates of female-to-male and male-to-female violence are far more equal, but these forms of aggression are far less severe, and less likely to result in serious physical harm.

The feminist argument that domestic violence is a problem of power relations, and that men need to be held responsible for their abuse of women and children, is an important one, and has been influential in shaping policies related to the criminalization of male perpetration of such violence. Women's Aid, in particular, has successfully campaigned for the public awareness of domestic violence, the establishment of women's refuges and changes in the law related to the criminal status of domestic violence. I would suggest, however, that all perpetrators of violence, both male and female, must take full responsibility for their actions, and that support should be available to all who have been harmed by this violence.

Clearly, female aggression does exist, and denying it is both unhelpful and dangerous. Women are capable of severe psychological, emotional and physical violence, the consequences of which can be profound. The taboo of female violence remains powerful and can blinker the public from seeing what is before their eyes, and prevent individuals from reporting their experience of abuse by women, especially women who are mothers. The impact of exposure to female intimate partner violence on children remains an under-researched area.

Furthermore, in cases where mothers are violent to their children, the harm that is caused to them psychologically and physically can be profound. The distinctions made by Johnson tend to obscure this significant problem, which has manifestations in the way that their children develop, including male children, who may grow up feeling that all women are fundamentally abusive and untrustworthy: 'Apart from IPV directed to a partner, feminist theory also ignores violence by women directed at children, probably because such violence falls outside the political view of being a response to an oppressor male' (Dutton, 2006).

Women are capable of extreme violence, in some cases even more so than men, and their primary targets are often their own bodies and those of their children, treated as narcissistic extensions of themselves (Welldon, 1988; Motz, 2001, 2008). Maternal violence, as well as neglect and abandonment, plays a significant role in the development of childhood disturbance and insecure attachments, alongside exposure to domestic violence and other forms of adversity.

Impact on the family

Domestic violence is a public health problem that affects all members of a family, not simply the adult participants. There is an urgent need to understand and prevent domestic violence, with its traumatic developmental effects and its power to damage current and future relationships for children. Violence often goes unseen by wider society, taking place in the private realm of the home or family, leaving only the most vulnerable as witnesses to horror. These witnesses are the children, without the language or authority to stop it or the psychic apparatus to process it.

My experience of working with violent men, women and families where violence is so common and severe that the children have been removed for their own safety, has been deeply disturbing. It has fundamentally changed my understanding of the family, and of the depths of suffering that human beings are capable of inflicting on one another, even where love and need are most intensely felt.

The uncertainty of these children's fates, away from the homes they know, no matter how abusive or neglectful, is a heavy weight on the minds of those who work with them, and the genuine feelings of bereavement, seen in both parents and their children, are evident, and deeply painful to behold. The notion of the strong traumatic bond that ties children to even the cruellest of parents is highly relevant to this work, and will be explored in terms of insecure attachments and the terror of abandonment that so many violent partners display.

The vulnerability of children, and their capacity to imitate, to protect and to take on the burden of suffering for their parents, alongside their helplessness at their parents' mercy, can be almost unbearable to witness. It is only the attempt to understand how their own early experiences have shaped these men and women, who have been perpetrators of extreme violence and neglect, that makes it possible to work hopefully alongside them. Just as ways of relating can be toxic, so too can they become healthy; the harmful effects of childhood experiences can be understood and mitigated. When violent men and women can make this link and think about, understand and connect with the damage they have both suffered and are capable of inflicting on others, real change becomes possible.

Marking and ownership: links with slavery

Violence may serve as a replacement for thinking: traumatic experiences and unbearable feelings are enacted rather than reflected upon, discussed and worked through. The dreaded experiences of humiliation, fear, shame and powerlessness are evacuated into others rather than being addressed and digested. Likewise, the feelings that are evoked in all professionals who encounter this distressing, shocking – yet ordinary and everyday – violence, can be seen not as obstructions to professionalism or irrelevant emotional responses, but rich information about what is going on in the couple, or in the family. These responses must be addressed, despite the temptation to ignore or get rid of them. When subjected to scrutiny, they can play an important role in deciphering what is going on in a violent relationship. The feelings projected into us are those that are felt to be unbearable by those we work with, and so our helpless, hopeless or terrified states of mind often reveal the underlying traumas that must be understood, and eventually made intelligible, to violent perpetrators and their partners. Only when this can be put into words and thought about can the emotional processing, which is a requisite for recovery, begin.

The impact of domestic violence on children: 'toxic families' hit the headlines

In 2009, two brothers (aged 10 and 11) subjected two other brothers, of the same ages as themselves, to serious brutality, including physical battery and sexual humiliation, for a 90-minute period. They received five-year sentences in April 2010. Although not all children exposed to domestic violence go on to re-enact the scenes with others, it is clear that one way of managing unbearable emotional and physical experiences is to try to get rid of them by subjecting another to the same or similar torture. These boys clearly identified with their own victims and took on the role of the aggressor in their violence (Freud, 1936).

The following newspaper report describes how the scenario of severe domestic violence forms the backdrop to serious offending by the children who witnessed the violence:

> Caught between a depressive, drug-dependent mother and a violent, obsessively jealous father, the boys grew up, in the words of a defence barrister, amid 'routine aggression, violence and chaos'. It was, he said, a 'toxic family life'.
>
> The court heard how the brothers regularly watched their father punch and kick their mother, sometimes while drunk but often when sober, driven by an incurable envy which saw him forbid her from even talking to other men. The brothers learned not to intervene, the court was told; doing so meant either the mother was hit harder, they were struck, or both.
>
> The mother, meanwhile, treated the boys as adult confidants, pouring out her 'intimate' secrets to them, the court heard.
>
> Once she threatened to leave home, prompting the father to promise he would track her down and slice her face 'to bits' with a knife.
>
> It was shortly after the court heard this evidence that the younger brother, who had remained impassive when his own cruelty was explained in detail, started to sob silently into his cupped hands.
>
> (Walker, 2010)

The question of blame was clearly answered by Simon Heffer (2010) in his article for *The Telegraph* entitled 'Edlington attack: We don't have to breed such savages: Parents such as those who bred the Edlington savages should be in prison, not the likes of Munir Hussain'.[1] Heffer clearly blamed the parents of these children for the development of their violence, but described this in harsh and unsympathetic terms.

In Chapter 3, I will outline in greater detail the mechanisms through which these young boys, and others like them, would have been harmed by their exposure to domestic violence. The tragedy of this case, and so many others like it, is that these boys appear to have had few legitimate ways of expressing their sense of pain, confusion and rage, other than to re-enact the violence to which they had been exposed. The moving description of the younger child bursting into tears upon hearing in plain language the level of sadistic abuse and threats to which his mother had been subjected, indicates that he has repressed his sense of horror and despair. It is as though he had no words to describe it, and simply, rather desperately, expressed it through violent action himself. The sadness he carries seems to burst forth when he hears this dispassionate recounting of cruelty towards his mother, the woman to whom children look for protection. Not only can his mother not protect him from maltreatment, when she is herself so abused, but he is called upon to protect her, leaving him, no doubt, with a terrible sense of powerlessness and fear. If the brothers intervened they were beaten, or worse, their mother was hit harder. The person who is powerful is the violent and savage father, who is then seen by his sons as the one to emulate. In some cases, children are called upon to participate in violence upon their mothers or other siblings.

It is apparent that such violent scenes leave a terrible imprint on young minds, and call their bodies into action, attempting to expel scenes of torture through recreating them. This may afford a sense of control and escape in what is otherwise an intolerable situation. How can children be called upon to act as either witness or confidant in such desperate situations without finding some outlet for containment and release? In a society where these families are supported, and the children either taken to a place of safety or enabled to voice their distress, one would expect that they would be able to break out of a repetitive cycle of violent re-enactment and find a way to process their experiences. When this is not provided, and children are left to their own devices, they may indeed find a savage solution; but this does not make them savages. These boys were reported to have been reared on a diet of pornography, violence and illicit substances, which clearly left them with a distorted view of the world and only their own, desperate, attempts at mastery and escape, to fall back on. It is striking how little compassion and understanding is shown to children who are caught up in adult horror stories when they react to these scenes with aggression and criminality by creating their own horror stories and re-enactments, where they play the role of the violent perpetrator. It is essential to understand how violence develops, without condoning or excusing it.

Mythology of domestic violence

In this final section of this chapter, I offer a critique of the accepted mythologies of domestic violence, and provide an illustration of a 'typical' violent relationship – with its characteristic cycle of abuse, forgiveness, reconciliation and re-abuse – and provide a psychodynamic explanation for the compulsive force of this pattern of relating.

Clinical illustration: Shane and Lucy: the repetition compulsion

This young couple, in their late twenties, came to my attention for assessment of their capacity to parent their four children, who ranged in ages from two to ten. They had a long history of domestic violence in their 11-year relationship, which began during Lucy's first pregnancy when she was 18. The children had been witness to this violence as well as subject to frequent and unpredictable moves of home, school and town. Two of the older children had been caught in the 'crossfire' of the violence and injured.

Both Lucy and Shane were healthy looking, well dressed and attractive, with no obvious signs of self-neglect or ill health. On the contrary, they were striking in their appearance, and Lucy, in particular, looked youthful and fresh faced, to the point where she was often mistaken for being her elder daughter's sister.

They had met in their late teens, when both were working in a local pub. They had been attracted to one another 'instantly' and moved in together shortly after meeting. Lucy had an older child, a daughter, with another man, who had left her during the pregnancy. Shane was two years older than her, and had paid her attention. He was also able to help her care for her daughter, then aged 14 months. Lucy felt that she had never got male attention from her stepfather, and had no contact with her natural father after a traumatic and sudden separation from him, so she had craved this male attention. She wanted her daughter to grow up with a father figure and found it hard, at times, to be on her own with a baby, when still so young herself.

Shane's mother had emotionally and physically abused him, greatly affecting his development and his capacity to trust women in general. In describing his early life and relationships to me, he clearly identified men as safe, secure and loving figures, in contrast to his mother, whom he regarded with hostility, and by whom he had been cruelly treated. His descriptions of his painful treatment at her hands were poignant.

Although social services had never been involved with him, he did recall that there was an outsider who wanted to intervene. She was a female teacher who had realized that something bad was going on at home and in whom he could confide. When recollecting this, he became very tearful and distressed, and it seemed that remembering someone understanding and being kind to him triggered a sense of vulnerability and longing for the care and concern of which he had been deprived by his own mother.

At times when he perceived Lucy as critical of him or making threats to leave him, his early experiences of feeling hated and rejected would resurface, which in the context of alcohol abuse would have destructive effects. Shane was desperate to find affirmation of self-worth through Lucy's love and could find evidence of being worthless in the slightest change in her behaviour, or in his perception that she loved someone else more than him. He would unleash his frustration and rage onto the target of his fury, the woman who could make him feel hurt, humiliated, 'small' and rejected, despite desperate attempts to secure her love and commitment. The more he perceived her to be threatening him with abandonment, the more enraged he would become, and the more destructively he would behave, using any means to secure a sense of his power and control and alleviate his terror of being left. He went into a mindless state of panic and rage. He believed himself capable of murder when in that state.

He described his mother as being 'a slag' and knew that she had been unfaithful to his biological father, describing her as repeatedly enjoying 'a Friday-night thing'. He saw women as being deceptive creatures, capable of seducing and abandoning the men who depended on them. He acknowledged his own risk of violence, and saw it as borne of feelings of vulnerability in relation to Lucy, and his own mother.

I put to him that at times he also felt like a worthless object in her eyes, as though he too were just 'a Friday-night thing'. The insecure, disorganized attachment he developed in relation to his mother was transferred onto all other women, from whom he desperately sought affirmation and love. Any hint of potential abandonment felt completely unbearable to him.

He described the role that alcohol consumption had played in allowing his anger to be unleashed. His reliance on alcohol was highly significant in his violent and self-destructive behaviour, and escalated the violence to an extreme level. He described how he would turn to the bottle to 'drown his demons', and saw the pub as a place where he could escape from the terrors of home. Here he would often find his father, and drink with him, sharing a pint and seeking solace in the temporary respite from conflict with Lucy. He would return home in a disinhibited and indifferent state, emboldened by his drinking, and this was when he was most likely to enact violence. Drink was his first port of call when distressed, and he had learned to associate it with a temporary escape; it became his 'safe base', a place where he could return to find comfort. He felt it inside him like a potent presence, almost caressing him from within, and filling him up with something other than the poisonous feelings he had towards Lucy. It was very hard for him to link this comforting, healing presence with the wildness it led to, though he understood it intellectually.

Shane was someone who clearly had impulsive traits and an antisocial personality, posing a serious risk to those with whom he was intimately involved. He persistently committed drink-driving offences, with open disregard for the danger this posed to others and to himself. At one level, he did not appear to have learned from his mistakes, and continued to place himself and others at risk. This did not make sense at first sight but could be understood as an unconscious request to be stopped by a strong paternal authority, symbolized by the law, and protected from the force of his destructiveness. He expressed relief when he was convicted for drink-driving, and even for his assaults, feeling that he needed to be protected from hurting others and himself.

Shane displayed emotional fragility in the interview, where he said he felt devastated by the loss of his children. It was evident that his violence increased at times of loss and at points where he feared abandonment. During assessment, he was tearful and poignantly conveyed his concern about all of his children, and hope that he could somehow demonstrate that he could offer them the degree of security and stability that they deserved. He seemed to relate to me in a guarded but respectful way, indicating something of his apprehension about women, and a desire to please.

Lucy often became his mother in his mind, as she threatened repeatedly to leave him. His sensitivity to potential abandonment and deep fears of being unworthy and undeserving of love were repeatedly activated by these threats, with disastrous consequences. His view of Lucy can be considered a symbolic equation (Segal, 1957)[2] in that she was not just like his mother, reminding him of her in a way that allowed him to see that she was not his mother, but, in his mind, Lucy literally **became** his mother.

Lucy was aware of Shane's hatred of his mother and saw that their relationship had been characterized by violence and domination from the beginning. She first decided not to prosecute him due to the guilt she felt in relation to him, saying she felt she owed him her loyalty. She regretted going back to him and taking him back after he had been violent towards her but said 'sometimes it is what you know'. After the local authority became involved, she decided to press charges against him and he was convicted for Aggravated Bodily Harm.

Although she talked about all her children with affection and concern, it was striking that Shane was the main person on her mind, and she seemed preoccupied with him. Clearly she still felt deeply affected by his treatment of her, and the way that she had returned to the relationship repeatedly. She expressed her sense of his absolute control over her, saying 'I'm under his control so fast, I fall into his arms . . . once I'm there I'm too scared to get away.' She described herself as being wholly without self-confidence while in the relationship with him, and said 'before he went to prison [for assaults on her] I was a dead person, in a four-bedroom house with four screaming children'.

Lucy was tearful as she described the nature of the violence and intimidation to which Shane subjected her: he would come home from work in the pub having had a problem there and would start an argument with her. It would be worst when he was 'half cut', as then he would be argumentative and violent, whereas if he were more drunk he might fall asleep, which is what she would long for. He would be really jealous of her and she could not enjoy going out with him because if she spoke to other men he would become very angry.

She described how he had thrown a bar stool at her on one occasion when she had been cleaning the pub and he was angry that she hadn't finished yet. He would typically follow her and she would try to remain calm. On one occasion, he had strangled her until she passed out. The children had been aware of how badly she had been hurt. He would take her phone away from her and so, on this occasion, she had run out of the pub, leaving the children asleep and gone to the police to press charges. She was tearful as she told me about this frightening ordeal, and described feeling overwhelmed with guilt about having promised the children she would not get back with their father, but always breaking this promise. She said now she 'never will get back with him' and felt she had built up a lot of confidence since he had been in prison. She had also been heavily influenced by the Freedom Programme, a programme developed by Pat Craven for women who have been subjected to male violence, which she said 'changed everything'. This programme is available locally to help women and children subjected to domestic violence, and she had attended six sessions of the course. Lucy saw that Shane had subjected her to total control and intimidation. He had cut all her avenues of social and family support, and she was moved to isolated areas, while he kept charge of all the family finances.

An entrenched pattern of violence and reconciliation was repeated throughout their relationship despite the involvement of social services, which issued care proceedings in relation to their four young children. Lucy would frequently initiate the reconciliation, even while her bruises were still fresh, feeling that she couldn't live without Shane, and despite her conscious awareness that his level of control and brutality was unacceptable. These reconciliations were against written agreements with the local authority and involved repeated deceptions and cover-ups – now the couple were united against a common enemy. The children were told to keep the relationship secret, and involved in these lies. The social workers involved repeatedly attempted to house Lucy in a refuge, to no avail, as she would contact Shane from these safe places and return to him, or ask him to come back 'home'. The family frequently moved home, repeating the pattern of Lucy's childhood, and also evaded social services, as they were sometimes hard to trace. They sometimes provided false or misleading information to social workers, throwing them 'off the scent'.

The children witnessed these displays of violence, reconciliation and active deception of social services. Furthermore, they were invited, implicitly, to participate in it, taking turns to protect either father and mother, at times identifying with the apparently helpless, abused mother, and then with the terrifying violent father, who would then become helpless, sobbing and desperate as he begged Lucy to forgive him. The drama and intensity of the parental violence would overwhelm any other consideration in the household, and the needs of the children were almost wholly ignored. The frequent changes of address were echoes of the nomadic existence of her own mother's father. She belonged to a community where homes were not considered permanent, or even essential. In one way, she related to Shane as though *he* were her home, and also treated him as one of her own children. The boundaries between the roles of mother, wife, daughter and lover were totally fluid, and she existed in a volatile and exciting maelstrom.

This dynamic reached dangerous levels for Lucy and Shane in that he operated like an 'intimate terrorist', to use the term coined by Johnson (1995). Intimate terrorism can be seen in extreme forms in cases of abduction, rape and imprisonment, like the case of Josef Fritzl, who kept his daughter and the children he fathered with her in a cellar in his house, an elaborate underground prison, for his gratification and sadistic use.

Shane repeatedly experienced the trauma of maternal abandonment, a sense of shame and being unloved. Ironically, he unconsciously recreated this scenario repeatedly in his attempt to undo it. He became increasingly desperate to control his partner, the unavailable object, to keep her with him, but his violence eventually led to her leaving him. For a while in his relationship with Lucy he had, in a sense, mastered this trauma, and reversed the situation that had tormented him in early life. If he succeeded, albeit temporarily, in keeping his partner under his control and prohibiting her movements, he could feel secure that she would not abandon him.

In this sense, he is like Josef Fritzl, whose unavailable object, his daughter, had no chance of leaving him, as his own mother had repeatedly left him, shut up in the basement of the house they lived in. Fritzl became the master of his trauma through this perverse solution and saw the children he reared in this basement as his mirror images, only this time locked in with a mother who could not leave, who stayed with them at all times. He could be in total control of the children and his daughter, the embodiment of his own mother in his distorted mind, and he could enact revenge on her through his sadistic abuse of her and the children. Additionally, sexual gratification was reported to have become one of the main outlets for him of the anxiety and disturbance he had experienced from early life onwards.

For Lucy, the sense of being loved as an object, albeit by an unpredictable, violent and also frightening partner, treating her with the same inconsistency and intensity as her own mother had, was vital. She had not developed a sense of herself, had no capacity to be alone, to draw her own boundaries of personal identity. She existed only insofar as she could see herself reflected in the need of another. Without that, she had no sense of self, or worth. She felt empty inside.

The impact on children of domestic violence

As described above, in the case of the Edlington children and in the case of Lucy and Shane, the needs of the children are sacrificed because of the entrenched dynamics of the violent relationship, with its destructive excitement. Lucy repeatedly invited Shane back home and contacted him even when she knew that the children would be removed from her care if this relationship resumed. While clearly not responsible for the violence to which she was subjected, she nonetheless re-established the relationship at points when she was safely away from Shane, and would have been able to offer the children the protection and care they required.

There is a powerful sense of a 'folie à deux', in that both partners are active in keeping the violent partnership alive. The children are forced to witness and become involved in the violence, and some will replay these scenes with one another and with other children. The risk of sexual violence increases for children who have been exposed to this form of conflict between their parents. Sexualized behaviour may serve as a form of psychic refuge, a comforting activity, and also another forum within which issues of power and control can be resolved for these frightened and emotionally overloaded children. Some may also have been exposed to sexual violence between their parents, and their behaviour may mirror this, as they attempt to make sense of the disturbing scenes they have witnessed. In Chapter 3, I explore the impact of domestic violence on children in greater detail, and outline factors that can ameliorate the adverse consequences.

The force of projective identification

One of the myths of domestic violence is that the power resides only with the overtly aggressive partner. This is a simplistic argument, although it appeals at a certain level, and helps those hurt in these relationships to escape the sense of being blamed for their involvement. The sense of shame they feel about the relationship is often overwhelming and so, if they worry that they will be judged or blamed for remaining in them, they may find it very difficult to acknowledge what is going on.

However, at a deeper level, when disentangling the unconscious as well as conscious motivations and fantasies that characterize a violent relationship, the notion of power is far more complex, and not simply a question of physical force and intimidation. This is reductive, and while physical intimidation is a frightening reality, it is not the case that all power resides in this; an unconscious agreement exists within the violent couple that unacceptable parts of oneself will be projected into the other person, and then seen to exist in them alone.

This unconscious contract allows a temporary respite for each person from the uncomfortable state of knowing about impulses and feelings that are not easily tolerated, or that are not permissible. So, for the violent man, the memory of being a humiliated, needy and vulnerable child is wholly unbearable. He treats the woman he is with as this part of himself and takes some pleasure in this. Perhaps this is why we find candid accounts of the satisfaction that intimate partner violence offers so shocking. It is hard to hear that violence can be pleasurable and gratifying, offering a psychic as well as physical triumph. He is clearly disavowing his own vulnerability in this way. One of the fantasies that operates, and motivates his destructive behaviour, is that through exerting his power, he will keep his object, his partner, close to him, scared of him, and most importantly, unable to leave him. He identifies his own helplessness and fear in his partner, and this, temporarily at least, offers him a sense of mastery and control. He is no longer the frightened child, who feels despised by Mother, abandoned by Father, and helpless in his own skin.

For the woman to feel so harshly, brutally and wholly dominated by her partner is at once horrific, yet, in another sense, offers a certain relief – any aggression or violence is not within her but is borne by this frightening man. He is the perpetrator of terror, and she is the good, innocent and helpless one. In fact, again, her own unacceptable feelings have gone underground, been disavowed and located in her partner, who can carry and express them. This is not to say that the woman who is brutalized has invited, caused or enjoyed this assault, and certainly, this is wholly absent at any kind of conscious level; but she has located (projected) her own violence in her partner, disavowed it in herself and then inhabits a role in which she is purely victimized. She can hate the violence, fear the pain, and wish for an escape, but at least she does not have to hold herself culpable for cruelty, rage and sadism.

At another level, she may gain assurance that she is needed, longed for and powerful. She sees that her partner turns to cruelty to try to control her, and just as this terrorizes her, it also affirms her central role in his life – he is desperate to keep her there, and enacts this terror through physical means and also through trying to infiltrate every part of her life. But, any sentient being knows that thoughts are one's own, that in the act of hating, the brutality and wishing to leave, the betrayal has already been committed, and indeed the very fact of separateness is one that the perpetrator cannot bear. This is an existential crisis: the perpetrator wants the victim to be his soul mate, his other half, and to remain in a kind of fusion with him, and any sign of independent thought or life has to be obliterated. The victim of aggression, although tyrannized, knows even in the moment of her pain that she is separate, is not fused with him, and can hate him for his cruelty. His repeated assaults can be understood as a frantic, manic attempt to destroy the fact of her separate, independent existence, and his psychic cruelty becomes a wish to form her into his image of her.

The projection of dependence by the violent partner into the apparently helpless victim, and of hatred, aggression and sadism into the partner by the brutalized woman is the dynamic that operates in these violent relationships. These apparent roles are in fact far more complex and, when explored, the respective areas of power and control can be delineated. This conceptualization does not make the violence any more acceptable, nor any less harmful, but it situates the relationship within the dynamic interaction of two people, both consciously and unconsciously contracted to perform certain roles for one another, to maintain a psychic equilibrium.

A central dynamic between violent men and their partners is often sexual jealousy; women may appear passive and helpless, but underneath may have more subtle forms of power and control. One of the ways that women can express their individuality, independence and autonomy is to have relationships, even if only in their fantasies, with other men. This is an intolerable situation for the violent, jealous partner, and he will torment himself with obsessive fears of sexual betrayal, again sometimes projecting his own infidelity onto his partner. The violence that morbid jealousy produces can be fatal.

When battered women kill their violent partners, the dynamics of projective identification are clear, and dramatically reveal how the projected aspects of the self can be suddenly – and violently – taken back, and how the roles of perpetrator and victim change, with fatal consequences. I described this in my work on female violence:

This dynamic is clearly evident in the battered woman, who becomes the sponge for her partner's feelings of inadequacy and self-contempt. She absorbs these feelings, becoming increasingly depressed and he, in turn, loses touch with his own feelings of vulnerability, finding his aggressive and sadistic feelings more acceptable, less frightening to acknowledge.

The moment where the victim becomes aggressor, where the battered wife becomes the killer, can be seen as the moment of rebellion, of challenging the polarized and distorted roles that have been created. Just as the aggressive partner has denied his feelings of vulnerability through the battering, cruelty and intimidation, the abused partner has been allowed to deny her own feelings of murderous rage: this rage has been suppressed and her partner has enacted the feelings for her, until this explosive moment. The fear of these intense emotional states, either of murderous rage or complete vulnerability and abandonment, are actually shared by both. The polarization within the relationship has enabled each partner to deny an important and feared aspect of the self.

> The relationship between abuser and victim is one in which both play an active part. The relationship is not the creation of one person alone, and it is the complex interaction between the two parties, and the participation of the victim in the relationship, which is the most complex and sensitive issue for theorists to address. There is a fear that to explore the role of the victim or her participation in an abusive relationship is to blame her for the abuse that she has suffered. To ignore her role in the relationship is to denigrate her and to assign her to a kind of incidental role in which she is wholly passive. The abuser perceives himself to be, and is actually, dependent on his victim. He needs to see himself through her eyes because his sense of potency and worth is derived from her devotion to and fear of him.
>
> (Motz, 2008)

The Hegelian notion of the master–slave relationship is resonant here, in that the obvious victim, the one who is most severely beaten and intimidated, is, in some ways, also the one who can have a greater degree of control and power in the relationship. The violent partner's perception is often that he is powerless, humiliated and out of control, and his violence, as well as intimidating others, is a kind of proof to him that he has lost all control, over his own impulses and his 'better self', his ego and superego capacities. The terrifying explosions of violence and abuse are shocking to those around him, his victims, but also to him. It is frightening to lose control of one's impulses to the point where murder becomes possible. Many perpetrators are also terrified by their own destructiveness, and traumatized by memories of their own violence, as well as violent scenes they have witnessed in early life. The victim, or 'slave', may be the one who feels less out of control, and in less psychic danger. She may have disavowed her violence into this savage and dangerous partner.

Finding hope

Working with people who have suffered terrible abuse and neglect in early life teaches practitioners never to prejudge individuals; their resilience can be surprising. Having read their files, absorbed histories of their traumatic childhoods, and prepared oneself to meet a clearly distraught and 'damaged' individual, it can be a shock when a composed person walks into the consulting room. It is so hard to reconcile the story, the history, with the current presentation of someone who appears lively and engaged. Their presentation is so discordant with the recorded history that, suddenly, all the apparent facts in the case seem under suspicion. We explore this further in the following section.

Clinical illustration: Redemptive couples

This incongruity between what I knew, and expected, and my experience of meeting someone who surprised me, was striking when I assessed a young woman, Chloe, for childcare proceedings in a small English Midlands town. She was sweet-faced, with a ponytail, and came from a family where abuse crossed the generations and the genders. Her mother and grandmother, aunts and uncles, sisters and brothers, all took part in sexually abusing children, and enticing others into their perverse and sadistic world. In this family, children were made to have sex with each other and with animals. In fact, Chloe's childhood was disrupted by breakdowns in care as she repeatedly sought sexual attention from adults and inserted objects into the orifices of animals she had contact with. She seemed to be enacting with these innocent creatures the violations and insertions that she had borne, with the dispassionate but compulsive quality that she had herself experienced. Her foster-carer, a woman of considerable patience and resources, had finally been unable to stand the abuse of her own animals, the pets she loved, and had requested respite care.

The level of depravity was hard to bear, both as an assessor and as a witness. The childhood history was a chronicle of abuse, neglect, disruption and trauma. Chloe's behaviour, including stealing from foster-carers and aggression towards their children and animals, could be seen as a series of protests against the multiple changes in her care, as well as an expression of her unspoken rage and disturbance.

In interview, Chloe begged me not to let her baby have the same life she had experienced – 'get settled, go into another placement, get settled, go into another placement' – and told me the story of her own disruptions and disturbances. She appeared childlike and innocent, and it was difficult to recall the fact of her serious sexual abuse, as she seemed to be so devoid of adult sexuality – a kind of overgrown toddler, longing to be loved.

I read the perverse and panicky decisions that had shaped her childhood with horror and disbelief. I noted in particular the desperate wish of her foster-carers to adopt her alone; but that this did not occur, as the local authority had not supported this adoption, stating that she needed to stay with her brother, who had sexually and physically abused her. The adopters, therefore, chose another child and she remained in care, where she was subsequently raped by her biological siblings, who had also been abused.

Her development had clearly been affected to an extreme degree, and she had suffered emotionally, physically and psychologically, making serious self-harm attempts throughout her childhood, and abusing others in her foster placement in a sexual way. She had said this was what had been done to her, and that she thought it was 'affection'; with little awareness of how it had affected the children she had touched. At times she hid under beds, and inside cupboards, and frequently wet the bed. In time, she had begun to engage in therapy in a secure children's home, where she had been placed because she had run away from her previous foster placements. At 13, she was placed with a long-term foster-carer with whom she developed a strong attachment. She showed great empathy for her distress and disturbed behaviour, and stuck with her, despite her aggressive and volatile moods and difficulty in managing feelings of jealousy about the foster-carer's other children.

At 18, she moved away from her foster-carer, who had continued to remain her main support and confidante, even after leaving care at 16. She was seen as a 'daughter' to this woman and also cared for by her husband. The local authority had provided respite care as, at times, Chloe had become challenging and difficult for the foster-carers to manage full time.

Despite this, she had clearly developed within a safe and caring environment and had been able to recover some sense of well-being and some awareness of the difference between affection and sexual attention.

I considered these foster-parents to have served as a 'redemptive couple' for her, and to have allowed her to achieve developmental milestones she had not been able to meet in earlier life because of the severity of her abuse. This allowed her to recover from her early traumatic experiences to the extent that she too was able to form a 'redemptive couple' of her own, with a partner who was able to offer her care, protection and respect. The package of support this young couple received from social services and child and family mental health services was intensive, and included supervision, support and regular family meetings to ensure that the couple were managing the needs of their baby and dealing with any difficulties of their own. This was a thoughtful and comprehensive response to the needs of this family, and enabled the child to stay with her parents.

As well as having had this life-saving experience of good substitute parental care in early adolescence, Chloe was fortunate enough to have met her current partner, with whom she had become pregnant. The two had never engaged in violence and their relationship was non-abusive, in stark contrast to Chloe's earlier partnerships, which had been exploitative and sometimes violent. In adolescence, predatory older men had targeted and exploited her.

Despite serious concerns about Chloe's history, the local authority was persuaded of the value of a comprehensive assessment in a therapeutic residential centre, where their parenting together could be evaluated. The conclusion of this parenting assessment was that they had sufficient strengths and awareness of potential difficulties to have their baby rehabilitated to their care, and were also encouraged to join an extended therapeutic programme in the community, offered by the residential centre. This allowed them to continue to address underlying difficulties while still caring for their infant. In this way, their needs were met and the welfare of their baby was also protected, as the parents' functioning directly impacted on her care.

Rather than simply being seen as disturbed individuals who had little hope of change or recovery, they were treated as parents in crisis, doing the best they could in difficult circumstances, who were able to make use of the resources on offer. Chloe's own background was not simply seen as evidence of her unsuitability to be a parent, with the inevitable repetition of a pattern of abuse and neglect, but as a difficulty to be borne in mind, and not prohibitive of her capacity to change and develop.

At times, this hopefulness can seem naive or misplaced and, indeed, there is some danger that a new baby becomes the vestige of hope, and identified as the potential saviour of the parents, the force for change in their lives in an unrealistic way. While sentimental notions of 'rescue' and wishful thinking alone should be guarded against, at the same time, it is also essential to retain some hope in the possibility of change. The intense love for a child and desire to break free of an abusive cycle can be a powerful incentive for change, and can be tested out through careful and methodical assessments of the parent's capacity to put this desire into operation. This desire can be a powerful incentive to engage in psychological and educational work to improve parenting.

Chloe and her partner were clear examples of the possibility of change in a couple who were initially assessed as high risk, and whose baby was taken into care at birth. I have called them a 'redemptive couple' because it seemed that the factors that allowed Chloe to care for an infant, despite her own extreme difficulties and disturbance in early life, had developed within her relationship, where she felt safe, secure and contained, allowing her to relate to her infant in a way that her own parents had not been able to relate to her. The presence of her non-abusive partner was invaluable.

In this introductory chapter, I have described the public health issue of interpersonal violence, outlined its prevalence and severity, and explored how destructive relationships develop and are maintained. Finally, I have suggested that, in some cases, healthy forces within a couple (and an internal model of a good parental couple) can enable partners to break a cycle of destruction and abuse.

2 Russian roulette

The dynamics of violent relationships

Set me as a seal upon thine heart, as a seal upon thine arm: for love is strong as death; jealousy is cruel as the grave: the coals thereof are coals of fire, which hath a most vehement flame.

Song of Songs

In this chapter, I describe the characteristics of violent relationships and the destructive power of morbid jealousy. I explain how emotional abuse, physical abuse and the desperate wish for protection combine to keep people trapped in highly destructive relationships. The roles of jealousy and possessiveness are often central in violent partnerships and reveal the way in which the controlled partner is viewed as an object – rather than a subject – in the relationship. The notion of a high risk-taking pattern, in which violence escalates and there is a danger of severe injury or even death – the Russian roulette element of these relationships – is one of the defining characteristics of such partnerships. The element of risk can, for some, even be part of the attraction. I outline the particular characteristics of violent relationships, and provide the context for their development.

While the criminal statistics point overwhelmingly to the fact that men are far more likely to perpetrate serious violence against women than women are to perpetrate such violence against men (Wykes, 2009), recent literature has indicated that the problem of female-perpetrated violence is under-documented and that cross-culturally it is also a significant concern, with one in five men reporting having experienced interpersonal violence (Desmarais *et al.*, 2012a). This was discussed in Chapter 1.

Here, I will discuss the dynamics of extreme coercion, control and abuse, and their manifestations in sexual and physical violence. The impact of physical force and abuse is deeply significant, and meaningful beyond the actual pain it inflicts, as it creates a relationship between the perpetrator and the victim where a sense of brutality and dehumanization develops as the aggressor repeatedly attacks the body boundary of the other person, intruding into their body – and also their mind.

Sexual violence is defilement of the most intimate and humiliating kind and is also designed to rob victims of their subjectivity and self-respect, asserting that they are quite literally the total property of another, to be used for their own gratification. In her study of battered women who eventually killed their violent partners, Angela Browne (2000) reported that, of all the forms of violence and force reported by these women, the one they were most reluctant to disclose was sexual violence.

In this section, I will describe and illustrate typical patterns of intimate partner violence (IPV) that fall predominantly into the category of 'intimate terrorism' as defined by Michael Johnson (1995) and that involve humiliation, physical and psychological abuse, sexual tyranny and the subjugation of one partner to the needs of the other. Johnson argues that there are distinct typologies of violence and differentiates between two different forms of intimate partner violence: one motivated by one partner wishing to control the other (intimate terrorism); and the other involving situational violence, which is lower-level and involves mutual violence, where women as well as men are often perpetrators.

I describe how interpersonal violence within a couple can become the norm. In a minority of cases, women are also aggressors, perpetrating violence against their partners and, sometimes, their children. That women can be violent, even sadistically so, to others in their household, including partners, remains socially unacceptable, but is a painful reality (Mills, 2008; Dutton, Nicholls and Spidel, 2005; Dutton and Nicholls, 2005; Dutton, 2007). While women are violent to a lesser extent than are men, when they are, their victims are more likely to be their children or intimate partners, rather than strangers. Their violence is also often directed against themselves in self-harm (Motz, 2008, 2009).

I explore the complex and painful area of unconscious choices and the 'repetition compulsion', describing how these destructive relationships have an addictive and compulsive quality which makes them powerful and, at times, impossible to leave. I outline the practical and psychological difficulties that women in these circumstances face when leaving their partners, and discuss how violence is associated with early experiences and current difficulties, with particular reference to an underlying sense of shame in men.

I discuss the symbolic significance of physical force as well as its actual power, drawing attention in particular to the sense in which marking victims is a way of signifying ownership. Through these marks, the violent partner expresses his wish to use and abuse his partner's body and the skin that encases it as he wants. It is as if he has the power to deface or deform his partner and attack her beauty. Unconsciously, and sometimes consciously, he brands his partner's body as his property. In this sense, the scar or bruise is akin to acid being thrown in someone's face; it serves to disfigure it permanently and mark it out as damaged.

Disturbing as this is to confront, it is clear that some people take pleasure in seeing the evidence of pain, power and will imprinted on the face or body of another. This temporarily alleviates their sense of invisibility and impotence. Their wish for revenge is fulfilled and they can feel triumphant at their defacement and mutilation of the victim. The violence of intimate partner terrorism may serve to restore honour, and a sense of power in the perpetrator, who is defending himself from underlying feelings of shame and dependence (Gilligan, 1997; Websdale, 2010).

When the perpetrator is persecuted by an inner sense of an 'alien self' (Bateman and Fonagy, 2012; Bateman *et al.*, 2013), or a feeling of being helpless and incapable of leaving a mark on the world, he or she requires evidence of potency. This sense of power can be found in violence, particularly through marking or disfiguring another person, even if only temporarily, serving as a kind of branding. The sense of triumph and excitement that leaving marks creates is not often talked about, but some perpetrators will admit to it, as well as to the feelings of shame, guilt and distress that can also accompany the evidence of what they have done. The soft, vulnerable skin of children, like that of women, is particularly easy to bruise and may appear provocative to violent adults, who seek to deface something that looks so fragile, pure and innocent.

This chapter includes a clinical illustration of the complex dynamics of a violent relationship. I then go on to discuss countertransference feelings in the therapist when working with someone who has left a violent relationship, but soon forms another one.

Scar tissue: marking the body

In this section, I discuss the symbolic and actual significance of the marks left by physical violence within toxic couples, and how the despair of being subjected to violence can actually lead to self-harm. Although this may appear paradoxical, self-harm may be a potent means of self-assertion, communication and the release of tension for someone who is the victim of abuse (Motz, 2009). I describe the role that these physical marks play within the violent relationship and also how they can serve as evidence of harm, making public the private violence that occurs between people, and the ways in which the flesh can become the signifier of complex states of mind. I make the distinction here between the fact of physical violence and its immediate impact, and the aftermath, in the form of bruising, scarring and branding. I will also consider the role that tattoos, and other deliberately chosen markers, play in writing on the body; literally and symbolically.

Bruising and its meanings

The typical image of domestic violence is of a man raising his fist to a woman, whose face is bruised. Her black eye serves as both the physical and symbolic evidence of his ownership of her body, and his power to mark it as his. The power of the emblem, the fact of the bruise, is significant. It speaks silently of the abuse that has been done to the person and may invite a concerned response by others or, as is so often the case, may be politely ignored, despite the obvious injury it denotes.

The beauty of the woman's face, or the child's, has been altered, and the marks may endure for some time. Some will choose not to go out in public; others will try to hide it under make-up or dark glasses. The bruised woman is now ashamed and fears the judgement of others, the questions that may be asked, and can be left with a sense of disfigurement. One of the practical consequences for the violent partner may be that he has now controlled and restricted the movements of his woman, and she will now be less attractive to others. He has achieved his longer-term aims through this act of defacement, as well as the temporary release of his rage, and can feel triumphant that he has inflicted injury. He has felt the physical release of aggression and seen the evidence of his power.

It is also possible for women to bruise their male partners, for homosexual men and women to injure their partners, and for parents and siblings to hurt younger children. Like other forms of violence, the injuries reveal psychic wounding that needs to be understood and responded to. It is akin to self-harm, in that it makes public that which has been private, and brings into the public realm the abuse and hatred (including self-loathing) that has been hidden in the private sphere of the home.

Non-accidental injuries, scars and evidence

The forensic use of bruising, scarring and other signs of violence is important, as it forms concrete evidence that can be used to convict perpetrators. For some, marks of abuse need to be hidden or disguised. In the highly publicized case of Baby Peter in the United Kingdom in 2009 (the toddler killed in his mother's care following prolonged brutality and apparent sadism by her boyfriend), prior to a visit by social services, his mother was reported to have smeared chocolate over his face to cover up the bruises. The image of the toddler with a chocolate-smeared face was frequently reproduced in the press, in a chilling reminder of the ease with which evidence of serious harm can be hidden.

A fading black eye is a dramatic and often shocking public sign of private violence. It is possible to decipher the marks and bruises, the residues of rage or sadistic assault, and use these signs to create a clear picture of how one human being can be subjected to the tyranny and cruelty of another. This work can be distressing for both therapist and client alike, and requires courage.

For some survivors of childhood violence, the marks that were made by others are remembered, and replaced by their own self-harm scars, in an apparent attempt at mastery of trauma. These marks may also serve as visual reminders of earlier violations and attempts by the individual to assert their ownership over their own flesh.

A person who has been treated violently by others will sometimes choose to mark their own body through self-harm, both to release tension and anger, and also to assert their ownership and control of their flesh. This can be viewed as unconsciously reflecting the psychic defence of identification with the aggressor (Freud, 1936), so that a part of them turns on another part of themself and treats it with rage, as an object to be defiled or written upon. They treat their own body with cruelty and violence, just as their abuser treated them. The former victim now occupies the mind of the perpetrator, though it is still her own body that is hurt.

Branding the body

The objectification of another's body can be a means to assert one's own status and subjectivity; that is, the perpetrator is the 'mind', and the victim is the powerless 'body' whose injuries are secondary to the gratification of the aggressor and his need to vent his rage and inflict pain. The marks and bruises he leaves on his wife, partner or child are tributes to this capacity to use their flesh as he sees fit, and to distance himself from their pain (or, worse, to enjoy it, as it can give him a sense of power, control or even sexual pleasure).

The parts of the body that are hurt are significant. Some batterers avoid hurting the face, as this can lead to questioning by external agencies, and result in detection, or even arrest. Thus, they take care to mark only those parts of the body that are not seen by the public; under clothes, in intimate areas. Websdale (2012) describes how men who go on to kill their partners often use strangulation, without leaving marks; this is often accompanied by sexual assault. Others will use rolled-up towels to hit their partners with, or use other weapons that are unlikely to leave marks. The nature of bruising is a clue as to how injuries are sustained, and carpet burns, cigarette burns and finger-bruising marks or imprints in sensitive areas of delicate skin (such as the inner thigh or upper arm), are telltale signs of physical violence. These traces show that force was used in holding or grabbing, and that this was of sufficient strength to damage the skin.

Such marks can be left in the context of an assault in which all empathy for the victim was lost, but in which the main aim is not to leave visible evidence of injury. This is quite distinct from those assaults that are designed to disfigure the victims so that no one else will find them attractive, or perhaps to leave them unable to see or desire anyone else. Some violent men acknowledge the thrill they get when they feel the soft flesh under their fist as they punch their partners in vulnerable areas, like the stomach, and it is clear that the sense of their powerful, destructive impact on this area excites them, and motivates them to hit again. These feelings of excitement signify disavowal of the pain and distress that they were causing, as the person they were hurting became, in their minds, only an object, or even just parts of an object, to be tormented and abused. For these men, the marks they leave may be incidental, and their main aim is to inflict pain and take control of their partner's bodies with no real thought of the bruising and other evidence of the assault: this is not the aim of their violence. For some, their awareness of inflicting pain on another person adds to the excitement, in a sadistic sense. There are other cases of calculated violence where marking and defacing parts of the bodies of their victims is the intended goal.

In a highly publicized and disturbing case that came to trial in the United Kingdom in 2012, a violent man, Shane Jenkins, gouged out the eyes of his partner, Tina Nash, in his final assault on her, that she believed was an attempt to kill her. According to her (2012) autobiography *Out of the Darkness*, he taunted her during this 12-hour-long assault that she would be blind and never see her children again. One of her worst thoughts was that his was the last face she saw. The 32-year-old victim of his vicious and sustained assault had been beaten until unconscious and was asleep when he gouged her eyes out. She woke up and felt she was being buried alive, 'suffocating under darkness'. After the assault she said that all she looked forward to was being asleep, because only then could she see her children's faces again, in her dreams.

After his horrific assault on her, she described how, initially, she longed for Shane to contact her and apologize for his brutal assault, still missing him, despite this escalating, and near fatal violence. She sensitively describes the dynamics of their relationship, and how she alternated between pity and hatred for him. In her autobiography, she outlines the impact of sustained verbal, physical and emotional abuse on her self-esteem and her other relationships with close family and friends, and how her fear of him, and shame about continuing to love him despite his violence, conspired to isolate her from sources of help. Her recovery from this relationship, and fight to retain care of her two young sons, is detailed in her courageous book.

Sadly, some two years after this assault, Ms Nash was again assaulted, by her new partner, who was subsequently charged and imprisoned. She is reported to have expressed the wish to have therapy and indeed, the tragic irony of her involvement in another dangerous relationship indicates the high risk of repeating patterns of violent partnerships and the increased likelihood of being re-victimized after a traumatic incident. The unconscious forces that lead people to form destructive relationships often require the intensive scrutiny and care offered by psychotherapy. Like Tina Nash, many other women find themselves repeating patterns of destructive relationships, despite their conscious wishes not to, revealing that the problem is more complex than simply the aggressive behaviour of one violent man and that they remain at risk of future violence.

The crime of gouging out the eyes of oneself or another, enucleation can sometimes be found in crimes of sexual assault. In this case, it seems that the kind of murderousness that this man, Shane Jenkins, felt, was akin to psychotic rage, although Ms Nash made it clear in her statement following his guilty plea, that she firmly believed he had not been mentally ill at the time of the assault. In her account, by the time of the assault, he had sensed her growing distance from him as the long-term impact of his abusiveness made her feel increasingly alienated from him, but with no way to escape from his domination of her.

While not formally classified as psychosis, the types of delusional convictions that morbidly jealous men can form about their partners, and the violence that can result, have a psychotic flavour and can be difficult to distinguish from the typical delusions, distortions of reality and nonsensical logic that characterizes psychotic episodes. This has been identified as a key factor in intimate partner homicides (Harris-Hendriks, 2000). Jenkins' act of gross assault appears highly sadistic and possibly fuelled by what Nash describes as his obsessive interest in zombie films and depictions of violent assaults, including acts of enucleation. It also illustrates the sense of rage, domination and ownership this man, and others like him, feel when they mangle, torture, suffocate and defile the body, and the mind, of their partner – the woman they supposedly love. The symbolism of taking away the sight of another is chilling, and serves as a metaphor for the ways that severe violence can effectively silence and blind those they target, preventing them from contact with the outside world, and imprisoning them in a hell from which there can be no apparent escape.

There are many ways in which violent partners isolate their victims, including: making them move home, away from close family; constant complaints about their friends and families; and, in this rare case, the removal of the sense organs through which other loved ones can be seen. They force their partners to choose between them and anyone else they love or care for.

That the assault left Tina Nash deprived of ever seeing her children again is significant. For some violent men, even the love that women have for their children is a source of rage and jealousy: they believe that the look of love should only be shown to them.

The association between intimate partner terrorism and a high degree of possessiveness and jealousy is well-documented. When the abused partner attempts to leave the relationship, they may be stalked, terrorized, intimidated or threatened until they are too frightened to carry out their plan. If they have left, their abuser may track them down and threaten them to the point where they feel they have to return. For some, staying may paradoxically be safer than leaving their violent partner; Websdale (2012) notes that a significant proportion of domestic homicides take place when the perpetrator is actually living in a separate location from his former partner. Those who remain in violent households out of fear of leaving often feel that they are essentially hostages to their partners.

Branding can be a dramatic and extreme manifestation of this attempt at total control and expression of complete objectification of the other. In a case illustrating the sexual violation and physical brutalizing of young girls, sexually trafficked and abused by men, one of the girls was branded by her abuser, whom she considered her partner, as part of her abuser's repertoire of intimidation, control and ownership:

> She told a court yesterday about being mutilated by a hairpin, saying: 'After heating it up for a little while, he stuck it on my bum. It was M for Mo and he said I belonged to him. He was branding me so people knew I was his.'
>
> *Daily Mail*, 23 February 2013

Violence during pregnancy

In pregnancy, a woman's body serves a vital function for another human being, shattering a man's fantasy that he is the sole occupier of this body. Violence in pregnancy is an indicator of serious risk in the future and has been associated with homicide (Shadigan and Bower, 2005; Campbell *et al.*, 2003).[1] Homicide is a leading cause of death in pregnancy (Chang *et al.*, 2005).

Intimate partner violence sometimes begins when a woman becomes pregnant, revealing envious and vicious attacks on the unborn child and the fecund body of the female. For some children and infants, the impact of intimate partner violence can already be felt inside the womb.

There are indications that pregnancy is a time of increased risk of domestic violence for women, and begins in pregnancy, but there is some debate in the literature about these findings.[2] While some empirical data assert that violence from men to their female partners often only begins in pregnancy, and that this is a high-risk time for these women, others dispute these findings. It is possible that injuries or abuse only come to the attention of medical services during pregnancy, as women have to attend for regular check-ups, and it is suggested that prior to the physical violence there are usually controlling behaviours present that have not yet become physical. There are indications that those women who have already been beaten will continue to be subjected to violence when they are pregnant, particularly if the pregnancy is unwanted or unintended:

> Pregnancy IPV is a significant problem worldwide, with rates varying significantly by country and maternal risk factors. Pregnancy IPV is associated with adverse newborn outcomes, including low birth weight and preterm birth. Many mechanisms for how IPV may impact birth outcomes have been proposed and include direct health, mental health, and behavioural effects, which all may interact.
>
> (Bailey, 2010)

The physical and mental health consequences of partner violence in pregnancy are well-documented:

> Increased health problems such as injury, chronic pain, gastrointestinal, and gynecological signs including sexually transmitted diseases, depression, and post-traumatic stress disorder are well documented by controlled research in abused women in various settings. Intimate partner violence has been noted in 3–13 per cent of pregnancies in many studies from around the world, and is associated with detrimental outcomes to mothers and infants.
>
> (Campbell, 2002: 1331)

Victims of violence in pregnancy are more likely to report having experienced all forms of violence previously, particularly severe forms, and have higher odds of experiencing serious adverse health consequences. It is suggested that victims who experience violence during pregnancy may be more likely to be in a current intimate relationship with an abuser who inflicts repeated and severe intimate partner violence (Brownbridge *et al.*, 2011). It must be borne in mind that the shame and fear of reporting and detection of such violence makes it difficult to determine precisely its prevalence or when it began. Methodological differences in research designs and population samples contribute to the ambiguity in this area. The problem of under-reporting violence in general population studies is likely to be a contributory factor too. As Jasinski (2004) notes in her literature review of the association between intimate partner violence and pregnancy:

> Estimates of the prevalence of pregnancy-related violence vary due to differences in research designs, measures used, and populations sampled. The debate about whether pregnant women are at increased risk for violence continues as hospital- and clinic-based studies find pregnancy a time of

increased risk for violence, whereas national studies do not find an association between pregnancy and intimate partner violence.

While studies that use hospital-based samples find a significant prevalence of first-time violence in pregnant women – for example, the results of 13 studies found that the prevalence of violence during pregnancy ranged from 0.9–20.1 per cent (Gazmararian *et al.*, 1996), other studies that look at national samples suggest lower prevalence rates. Notably, analysis of population-based data from the Centers for Disease Control and Prevention's (CDC) (1999) Pregnancy Risk Assessment Monitoring System (PRAMS) 1996 Surveillance Report (Beck *et al.*, 2003), found reported rates of pregnancy-linked abuse to be much lower than studies using hospital-based samples, ranging from 2.9–5.7 per cent among several thousand women across 11 states (Gazmararian *et al.*, 1995). The estimated 1998 PRAMS prevalence rates of physical abuse by husband or partner during pregnancy, which CDC reported for 15 states, ranged from 2.4 percent to 6.6 percent (General Accounting Office, 2002).

In 2005, a study published in the *American Journal for Public Health* (Chang *et al.*, 2005) conducted by the US Centers for Disease Control and Prevention, reported that homicide was a leading cause of traumatic death among new and expectant mothers, with higher risks for women who are younger than 20, or black. It was the CDC's first national look at pregnancy and homicide, and documented 617 slayings from 1991 to 1999. However, that number significantly understates the actual toll, because many states do not have reliable methods for tracking such deaths, researchers said. The CDC study was welcomed for recognizing an overlooked phenomenon. Using data from more than 30 states, the CDC found that homicide ranked second, after car accidents, in the trauma deaths of pregnant women and new mothers. The study looked only at 'injury deaths' and drew no comparison with deaths from medical causes.

There are clear methodological difficulties in obtaining data that address the question of whether a woman's risk of assault by her intimate partner will increase during pregnancy, and it is evident that pregnancy must be viewed alongside other risk factors for IPV. These other risk factors include socioeconomic deprivation in the couple, low social support for the abused woman, and substance and alcohol misuse in the abuser: 'One factor that has emerged as a consistent risk factor for violence is low socioeconomic status (measured with educational levels, income, and/or employment' (Jasinski, 2004).

The increased risk of women with low socioeconomic status being treated violently in pregnancy may be created by the combination of raised stress levels and restricted avenues for leaving the abusive situation; these women find themselves financially, socially and emotionally dependent on their partners. When tensions in the relationship escalate, they are not in a position to leave, even in the face of violence.

Consequences of pregnancy-related violence include later entry into prenatal care, low birthweight babies, premature labour, foetal trauma, unhealthy maternal behaviours, and health issues for the mother. Clearly the impact of this abuse on the mother's state of mind and on her body may also interfere with the development of her foetus.

No consistent research findings indicate that foetal health is necessarily affected by violence, although there are obvious ways in which it can be. Severe cases of physical abuse are known to have direct effects on the foetus; for example, foetal injury or death associated with trauma to the mother.

In addition, foetal health may be affected indirectly by maternal stress, smoking, or alcohol or drug use – all of which might be responses to the violence itself. These conditions and behaviours are known to be associated with poor outcomes such as low birthweight, intrauterine growth restriction, and foetal alcohol syndrome (FAS).

Women in abusive relationships can find it difficult or even impossible to fulfil prenatal care recommendations such as frequency of visits, prescribed supplements, nutrition, the prevention of sexually transmitted diseases, or attending substance-abuse recovery programmes. Given the real risks outlined above of intimate partner violence during pregnancy, it is essential to understand how and why such violence develops when it does. The meaning of pregnancy for partners is important to outline; this is the aim of the following section.

Pregnancy as perceived provocation

There is clinical evidence that some men feel deeply provoked by pregnancy and engage in a battle for ownership of their partner's body, competing against their unborn child for primacy. This rivalry is not always something that they are consciously aware of, but men often disclose feelings of being abandoned and unwanted when their partners became pregnant. In terms of an attachment-based model of domestic violence, this represents a significant threat to the man, who has a fearful and insecure attachment to his partner, and his characteristic response to threat is to become angry and aggressive (Dutton *et al.*, 1995). The trigger for the abuse is the fear of loss, which activates the loss, fear and rage components of the attachment system (Hudson-Allez, 2011).

Women who have been subject to violence offer clear and vivid memories of how they were first assaulted when pregnant, and how the blows were often aimed at the stomach and between their legs. I have met several women who miscarried after violent assault and who blamed themselves for their association with their violent partner, as though they had chosen to have their unborn baby harmed or even killed.

Envy of the woman's love for the baby growing inside her, and the fear of being displaced, can reawaken feelings of murderous rage in men who have themselves felt pushed out, unwanted and unloved. These men feel excluded, tormented and deeply jealous of their partner's procreativity and the possibility of loving another. This can lead to violent assaults on a woman, targeted at her stomach and the baby growing within. If women do not seem as interested in or available for sex with their partners, this can also be felt as a rejection, and justification for assaults.

Others feel jealous and suspicious of the unborn baby, to the extent that they imagine it is the product of sex with another man, and therefore a symbol of their partner's betrayal. It is as if they have forgotten or cannot believe that they produced this baby and have somehow disconnected from the pregnancy altogether; this may indicate an unconscious primitive fear of reproductive sexuality and sense of alienation from the woman's pregnant body. There is no sense in such a man's mind of a procreative couple, so the pregnant woman is seen as doing something on her own, without him, perhaps in union with someone else. The unborn child is a threat, and possibly proof of sexual betrayal: the baby is a source of shame and humiliation.

When seen as evidence of another man's possession of the woman's body, the unborn baby becomes a target for assault, and the pregnant woman is viewed as provocative and mocking. In cases where the man goes on to kill his partner and at least one child (familicide), the perpetrators often have an entrenched, delusional belief that the baby is not theirs (Websdale, 2010).

For one woman, whom I will call Melissa, her pregnancy heralded the first of many brutal assaults, always directed at her stomach and genital area. When Melissa required hospital admission after the threatened miscarriage of her 16-week-old foetus, she decided to make a police statement. When questioned about the charges against him, her partner asserted his concern for the unborn baby and described his conscious wish to father a healthy child and to provide care and protection for his wife, apparently unaware of how this contrasted with his clearly murderous unconscious desires and life-threatening behaviour. He was prosecuted and attended a domestic violence course run by the probation service. Although Melissa refused to have him back, she allowed him some access to their baby. She also accepted his apology and explanation that the course had taught him that he had, unwittingly, become deeply possessive and controlling of her, linking his fears to his own experiences as a battered child, and continuing to assert that, at least at a conscious level, he had wanted to protect rather than to hurt their child, and her. She said that it was as if 'this pregnancy had sent him mad'.

The likelihood of an increased risk of violence in pregnancy for some women, particularly those with a history of victimization (Jasinski, 2004), places a particular burden of care on midwives and health visitors, who are responsible for the welfare of pregnant women and newborn babies, and tasked with identifying signs of domestic violence and risk to mothers: 'Health care providers who have received training are more likely to screen for violence; however, very few providers have received training as part of their medical education' (Jasinski, 2004: 48). This puts them in the complicated role of detective with statutory duties, as well as carer, and can lead to a sense of being involved in the complex domestic situation either as witness or confidante. Silence means collusion, but reporting can feel like a betrayal. This mirrors the conflict of the woman, who is in a relationship she may want but also fears, and her sense of helplessness and paralysis.

Intimate terrorism: the livid coercive partner

There are cases of interpersonal violence where the end result is murder. In such cases, it is very likely that the whole household has previously been subjected to the form of control, cruelty and tyranny that can best be classified as 'intimate partner terrorism' or 'livid coercion'. This is violence that involves the wish to control, and is not mutual; although the vast majority of intimate terrorists are men, Dutton (2007) also found that some women can act as intimate terrorists too, strictly controlling their male partners.

Websdale (2010) gathered data on 211 cases of familicide and examined over 400 fatalities in which members of a family, usually the mother and at least one child, were killed, using a variety of methods to compile his research and its findings. He proposed a continuum of interpersonal styles of those who have committed familicide with the 'livid coercive' group (those who use domestic violence habitually before killing) at one end, and 'civil reputable' individuals (who, superficially at least, are engaged in more socially desirable patterns of interpersonal and family relationships) at the other. Excessively strict and occasionally abusive, the livid coercive individual bases his self-worth on his authority as head of household. If the wife and family rebel against the husband's control or attempt to leave, the husband may attempt to assert his dominance through violence. This category is linked with Johnson's (2008) classification of 'intimate terrorism'. The other type, the civil reputable killer, invests his entire self-worth in his status as a family man and as a provider. If his finances deteriorate, he may develop depression and consider suicide. Not only does he finally kill himself, he also feels compelled to kill his family to spare them the shame of his suicide and their probable poverty.

Why don't battered women leave?

Angela Browne (1987) points out that the question 'Why don't battered women leave?' is based on the erroneous assumption that leaving will end the violence. In fact, leaving is the point of greatest risk for women.

Browne describes the cycle of domestic violence, where tensions escalate to the point of an actual physical assault, followed by acts of contrition, pleading and a period of calm, before the cycle begins again and another act of aggression takes place. During the contrition and remorse phase of the cycle, the abused partner feels hopeful and agrees to forgive her partner and give him another chance. This maintains the status quo of the relationship. Dutton (2007) further elaborates on this and situates the relationship in the context of two individuals with insecure attachment, whose partnership reflects their own unmet needs and deepest fears of abandonment, betrayal, rejection and loss. He suggests that the presence of personality disorder in either or both of the partners is also an important risk factor, and it is well established that personality disorders are themselves characterized by unstable relationships, and often, a history of deprivation and trauma.

Browne studied abused women, a minority of whom went on to kill their abusers. Her study consisted of 42 female homicides and a comparison group of 200 victims of domestic abuse who did not kill. Fifty-three per cent of women in the group who did not go on to kill their violent partner had left their partner by the time she interviewed them. She points out that these women will not easily be identified as battered wives because they left the relationship after the first or second violent incident, and often will not have discussed their experiences with anyone, out of shame, guilt or self-blame. In the homicide group, a significant proportion of women had left their violent partners in the past, and some had even been separated or divorced for several years before the fatal incident. Browne (1987) outlines three important reasons why women do not, or cannot, leave their violent partners:

1.   practical difficulties in effecting separation;
2.   fear of retaliation;
3.   the effects of severe abuse on the victim.

This question of why women do not leave violent relationships assumes that women who are in situations of domestic terrorism have the choice to leave, that they have alternatives, and that leaving is safer than staying. However, all of these assumptions may, in fact, be wrong.

The notion of choice is highly complex and raises important philosophical as well as psychological issues. While I would argue that all individuals who are embroiled in violent relationships could reach the point (with practical, cultural and emotional support) where they feel that leaving is possible and within their power, there are many reasons why the notion of 'choice' may simply not be applicable. Some of these are to do with cultural and religious beliefs that prohibit women from leaving marriages, and even sanction coercion and control within marriage, as well as threatening those who do leave with social and familial isolation and exile, or with the punishment of death. Others may have reached the point of 'psychic death', where they feel so helpless, and hopeless, that the possibility of changing their situation is beyond their conception. In cases of economic dependence on the abusive partner, leaving may not be viable, particularly in the absence of family support, without alternative accommodation, and with childcare commitments that prohibit employment. Many women in abusive relationships also value their partners' relationships with their children and could not imagine subjecting them to separation. The impact of exposure to abuse on children is often denied or minimized, making it even harder for parents to consider that, for some children, separation from the parent who is abusive may be desirable. The degree to which children are affected by exposure to abuse, even if not direct victims of it, has recently been explored in depth and reveals that this exposure has significant potential to harm (Dube *et al.*, 2002; Callen and Farmer, 2012).

The case of honour killings (further discussed in Chapter 7) is a tragic example of the lack of real choice within certain social and religious groups (unless, of course, one adopts a brutal existential position where choice is viewed as always possible, even if certain death is a consequence of one's chosen course). How easily can a woman with children, who does not want to leave them motherless with a violent father, be said to 'choose' to leave? And even if death is not a likely consequence, its threat may be enough to take away the sense of choice, since fear is paralysing.

As Ewing (1991) described, the sense of having no choice but to stay, is itself an effective form of imprisonment, evoking the phenomenon of learned helplessness, where creatures subjected to punishment they cannot control eventually give up any sense of control, even in those situations where their action *could* be effective and prevent punishment or harm. I discuss this elsewhere in relation to battered women who kill (Motz, 2008).

Emotional, sexual and physical abuse and their consequences: fear of leaving

Apart from the pragmatic complications of leaving a partner who is the father of one's children, and/or the breadwinner, domestic violence and extreme control have serious psychological and physical impacts that contribute to women staying in their situation. Sometimes, too, there are few practical alternatives, apart from temporary lodgings in refuges or with friends, and there are overwhelming reasons to stay put, including the fear of antagonizing the violent partner, the fear of bringing shame on the family, the children's divided loyalties and feeling that the home belongs to the family and should not simply be evacuated by those who are trapped there.

The perpetrator can use repeated threats, harassment and stalking to terrorize his partner. These tactics are designed to prevent them from leaving, and can intensify at times of separation, leading to the period after separation being one of greatest risk for those leaving abusive relationships. For some, the harassment and intimidation continues for years after the relationship ends, and even the protection of restraining and no-contact orders is ineffective in stopping this predatory behaviour.

The long-term impact of domestic terrorism is to destroy a sense of agency in its victims, who begin to take on the roles assigned to them by the perpetrator, as objects to be controlled and maltreated. Ewing (1991) describes this kind of state as one in which a psychic murder has taken place, in that the victim has been left with a sense of helplessness, no self-esteem and a sense of profound despair. He cites this kind of psychological assault as a justification for killing a violent partner, describing such a response as defensible on grounds of 'psychological self-defence'. This refers to the sense of psychological extinction that accompanies years of emotional, physical and even sexual abuse.

The dangers of hope

In situations of IPV, hope is dangerous. Women who have been subjected to severe abuse may still cling on to the hope that their partners will change, and that this change will last forever. Staying with someone they love, who can become transformed into an apparently alien other, remains the preferred option, and it is easy to understand how the violence is seen as an aberrant event, whose memory has to be wished away or denied. How can terrible aspects of experience be incorporated into daily life and kept alive when people need to survive and tend to their ordinary activities? Those aspects of unbearable reality tend to be banished to the back of victims' minds, as they cannot be readily incorporated with the lived known. In other words, the need for loved ones to stay close is so deep, and the need to maintain the status quo so ingrained, that violent or frightening ways of behaving tend to be viewed as isolated, unusual and encapsulated bits of experience.

The full implications of living with a violent partner, and the realization that aggression may be the norm rather than the exception, are dislocated from conscious awareness. We know that this is how the mind works in relation to unwanted or unacceptable facts, and that we are essentially programmed to carry on, to deal with unwanted and painful events and experiences by forgetting, minimizing and normalizing them. So why is it surprising that, despite repeated encounters with horrific violence by their partners, women (and men) would rather stay with what is known, than risk leaving? Aside from the practical fears of what rage their leaving would unleash, the effort of changing the familiar, if brutalizing, environment, for the unknown, is daunting.

The wish to forgive and to transform is associated with higher-level moral processing. Society values this attitude and particularly endorses it in women, certainly within traditional patriarchal cultures. It is therefore unsurprising that the hope of change and feelings of forgiveness are powerful forces that lead people to remain in dangerous places, with violent partners, working frantically to make them safer or trying not to provoke their rage.

As I discussed earlier, understanding the nuanced nature of violence in partners, the awareness that there are fears and terrors that can drive people to wish to control others so wholly, is another factor that can stop women from leaving violent men, and men from leaving violent women. Like good psychotherapists, they understand that underneath the aggression there is so often fear, isolation and emptiness, and that violence is the way in which such people communicate this need without losing face. There can be a feeling that to transcend one's own pain and humiliation, to forgive and understand the violent partner, is the 'best' way to act. When this self-sacrificing attitude is socially sanctioned and the partner also offers affection, attention and even care, at some times, it can be hard, if not impossible, for a battered partner to find a different voice, and to allow their own sense of outrage to surface. The desperation for love and care, that is arguably strongest in those who have been deprived of it in early life, can lead to a greater fear of leaving even the most abusive relationship. Furthermore, those who were abused in early life and carry a sense of shame in relation to this, will find this shame reactivated in their violent adult relationships, and this makes it a familiar pain that, in a perverse way, confirms their fears about themselves: they are confirmed as worthless, deserving of pain. Shame is a powerful force in maintaining violent relationships.

> For people who are used to brutal treatment through their own early lives, or who have become accustomed to it through their relationship with a violent partner, the expectation is that it will continue, that somewhere they even deserve it, and that despite the hope that it will stop, they feel they can manage it. A split between mind and body, or dissociation, can operate that allows the victim to feel that they are not really being hurt by the aggression, that they can rise above it. In this sense they are surviving, and transcend it, but the cost is that, in so doing, they have also become split off from parts of themselves and learn to rely on this dissociated half-alive state. A part of them is witnessing the horror to which they are subject, but has become mute, and distant as a means of surviving. Violence serves as a powerful tool for dehumanizing the other, making them an object, to be owned, abused and manipulated. The development of dissociation in victims of trauma can be one part of the constellation of symptoms of post-traumatic stress disorder, and while partly protective, it also cuts off experience and leads to destructive behaviour. Some use drugs and alcohol to try to generate a sense of aliveness in this cut-off state, while for others self-harm can be used to bring back a sense of reality at times of dissociation.
>
> (Motz, 2009)

Violence, antisocial personality disorder and the alien self

Violence can seem incomprehensible to some, particularly those fortunate enough never to have been subjected to it, but may be understood as a maladaptive psychological solution and communication. It is essential to try to understand the mind of the person who inflicts it, their sense of having no alternative to aggressive, even murderous, action and their rigid belief in their right to attack the body of the person they love.

Bateman and Fonagy (2004) offer a model of mentalization, defined as 'the process by which we make sense of each other and ourselves, implicitly and explicitly, in terms of subjective states and mental processes' that develops through a secure attachment with a parent who can reflect the infant's mind to them. This enables the growing infant to gain a sense of both their own mind, and that of other people: a prerequisite for empathy. Fonagy and Bateman have developed a treatment model based on mentalization to help individuals learn how to mentalize through the safety of a secure therapeutic relationship, and have demonstrated that this treatment model reduces rates of self-harm, suicide attempts and other impulsive behaviour in people with borderline personality disorder.

They have shown that failures in this capacity can result in aggression, relationship domination and interpersonal alienation. The person cannot identify, process and make sense of their feelings and thoughts, and instead converts them into action, often violence. They are also prone to interpret other people's behaviour as threatening, and respond accordingly. Such individuals are often considered to have antisocial personality disorder (ASPD) and manifest what they consider 'the alien self'. This is the person who cannot relate to others or himself, who has profound difficulty in understanding either his own mind or that of another. In the following excerpt, Bateman explains how unacceptable aspects of the self, which cannot be mentalized, are projected onto others:

> In ASPD, the alien self is firmly and rigidly located outside – a partner may be seen as mindless and subservient – 'women need to be treated like dogs at first. They need firm training and only gradually can they be let off the lead'; a system is portrayed as only authoritarian and attempting to subjugate through unwarranted attention – 'the police pick on me, follow me about and think they can dominate me'. These characterizations stabilize the mind of the patient. Doubt and uncertainty are not apparent. Any threat to the schematic representational structure, for example a partner demanding an unacceptable level of independence, police suddenly becoming helpful and friendly, leads to arousal within the attachment system. This triggers an inhibition of mentalizing that in turn leads to anxiety about loss of control of internal states and a threat of the return of the alien self. With an imminent collapse of the self, the need for the other as a vehicle for the alien self becomes overwhelming.
>
> (Bateman and Fonagy, 2012)

Clinical illustration: Russian roulette: Stacey – a woman addicted to violent relationships

Stacey was a 33-year-old woman whose elder four children had been removed from her and been taken into care, and who had recently given birth to a son, Abraham. The three oldest were placed with her parents, and the youngest son was now in foster care, with her baby. I met Stacey at two very different points in her life: one where she had identified that her violent partners destroyed her chances of parenting her children and developing her own sense of herself, and had vowed to put her son, Felix, first. The next, some five years later, marked her return to a state of violent abuse, unplanned pregnancies, alcohol dependence and neglect of her children.

Stacey had initially confided her hope in me, and the older children, that she could lead a different life, one free from the reign of terror she and her children had endured. Despite a short-lived period of freedom from this state, she had returned to a brutal relationship with a man who had a long history of violence, including a Schedule One Offence: an offence against a child for which he had been convicted. This had been a brutal assault on his own son, who was living with his ex-partner at the time. It was difficult for me to process the shock of her return to her state of self-neglect and reversion to a violent relationship.

The baby she had fought so hard for when we first met, Felix, was now a traumatized little boy, aged six. He had witnessed scenes of frightening violence and had often been neglected by his mother during these times of crisis and when she was preoccupied with her own wishes and needs; she sometimes forgot about his presence during fights, and, at other times, left him in the care of her partner when she went out to the local pub, where she worked part time. She was dependent on alcohol and said she used it to help her manage the stress of daily life. On one occasion when she had left Felix with her violent partner, he had threatened Felix with a beating with a dog lead and 'teased' him by locking him in the cupboard for several moments, saying he wouldn't let him out until he was better behaved.

Felix frequently wet the bed and was socially very anxious, described by his school as 'fearful' and 'a loner', despite having been a settled and sociable baby and toddler. He and his mother had been alone together from when he was nine months old until he was 16 months, when she had tried to live without the involvement of a partner, and had not abused alcohol. It was during this time that I first met Stacey, who was determined to manage as a single mother, and stay away from abusive relationships.

As he grew up, she re-entered new, violent partnerships and he was described as constantly worried about his mother's safety and always wanted to be with her, clearly feeling anxious and afraid whenever he separated from her. Stacey herself was prone to angry outbursts and freely told me that she 'gave as good as I get'. It soon became clear that, while she was often badly battered in the incidents, she would retaliate physically, describing it as 'helpful to release the stress'. She told me that sometimes she would feel so angry at her partner, and so suspicious of him, that she would 'take it out' on her son and threaten to hurt him. At other times, she had picked him up and held him close to her, rather like a human shield. This seemed to be an attempt to stop the physical attacks on her; she felt guilty about this, but felt that it was the only way of getting the battering to stop. From early in Felix's life, he was literally caught in the crossfire.

Stacey had not undertaken the counselling I had recommended after I had first met her as being essential to enable her to process her previous experiences and care for Felix. This would have helped provide her with the ego support she required in order to be able to parent Felix and any future babies, including Abraham, and care for herself. Within months she had found a partner and was back in the familiar world of fight, generally triggered by mutual jealousy and suspicion, followed by reconciliation. It was as if the most compelling option was to revert to a familiar, if destructive, state of virtual imprisonment within a volatile and dominating relationship. She would be violent too, not simply a victim of physical intimidation and brutality but in some ways a willing partner, as she admitted feeling that she 'got a buzz' from the drama. The state of captivity she had in some ways chosen was one in which she reverted to a way of being and relating that felt enlivening and real, rather than difficult and false. The life she was expected to lead was one where she would engage in counselling, stay in a mother and baby unit to learn parenting skills, and then learn how to function as a single parent.

Stacey described herself as 'learning disabled'. In a sense, her description was apt, in that she did have profound difficulties in learning, but it seemed the problem was not a cognitive one *per se*, but a kind of paralysis in her emotional and imaginative functioning, where she couldn't give up the habitual, familiar and destructive pattern of her intimate sexual relationships. She could not necessarily put her thoughts and feelings into words, or give vivid accounts of what happened in her early life, but her behaviour and compulsive attraction to particular types of relationships indicated a sense of relentless, compulsive repetition, as described in Freud's 1914 paper 'Remembering, repeating and working through': 'We may say that the patient does not remember anything of what he has forgotten and repressed, but acts it out. He reproduces it not as a memory but as an action; he repeats it, without, of course, knowing that he is repeating it' (1914: 150).

Stacey's own experiences in childhood and adolescence had left her with an impoverished sense of her own inner resources and a tremendous need to be in a relationship with a man, even one who treated her violently. During our interview, she said that her central problem was that 'Mum and Dad aren't here', living far away. She felt very lonely at times, and became emotionally overwhelmed. It was difficult in this interview, as in my previous assessment, to get a full history from her, and she described her parents – currently – as positive factors in her life, where she felt wholly supported by them, and they were 'there for her' although, while growing up, she had been the 'black sheep' who was often farmed out to other relatives and left to get into trouble at school and in the village where she grew up. She had a disrupted early life and insecure attachments to her parents, who seemed to prefer her siblings to her.

At times of crisis in the present time, she would go to her parents' house, and was pleased that her older children were in their care. She felt that during 'hard times' she couldn't focus on the needs of her children, but assured me that she could learn to manage without being in a relationship with a man (although she acknowledged that this had not been possible for her in the past). She was open about her fear of being alone, and her attraction to men whom she initially saw as strong and protective, but who turned out to be violent and abusive. She described a sense of safety within these relationships and a 'buzz' that came from the intense emotions she experienced with her partners, and how the whole world seemed to stop and stand still, leaving her all alone with her man. It would feel, she said, like a dream, like the kind of fairy tale she had loved in childhood, but then it would turn nightmarish and her 'Prince Charming' would turn into an ogre, and she would go from being the beautiful princess, to the wicked witch, filled with ugly fury and despair.

At times, Stacey also felt overwhelmed by an unmanageable anger that she had to discharge, becoming bad tempered and even violent to Felix, indicating something of her own difficulty in feeling that strong emotions could be understood and contained. Her history indicated that she had always found interactions with others difficult and had trouble managing her impulses or acting on the advice of others. She identified strongly with Felix, seeing him as a shy, overly sensitive child – much as she had been. She missed him terribly once he had been taken into care, aged five and a half, but saw how she had damaged him by exposing him to violence and neglecting his needs.

In addition to her psychological difficulty in managing her feelings, she was convinced that she couldn't learn, though formal assessment in my earlier report demonstrated that this did not reach the level of learning disability, but fell within the low-average range of intelligence. It seemed to have the aspect of traumatic 'shutdown' that Sinason (1986) poignantly describes in her seminal paper on mental handicap as a secondary consequence of trauma. What could not be expressed or articulated seemed destined to be acted out and repeated.

Clinical illustration: discussion

Stacey struggled to learn from experience, had unmet needs from her early life, an impoverished capacity to regulate her emotions or delay gratification, and an impulsive aspect to her personality – all of which led her into unsuitable, often abusive relationships. She seemed to have become addicted to the excitement and drama that these relationships appeared to offer, and has continued to enter into such relationships without regard for her own safety, or that of her children. Once she entered into such a relationship, she was increasingly less able to see its abusive aspect, and became desensitised to this. Her view of an independent life, without the apparent excitement of this relationship, was that it was not worth pursuing, and she overlooked those aspects of herself that could eventually offer her the peace of mind and emotional stability her children desperately required.

She reported being lonely at night and wanting to contact her ex-partner, but knew this was wrong and that she needed to 'be there for the children' and not allow a violent man into their lives. Her apparent awareness of this was, however, strongly at odds with the behaviour she displayed and her real difficulty in staying away from men who had been violent towards her. Her impulsivity was evident during clinical presentation, where both now and earlier she seemed to rush through things and felt anxious to get away; this tendency also seemed present in her decision-making in relation to men. She viewed all partners as potential rescuers, who could offer her sanctuary (see Pat Craven's (2008) *Living with the Dominator*). Unwittingly, she exposed her own children to the disruption and neglect that she herself had experienced in her early life, and did not give them a sense that she was 'there for them'. Her son Felix, with whom she strongly identified, had already developed serious disturbance, and had difficulties in learning and concentrating.

Clinical discussion: parental distress and the impact on children

The impact of parental disturbance and consequent neglect on children's development is well documented in the literature and will be further discussed in depth in Chapter 3 (Dube *et al.*, 2002; Glaser, 2001). The NSPCC (Lazenbatt, 2010) identifies the impact of domestic abuse on children: 'Domestic abuse can directly and indirectly affect children, even before birth. It is likely to have a damaging effect on their health and development, with children under one at the highest risk of injury or death' (McVeigh *et al.*, 2005; Goodall and Lumley, 2007). Domestic abuse, adult mental ill-health problems, substance misuse or racism from a care-giver may be factors underlying the physical, sexual and emotional abuse of children within the family.

Women who are depressed and anxious, fearful for their own safety and that of their children, are less likely to be emotionally available to their children. My clinical experience over the past 24 years of working with highly disturbed mothers, supports the finding that children whose mothers were using them for their own narcissistic gratification (i.e. to make them feel loved and cared for, seeing them as objects or extensions of themselves, rather than independent beings in their own rights) were more likely to have serious psychological difficulties as they developed, including feelings of worthlessness, self-harming activities and depression.

The extensive literature on attachment disorders (Music, 2011) highlights the extent to which patterns of attachment between primary caregivers and their children affect children's psychological development and can influence how they go on to parent their own children. Insecure attachments, to a mother or carer who is unpredictable and often emotionally unavailable, lead to a sense of confusion and unhappiness in children, who grow up without a sense of inner security, or feeling that their own strong emotions, such as anger and fear, can be managed safely by an adult. They may have a deep sense of unmet needs that leads them to form unsuitable, impulsive relationships, but find it hard to sustain these or any other relationships.

Countertransference feelings with women who return to violent partnerships

With Stacey, described above, I found myself feeling despair and anger at her return to a highly toxic relationship in which the baby she had fought to care for was once again sacrificed for the sake of her desire to be 'brought back to life' with a frightening man. What she took to be a deathly state of isolation, alone with her infant son, was – to my mind – a reflection of her inability to appreciate peace and safety and to allow herself to find some kind of redemption through caring for her son and herself. She left me feeling betrayed, as if my attempts to help her achieve rehabilitation of the baby into her care and secure help for herself had been futile, and that she had deceived me. I had wanted to believe her, and she had convinced me, and possibly herself, that true change was possible. This was backed up by desperate assertions that she would 'fix herself' through therapeutic interventions, literacy classes and women's support networks, including parenting classes, which she never actually attended.

I reflected on my strong sense of betrayal and hurt and its intensity, since this was not characteristic of my professional encounters with mothers in care proceedings, and seemed particular to Stacey, indicating that something was being communicated to me that 'belonged' to her. Eventually, I came to believe that she too must have been 'fobbed off' with similar apologies, convincing promises to change and leave violence behind by her partners, who simply reverted to form. Through projective identification, I was left feeling like the shamed partner of a violent man, with my hopes dashed and my trust betrayed. I also felt for the children, whose wishes for safety and desperate hope that their mother would stay away from violence were ignored.

It was important to distance myself from this overwhelming state of emotional overload in order to sit with Stacey and engage with her 'without memory or desire'[3] of my own. My feelings of despair, anger, futility and helplessness were useful in giving me a window into how she felt at times of beatings and reconciliation, and how the children could feel whenever she took back her partner. These powerful emotions could inform me about how Stacey felt, and how she made her children feel, but it was important that they not dominate my mind to the point of being unable to think and reason. It seemed significant that I struggled to think at moments in the meetings with her, mirroring the state that she described as her 'learning disability', possibly borne of a wish not to think and a need not to know. As with Tina Nash, it was hard, if not impossible, to imagine that Stacey would enter into another violent relationship, having suffered so deeply at the hands of her previous abusive partner. This thought was quite unbearable.

The force of the repetition compulsion, described earlier in this chapter, and more fully by Freud (1936), is such that a kind of unthinking search for familiar, destructive relationships dominated Stacey's life, and cost her the care of her children, time and time again. Her notion of romantic love, and hope that the dramatic fights she had with partners confirmed the passionate intensity of the relationships, left me with a sense of real despair, and ultimately destroyed her capacity to learn from experience. The sentimental notions of love as a rollercoaster, and confusion of morbid jealousy and control in her partners with devotion and care, combined to leave her repeatedly disappointed and increasingly desperate.

The currency of romance for Stacey was found in beatings and apologies, accusations and reconciliations, and an overwhelming cycle of physical fights and reconciliations, sometimes accompanied by visible bruises or even broken bones, and compensated for with flowers bought for her by her partner. On one occasion, during the second evaluation, she had attended an interview with me with a freshly blackened eye that was distressing to see, and which she had not concealed with make-up, determined at that time to show me how destructive her boyfriend was. On the way out of the office, she found an extravagant bunch of flowers waiting for her, along with a card with an elaborate apology. Stacey was clearly moved by this display, showing me the bouquet. This dramatic and public gesture seemed to meet her need for witnesses to her situation and a desire for symbols and concrete signs of devotion. While this gesture seemed to me in place of actual tenderness, intimacy and concern, it seemed that she valued it highly. I felt protective of her, and thought the flowers were a dramatic and inauthentic display of remorse, designed to seduce her; but, for her, this world of action and reaction was the one where she felt most alive and cared for.

Again, it seemed that events from her early childhood, even some that she could not consciously remember, were being repeated. The details and emotions related to early experience – including fear of abandonment, as she witnessed her violent parents fighting – were too disturbing to allow into her conscious memory. These memories were repressed, but my request to read her case files revealed that she had been subjected to similar situations to the ones to which she had repeatedly exposed her own children, including witnessing violent scenes. She appeared compelled to seek out familiar situations as, at some level, this type of relationship appeared to be 'normal' and through repeating these patterns she could feel 'at home'. This illustrates the repetition compulsion, and shows how she was caught up in such a repetition while being quite unaware of this. In the throes of these re-enactments, she was unable to bring to awareness what was going on, or find a way to work through it. Bowlby's notion of the importance of secure attachment on later development was also evident in Stacey's case, in that she had not experienced a 'safe base' in her early life.

The therapeutic intervention I had recommended could have offered her an opportunity to gain some distance from this pattern and to reflect on it and modify it. Indeed, within a psychodynamic treatment I would have expected her to repeat this pattern in her transference to the therapist, and this would have been a central tool for change, as she would have anticipated rejection, harsh criticism and ultimate abandonment, alternating with seduction and dramatic reconciliations. I would expect her to relate to me as an unreliable object and to create situations where it would be difficult for me to be with her, or in which I would be overwhelmed with violent feelings, and provoked to anger. This is the type of transference and countertransference that is familiar when working with survivors of domestic violence, and that can fruitfully be worked through, providing rich information about patterns of relating.

One of the more disturbing aspects of countertransference is the sense of anger at the apparent passivity of the person who is entrenched in a violent relationship, and a feeling that they have abdicated responsibility for their own lives and any sense of hope. This is a reflection of the state to which they have become accustomed, and the therapist can feel, at times, in identification with the aggressor: angry and impatient, perhaps even sadistic towards this clearly pitiful person. At other points, the therapist feels helpless and that change is impossible, feeling like a victim herself. These moments in the therapy mirror what happens within the violent relationship and can be used to explore underlying conflicts and fears, to help the client to reclaim her own authority and agency, to see how she is participating in the destructive relationship and how to disengage and face the loss of this familiar way of relating and the terrors that underlie it. Sadly, in this case, Stacey was unable to undertake this work I had recommended by the time I saw her for a second evaluation.

While being repeatedly placed in situations of domestic terrorism was frightening and unpleasant, they actually allowed Stacey to act out familiar scenarios that she equated with care and affection, and in which she could express her inchoate feelings of need, desire and anger. What seemed to be more terrifying for her than repeated violence and loss was having to think about and give voice to these experiences, through therapy or counselling, or to be confronted with vulnerability and helplessness through childcare. So it seemed that, for Stacey, remaining in an 'exciting' cycle of violent action, with frequent separations and reconciliations, allowed her to escape from her underlying sense of despair and emptiness.

I heard from Stacey some three years after our last contact, when she informed me that she had now moved area, had obtained a lifetime restraining order against her violent partner, and was actively engaged in the Freedom Programme. She was determined to maintain her freedom from abusive partners and to fight for rehabilitation of her two youngest children, who were themselves engaged in therapeutic work in relation to the damage they had suffered under her care. She now saw herself as a freedom fighter and recognized that she had the potential to build a life for her children that would be safe, stable and secure, with the help of her extended family, including her parents. Although her parents were not ideal carers, they seemed to have resolved their earlier conflicts to some extent (largely through her father addressing his alcohol dependency), and were able to offer some form of stability to their grandchildren and to Stacey herself. It was possible that they were now able to offer her some sense of a 'safe base' to which she could return, as well as helping her to resist the temptation to seek out new, risky partners.

This sense of a reliable place to go, and a safe base from which to explore, could also be offered in the form of a robust therapeutic relationship, which she now said she was ready to begin; she was on the waiting list for weekly individual psychotherapy.

While I was aware of the 'dangers of hope' in myself, wishing for a 'happy ending' for Stacey, it was nonetheless heartening to learn of her progress, and the possibility of a reconciliation between this mother and her children. Although caution and child protection must remain at the forefront of practitioners' minds, it is important to allow some hope to be kept alive in both therapist and client, if positive change is to occur.

3   Action replay

The intergenerational transmission of violence

[T]he patient *remembers* nothing of what is forgotten and repressed, but . . . he expresses it in *action*. He reproduces it not in his memory but in his behaviour; he *repeats* it without of course knowing that he is repeating it.

(Freud, 1914)

In this chapter, I explore the physical and psychological impact of exposure to domestic violence on children. In a significant proportion of domestic violence cases, children are present in the household. Recent statistics compiled by the United States Bureau of Justice relating to non-fatal intimate partner violence (IPV) demonstrate how often children are exposed to such abuse.

On average, between 2001 and 2005, children were residents of households experiencing intimate partner violence in:

- 38 per cent of incidents involving female victims;
- 21 per cent of incidents involving male victims.

Children whose parents or carers are in violent relationships are also more likely to be victims of direct physical abuse themselves; some definitions of domestic abuse and violence include physical assaults of children by parents, or between siblings. In this chapter, and throughout this book, I use the term 'domestic violence' primarily to denote intimate partner violence.

In this chapter, I outline the impact of trauma and neglect due to violence on the developing brain and on the blueprint for future relationship patterns. I use clinical material as well as empirical data to illustrate how children are affected by their parents' styles of interacting, and also how their early experiences are re-enacted in later relationships, though this may occur without their conscious awareness.

The evidence from attachment theory, social learning theory (both discussed later in this chapter) and psychoanalytic models of development, suggests that the templates for later relationships are drawn up in early life. These templates then shape the children's intimate partnerships in later life. An exact repetition of the parents' relationship(s) is, of course, not inevitable, but the nature of early attachment experience is highly significant in shaping later relationships. This is explicable in terms of neurological, psychological and social development.

Exposure to violence profoundly impacts on a child's sense of boundaries, on notions of acceptable behaviour, as well as on her capacity to learn and to think. Disturbances in attachment that can result from this exposure, as well as the traumatic aspects of exposure to the abuse itself, have long-lasting consequences. It is clear that human development is adversely affected by violence across the entire lifespan, over a wide range of domains including the social, emotional, cognitive and interpersonal.

Families under siege

Every year in the United States, women are subject to approximately 4.8 million intimate partner-related physical assaults and rapes, while men are the victims of approximately 2.9 million intimate partner-related physical assaults (Tjaden and Thoennes, 2000). In the United Kingdom, on average two women are killed every week by their current or ex-partner: between 2009–2010, 94 women and 21 men were killed by their current or ex-partner (Callen and Farmer, 2012). The hidden victims of this violence are often the children.

Impact on children of domestic homicide

In the first four days of 2012, there were three national reports in the United Kingdom of fatal violence in the family, in which the father was the perpetrator. These events are shocking, gripping and sadly predictable, as the Christmas period is itself a time of increased risk of violence. Tension created by high expectations of the holidays, the proximity of family members who might ordinarily not spend much time together, and the increased availability of alcohol, can all contribute to this phenomenon.

Such crimes are often the fatal outcomes of the forces of jealousy, humiliation and rage in partners who believe they face some form of abandonment. In Chapter 2, describing the characteristics of violent partnerships I outlined the toxic and controlling dynamics in which a form of 'Russian roulette' is played out, sometimes with lethal consequences. Recent literature has identified personality disorder in the perpetrator, rather than mental illness, as a significant risk factor (Dutton, 2007). Others suggest that it is their failed attempt to control their partner or the risk of tremendous shame and loss that drives these perpetrators to murder (Websdale, 2010).

Tragically, domestic violence can result in the death of a family member; in intimate partner violence, the victim is far more likely to be the female than the male. Intimate homicide by a male of his female partner or ex-partner is known as femicide. In their study of these killings in the United States, Campbell *et al.* (2003) identified factors that significantly increased the risk of intimate partner femicide prior to the incident. These included: the perpetrator's access to a gun and previous threats with a weapon; the presence of the perpetrator's stepchild in the home; and estrangement, especially from a controlling partner. Significant factors found in the homicide incident itself included: the victim having left her abuser for another partner; and the perpetrator's use of a gun. Other significant risks included stalking, forced sex, and abuse during pregnancy (Campbell *et al.*, 2003).

The situation of homicide followed by suicide is one of the most tragic that can befall a family. Children who survive the attacks by their parents (in 77 per cent of cases, the father), lose both parents, as the perpetrator turns the murder weapon on himself after killing the mother. In cases where one parent kills the other, the children effectively lose both parents, as the perpetrator is generally incarcerated – either in prison or psychiatric hospital – and contact may be severed. They are then doubly bereft. How can anyone make sense of this, least of all a young child who is almost wholly dependent on her parents?

I have worked with adults whose fathers killed their mothers when they were children, and they suffered enormously, not simply as a result of this trauma, but also because of their exposure to the violence and terror that typified their parents' relationships even before the murder. In one case, an adult son became obsessed with the need to avenge his mother by killing his father himself. A violent man with a profound difficulty in expressing vulnerability, he came to see me for therapy to work out this wish to kill. In the course of the psychotherapy, he revealed that he had spent much of his childhood hiding away from the scenes of horror enacted before his eyes, and had also been hospitalized for several months before his second birthday for a series of operations. He believed his parents had not been in contact with him much during this time, and also had a hazy memory of a brief period of time in care. His attachment could best be described as insecure avoidant, as he tended to minimize the potential emotional impact of this, or other salient experiences, and to say dismissively about conflicts: 'This means nothing to me' – despite showing evidence of major difficulties in forming intimate relationships or managing aggressive impulses. Although he did not go on to kill his father, our two years of work ended abruptly when he was charged with assault on another family member and I was required to attend a child protection conference. He saw this as a betrayal, and perhaps also felt too ashamed to return to the clinic, believing he had been publicly humiliated.

In another case, I worked therapeutically with a highly disturbed adolescent who had witnessed his mother's murder by his father. He was depressed and suffered from severe levels of post-traumatic stress disorder (PTSD). He self-harmed severely, and came to the attention of forensic psychological services; not for violence, but for shoplifting. He had stolen an expensive leather jacket, in what appeared to be an uncharacteristic act of delinquency. As we worked together, it became apparent that he felt racked with guilt for not being able to protect his mother from the abuse she had suffered for years; it seemed that his offence reflected an unconscious wish to be caught and punished for his underlying feelings of profound guilt. The symbolism of the jacket was also apparent, as he loved how it felt: it was a form of second skin, a beautiful protective layering, like the touch of a mother. This young man felt that he was in desperate need of comfort and care, and did not know how to contain his grief and anxiety. He appeared to identify with his battered mother, who had suffered for years with depression, linked to the intimate partner violence to which she was subjected, rather than with his father, the violent aggressor in this case. He engaged well in this supportive psychotherapy and later sought out specialist PTSD counselling, which proved highly effective for his residual symptoms, including recurring nightmares of the night of the murder.

The conflicting feelings for both men about their remaining parent were terrible to encounter, as they saw any forgiveness of their father – on their part – to be a form of collusion with their mother's killing, and so were left effectively orphaned. In other cases, the resilience of a child who experiences the death of one parent at the hands of the other is protective. A secure early attachment experience can provide the child with a sense of emotional containment and integration that can help sustain her even in the face of catastrophe (S. Redfern, personal communication, April 2013). Children who experience this trauma can be helped by having contact with their remaining parent if this is planned carefully and their grief explored and worked through carefully in psychotherapy (Harris-Hendriks, Black and Kaplan, 2000).

This chapter is devoted to exploring how this exposure affects children and can influence their own intimate partnerships in adulthood, and includes a clinical illustration to highlight key points.

Psychological assessment of violent couples

I come into contact with violent couples through my work as an independent expert to the family courts; I conduct assessments of their parenting capacity and psychological risk factors. I am often asked to address issues of interpersonal violence between parents. Part of the psychological assessment of violent couples, and the impact on children, includes close examination of how the parents' earlier experiences are repeated in later life, and consideration of what could help this destructive pattern to be modified.

To undertake this evaluation, I meet each partner individually to explore their early experiences, attachment styles and any history of trauma, including their exposure to intimate partner violence. I assess the couple together to observe the way they speak and relate to each other, and to witness how their attachment styles interact. I pay close attention to how they describe their pattern of arguments and their resolution, what they say about how they met, and what first attracted them to one another, who does the talking, who is more passive, where the 'flash points' are, as well as asking detailed questions about the children in the household and how they perceive them. I may use formal psychological assessment tools to assist in identification of particular difficulties, including intellectual disability, mental health issues or personality disorders. Structured assessment tools can serve as guidelines for determining risk, but are only ever used as an adjunct to clinical assessment.

The most important tool in the assessment is paying close attention to the parents in the room, listening carefully to their narratives about their history, observing their interactions, as well as thoroughly reading all available documentation from as many sources as possible. Charting the emotional landscape of the relationship is the richest form of evaluation. I consider what aspect of each is projected onto the other in order to maintain an acceptable sense of the self; who is being asked to do the work of aggressor; and who takes on the subservient, frightened role. I consider the shared unconscious fantasy (Clulow, 2009) that may be underlying their particular relationship. As well as taking a careful history in relation to violent events, jealousy and controlling behaviour, understanding of the other person's subjectivity, and capacity to retain their autonomy, I consider the degree of empathy and compassion each has towards the other, and in relation to any other significant family members, including children.

The descriptions of emotional and psychological difficulties in the children, including PTSD and their own statements about their feelings, are important indicators of the quality of their home life, and the impact of exposure to intimate partner violence. In some cases, the children are most secure in the company of another significant attachment figure, such as an aunt or grandparent, who offers them a safe place to go, away from the domestic war zone. These sources of comfort and sanctuary can be protective against the adverse impact of exposure to this violence.

When partners have experienced secure attachments in early lives, and can tolerate separations and resolve conflict, difficulties with parenting and with managing loss and pain can be addressed without recourse to violent action and desperate states of mind. However, when one or other partner has had a traumatic early life, involving insecure and disordered attachments with primary caregivers, their capacity to engage in intimate partnerships can also be disordered, with traumatic consequences. As described in Chapter 2, exposure to frightening or violent parents does not allow infants to develop a sense of their own mind or to learn to regulate their feelings. This absence of reflective functioning in the face of frightening parents can lead to the development of the 'alien self', who is more prone to acts of violence.

Even in these evaluation interviews, it is possible to get a real sense of the quality of the emotional tone of the relationship, and the way that the children are viewed. The interview situation itself can act as a kind of mirror of what goes on at home, when not observed. At times, it is as though the children are entirely forgotten as they fade into the background of lively and detailed descriptions of the couple's own struggles. As well as bearing in mind the unconscious 'contract' between this couple, I assess current social and economic factors, as well as the historical risk factors that can increase the risk of any particular individual becoming violent – that is, the parent's own early experiences of care, abuse or deprivation. In his illuminating account of how fearful preoccupied attachment styles in partners can potentiate violent relationships, Clulow (2001) highlights the importance of understanding the development of interpersonal violence in the couple – by reference to both the individual's experience, and how their close proximity to another person, in another central attachment experience, can reactivate their own disturbed, disorganized attachment systems. This relational account marries both attachment and psychoanalytic understanding of individuals, and offers a coherent model for (1) the development of difficulties in forming secure relationships, and (2) the transmission of this to the next generation.

Their own attachment system is operating in partnership within the couple and the interaction or 'dance' between the two will shape the way the couple operates, particularly at times of stress, threat or loss, when the attachment system is activated. Even in an interview situation, the transference reaction will create a degree of arousal so that the individual's style of relating to others will become apparent; this offers a valuable window into his or her internal world.

Jealousy about one partner's care of a child, and perceived preference for this child over the partner, can be a trigger for violence. In some cases, the children have one biological parent and a step-parent; the fact that they are not the biological child of this carer can also have a significant impact on how they are both perceived and treated. On occasion, the assessment of a violent couple, for care proceedings, reveals that biological parentage is not what it was assumed to be, as secrets about parentage come out. This information can be explosive, and may have significant consequences for those involved. The process of investigation and close file reviews may reveal these secrets, or the fact of external intrusion itself can lead to family breakdown and parental separation, in which issues of paternity emerge.

Clinical illustration: Secrets in the family

A clinical illustration of the unexpected exposure of the truth can be found in further exploration of Shane and Lucy, whom we introduced in Chapter 1. This family had been 'on the run' from social services, moving location and disengaging from services until one violent incident, after which Lucy ran away from Shane, taking the children with her. Her eldest son, Owen, the only child who was not Shane's natural son, but believed he was, tripped up, and then Shane fell over him. The child sustained a minor injury and the police were called, finally arresting and charging Shane with grievous bodily harm (GBH) for his assault on Lucy.

Owen, aged ten, was guilt-stricken, believing he had caused his father to be arrested, and that the reason he was taken into care was because he had done something wrong. He turned the blame on himself, as a way of not blaming his parents. Furthermore, he was separated from all but his youngest sibling, as the others were too disturbed to share a placement with him. This was seen by him as further punishment. He felt that he deserved such punishment, and found it hard to accept the kindness and care offered by his foster-carers, although he flourished at school with their support and was also able to sleep better and gain weight; he had become thin and malnourished, reflecting his level of stress at home. His needs had clearly been neglected, as his mother and her partner were totally preoccupied with the intensity of their violent relationship. He adored his mother, whose affection he craved, and who could be very loving to him.

As a result of the family breakdown, and Lucy's eventual separation from her entrenched relationship with Shane, she decided to tell Owen that Shane was not his natural father, though he had raised him as his own child from the age of 18 months old. This was a double blow to the child, who had lost his siblings and parents, and now had to face the confusing fact that the man who had been so violent to his mother but loving to him was not his actual father. For Shane, too, this news was devastating, as he considered him a biological son, and now felt doubly bereft, of his children, and of the relationship that he and Owen had enjoyed. I felt that the timing of the revelation was an act of revenge by Lucy, in which she wanted to sever all ties with Shane, and that telling the child, and Shane, this news was an attempt to effect separation. She did not want to consider this possibility, and felt she had been burdened with a secret that was hard to keep.

When I next saw her, Owen had been informed of this truth, and she felt he had taken it well. She seemed not to want to consider how it might have affected him, in ways he could not or would not articulate. In fact, he was thriving in foster care, away from the disturbance and chaos of Shane and Lucy's relationship.

Clinical illustration: discussion

It is not possible to comment on whether or not Lucy's disclosure was the right decision to make, but it did strike me as a poignant illustration of the way that such crisis points, and the assessments that are conducted, often serve as catalysts for uncovering explosive secrets. In this case, I concluded, sadly, that neither parent was able to offer safe care of the children.

The impact of intimate partner violence on children

Watching people tear one another apart, psychologically and physically, is a horrifying situation; those who witness violence can be traumatized by what they have seen or, alternatively, might become desensitized to it, and see it as normal, predictable and acceptable. The defensive response to such exposure can be to 'shut down' emotionally or to become hyper-vigilant, and overly aroused, displaying anxiety and agitation. Observation of infants exposed to trauma (or unpredictable and intrusive parenting) reveals typical responses that serve to protect them from painful experiences.

Children who witness abuse and degradation are particularly susceptible to learning to repeat this behaviour and to find ways of 'normalizing' it, tending to imitate the ways of relating to other people that they observe. They learn from their parents or carers, whom they most admire and on whom they depend. Children exposed to intimate partner violence may also be more likely to tolerate violence towards themselves in later life, or to view it as an acceptable means to assert one's power and to get one's way. Exposure to abuse that is not violent, such as emotional threats and manipulation, verbal and sexual abuse, is also toxic.

Exposure to intimate partner abuse in childhood is linked to a plethora of risk factors, including depression, anxiety and the increased likelihood of being the victim of physical abuse oneself (Jaffe, Wolfe and Wilson, 1990; Wolfe, Jaffe, Wilson and Zak, 1985). Children who are victimized directly through physical harm can be severely traumatized and physically endangered. Their awareness of the adult's intention to harm them is terrible, and can leave them with an indigestible sense of being hated, and of being the unwitting 'poison container' (deMause, 1990) for a parent's own toxic feelings. That their parent, the person on whom they rely, wishes to hurt and frighten them, is confusing, and renders their attachment to them conflicted and disorganized. Likewise, a child who is not directly abused, but who watches one or both of his parents physically harm the other, is also likely to develop a disorganized attachment style, in which his feelings of love for the abused parent, and concern for her, co-exist with fear, confusion and, at times, a sense of helplessness, as he is unable to protect her from the damage she suffers.

This is clearly a gross distortion of what Bion (1962) describes as the requisite relationship between parents and children of 'container and contained'; in this situation the caregiver (mother or father) is able to act as the container for the indigestible and frightening experiences of the infant, and to feed back these fragmented bits of experience in a digested and detoxified form, as the building blocks of meaningful thought and symbolic processes.

Between the volcano and the void

The significant impact of witnessing domestic violence on children, and the consequences for their development in adolescence and adulthood, will be explored in some depth in this section. As described earlier, children who are reared in such households are also at increased risk of physical abuse, as well as neglect; the serious consequences of neglect and the implications for future harm are not as readily identified as those of physical or sexual abuse, but are equally serious. One of the consequences can be the development of an attachment disorder, which severely disrupts the child's psychosocial development, capacity to empathize with others, and ability to achieve intimacy in relationships in adulthood (Hornor, 2008; Zeanah and Gleason, 2010). This can be understood in the following terms: 'an attachment disorder is warranted when a child who is developmentally capable of forming attachments, does not, because of an aberrant caregiving environment' (Zeanah and Gleason, 2010: 31).

The violent parent can be likened to a volcanic force of dangerous, molten activity that explodes and frightens, and the depression and fear of those who are harmed (including, most typically, the mother) represents a void. In her state of distraction, distress and fear, her mind cannot be reliably available for the child. Instead, the child may try to 'hold' the mother in mind, and have a pervasive sense of responsibility and hyper-vigilance, being overly attuned to subtle changes in her mood. This disrupts the development of the child, who seeks to discover her own mind through her mother's responses to her, as the psychoanalyst Donald Winnicott so acutely observed in his important (1967) work on mirroring. The child psychoanalyst Alice Miller describes Winnicott's theory in terms of how the mother offers her infant a reflection of his or her own mental states, which can then be taken in. This can be understood as the beginning of the development of the infant's mind. If the infant only ever sees its mother's own fears or pre-occupations when they gaze at one another, he will develop a 'false self', related not to his own needs and desires, but in response to the wishes and fears of the mother; her projections onto him.

> The mother gazes at the baby in her arms, and the baby gazes at his mother's face and finds himself therein . . . provided that the mother is really looking at the unique, small, helpless being and not projecting her own expectations, fears and plans for the child. In that case, the child would find not himself in his mother's face, but rather the mother's own projections. This child would remain without a mirror, and for the rest of his life would be seeking this mirror in vain.
>
> (Miller, 1981: 32)

The roles of volcano and void are not rigidly allocated by gender and, in some cases, it is the mother who serves as the volcanic force and the father who is the non-abusive partner, more vulnerable to the preoccupation and depression characteristic of victims of violence. A mother's rearing of her children is of crucial importance. Mills (2008) suggests a link between a critical, emotionally abusive mother and her son becoming physically abusive to an intimate female partner in adulthood.

The lack of mirroring by these parents can lead to the development of the 'alien self' described in Chapter 2, where the mother or father is frightening and violent and thus incongruent with the infant's own feelings, the infant internalizes an alien self that leads to disorganization and disorder of the attachment system. This leads the child to develop aggressive or self-harming behaviours in later childhood and adolescence: for girls, self-harming and internalizing behaviours are more likely, while, for boys, aggression and conduct disorders are more common manifestations of disturbance. Conduct disorder (CD) is a group of behavioural problems where a child is aggressive, antisocial and defiant to a much greater degree than expected for the child's age. Characteristics of conduct disorder include: fighting and physical cruelty, destructiveness, lying and stealing, and truancy, including running away from home.

The adverse consequences of exposure to domestic violence in children have been demonstrated extensively in the psychological literature, and will be explored in further detail later in this chapter. In families that experience intimate partner violence, the children are far more likely (60–75 per cent) to experience physical abuse than in families where it does not occur (Dube *et al.*, 2002). The psychological consequences of this maltreatment on their sense of self and capacity to relate intimately to others are also significant. Identification with the parent, as victim, perpetrator or both, has grave implications for both boys and girls. The risk of developing adverse behaviours increases for children who witness intimate partner violence.

When violence is an everyday occurrence, and parents hurt one another routinely, it becomes the currency of communication in daily life. A child who grows up in this environment is at increased risk of neglect, physical abuse, emotional harm and other adverse consequences; he or she is also more likely either to anticipate violence towards themself as the norm, or to turn a blind eye when they see it being directed at another.

Developing forms of protest against violence, while it might be manifested through fear, anger or disturbed behaviour, is preferable to a defeated state of acceptance, where the child grows up expecting to be hurt, and is resigned to this, sometimes seeking it out. In adolescence, both girls and boys from violent homes can find themselves feeling dissociated and cut off, unable to trust themselves to form intimate relationships. Across the genders, the impact of exposure to parental violence, or intimate partner violence where one of the partners is a parent, has been shown to be more harmful than exposure to verbal aggression between a parental couple.

Internalizing blame as a child's defence

Yakeley (2010) provides a rich analysis of the way that children who are exposed to violence sometimes internalize it, and repeat it in their own adult relationships. She offers insight into how their later toxic couplings offer a solution to longstanding psychic conflict. The burden of guilt that children carry for feeling love for their violent or abused parents, and their need to preserve them as 'good', leads them to take the blame onto themselves, as Owen demonstrated in the clinical illustration above. This, in turn, can increase children's risk of entering similarly violent relationships to relieve them of guilt.

Yakeley draws on the notion that the abusive partner locates his denigrated vulnerability in the woman he hurts (Motz, 2008), and that she, in turn, projects her own aggressive wishes and feelings into him. She describes why a woman would allow herself to become the receptacle of his violent impulses:

> Many of these women, because of their own early histories of abuse, neglect and attachment difficulties, may already have an image of themselves as damaged. Many will also have witnessed parental violence and seen their own mother as victims. Feelings of anger and aggression towards the abusive partner are associated with intense guilt and so are split off and directed against themselves, so that the parent is preserved as a good object. Becoming the recipient of abuse in relationships as an adult both appeases the battered

woman's sense of guilt for her aggression towards her own caregivers and also recreates the abusive relationship of her parents.

(Yakeley, 2010: 81)

The shared projective identifications of the couple perpetuate the destructive cycle of violence. The child needs to retain his belief in his parent's innate goodness, and will place blame and guilt on himself; this sense of his own 'badness' and need for punishment can persist into later life, and shape his choice of partners.

The question of identification with the parent of the same gender is also highly pertinent here. Freud describes how boys may grow up identified with their father, as the aggressor. He offers a clear account of the vital process of identification in boys:

> Identification is known to psychoanalysis as the earliest expression of an emotional tie with another person. It plays a part in the early history of the Oedipus complex. A little boy will exhibit a special interest in his father; he would like to grow like him and be like him, and take his place everywhere. We may say simply that he takes his father as his ideal.
>
> (Freud, 1921)

The impact for the boy who sees his same-sex parent behave violently towards his mother, or himself, is profound, as he internalizes this image of masculinity and associates it intrinsically with violence and abuse.

Violence towards a child can inscribe a sense of absolute despair in the child as she becomes a psychic and physical container for poisonous feelings and the recipient of hate. These are overwhelming, unbearable, incomprehensible feelings. As Grosz describes: 'For a small child, violence is an overwhelming, uncontrollable and terrifying experience – and its emotional effects can endure for a lifetime. The trauma becomes internalised, it's what takes hold in the absence of another's empathy' (2013: 9). It is introjected into the child's mind and body and causes a breakdown of functioning – reason cannot justify that a good parent can behave like this, so the child must warrant this degree of hatred: they are bad. And nothing can stop the violence, whether begging, pleading or prayer, leaving the child feeling helpless.

The violent couple in the mind

One of the consequences of exposure to domestic violence is that children caught in the crossfire grow up with the image of their parents fighting: the couple who appear to have chosen to be together, and who may claim to love each other, are also in battle. When this association is imprinted on their minds, violence and intimate relationships become intrinsically connected. The loving couple is also the warring pair, and within this there may be little space to attend to children, to speak and reflect together, as extremes of emotion are played out through physical injury and retreat. This can be an unconscious or conscious awareness, and the danger is that – at some level – it becomes the prototype for intimate relationships.

As the child grows up, there is an increased risk that in adulthood he or she will repeat these behaviours and similarly use action to express feelings, especially destructive ones; this is what I have termed 'action replay'. The term may also be used to refer to the ways in which the scenes of violence, and the ways in which the children were aware of them, are repeatedly played in the mind's theatre, sometimes in a traumatic sense, as intrusive memories that cannot be managed, or as the scripts for the child's own method of managing conflict or unhappiness. As they develop, they may rely on the language of the body, rather than words, to express themselves and repeat the scenes they witnessed.

As the process of learning to reflect on one's own mind and that of other people is so severely disturbed by an exposure to violence in childhood, it is also more likely that these children will develop major difficulties in empathy and in mentalization (Bateman and Fonagy, 2010; Yakeley, 2012), and will use bodily action to express their feelings: violence against themselves and others becomes the way of managing strong emotions. Their capacity to use language and symbolism is restricted by the damage done by this early exposure to violence, and its effect on their capacity to process experience. These children miss the reflections of their own mental states that would ordinarily be offered by their parents and easily become anxious and overwhelmed. They may struggle to name emotions or to put things into words, instead using their bodies to communicate their feelings through aggression, self-harming or somatic complaints.

Of course, not all these children will grow up to recreate this pattern, but even for those who do not, the sense of fear and danger that such violence created in their early lives can make intimate relationships feel frightening, or even undesirable. The helplessness of the child in the face of adult rage is a profound experience, and one that can take hold in a child's memory in a highly destructive way. It is clear that the consequences of exposure to domestic violence can be highly significant for children, and this sometimes begins even before their birth (see Chapter 2 for a discussion of violence in pregnancy).

Because the psychological effects of intimate partner violence are so profound, the implications for children who are reared within this situation are often grave. The quality of the care that they receive is highly likely to be affected by the fact that one of their caregivers is suffering from the psychological consequences of violence and emotional abuse, and this will have an impact on the whole family system. A child does not have the intellectual or emotional apparatus necessary to process this dramatic and distressing situation, and will make sense of it in her own way, which may mean that she blames herself, or believes (falsely) that she should be able to protect the injured parent. The sense of helplessness and impotence that results from this perceived failure to protect leaves the child with feelings of guilt and shame that can be difficult to process or relinquish.

At what point is exposure to violence recoverable from, and when does it create such a high level of disturbance that there is no way back? The notion of a critical age for healthy attachment is supported by the data. There is growing evidence for the existence of a critical age for neurological and psychological development, and, thus, for the long-lasting impact of the exposure to traumatic situations on the infant's brain. There is also a substantial body of data that indicates that attachment disturbances of a profound level in early infancy can leave children without the capacity to form secure relationships in later life. This constellation of difficulties is known as an attachment disorder; such a disorder has serious implications for the development of healthy relationships with peers, intimate partners and, in turn, with offspring, creating an intergenerational transmission of highly disturbed attachments.

Empirical evidence for the association between witnessing intimate partner violence and adverse consequences for children

In their large-scale study of over 17,000 users of health services in the United States, Dube and a team of researchers identified the long-term consequences of 'adverse care events' in childhood, including the effect of witnessing intimate partner violence, in order to determine how best to integrate healthcare services so that the children of abused parents (in this case women) are also screened and treated for difficulties. They argue that the focus on particular life stage and presenting difficulty of those who appear at healthcare services – i.e. paediatrics, substance abuse in adulthood, victims of physical abuse – detracts attention from the way in which these problems interact, and the likelihood of IPV actually increases the risk of the other difficulties. In their study, they found that the presence of Adverse Consequences in Childhood (ACEs) was dramatically related to the experience of witnessing intimate partner violence, and identified a clear need for integrated services, to allow practitioners who see children with such difficulties to consider the possibility of domestic violence towards their mothers, and those who see mothers who suffer IPV to enquire about, and intervene, with their children.

> Children whose mothers are treated violently are more likely to suffer multiple forms of abuse, neglect and serious household dysfunction. Many studies on the consequences of witnessing IPV and experiencing childhood abuse have found deleterious effects on their children, ranging from behavioural problems in childhood and adolescence to greater psychopathology as adults (Jaffe, Wolfe and Wilson, 1990; Wolfe, Jaffe, Wilson and Zak, 1985). We found that among the abuse categories, physical abuse had the highest increase in prevalence as frequency of witnessing IPV increased.
>
> [. . .]
>
> Practitioners who identify and treat victims of IPV must inquire about any children involved and those who identify and treat abused and neglected children must inquire about the possibility that the mother may be the victim of domestic violence. Without such integrated services children who witness IPV are likely to continue to be at high risk for abuse, neglect, and

exposure to other potentially traumatic experiences, and be at high risk for health and social problems, such as substance abuse and depressed affect, later in life.

Intimate partner violence (IPV) damages a woman's physical and mental well being, and indicates that her children are likely to experience abuse, neglect and other traumatic experiences. . . . Identification of victims of IPV must include screening of their children for abuse, neglect and other types of adverse exposures, as well as recognition that substance abuse and depressed affect are likely consequences of witnessing IPV.

(Dube *et al.*, 2002: 3)

Even though children may not be direct victims of physical abuse (although the risk of this is increased in families where violence is present), there is still a significant impact on them of exposure to IPV. This is mediated through their mother's distressed mental state and the various coping mechanisms she may employ to manage her feelings, including alcohol or substance abuse. Unwanted pregnancies, youth and HIV status in the mother are also risk factors for IPV in pregnancy, and these may also be significant features in their parenting styles and difficulties, with serious implications for their children.

The risk of physical violence, neglect and emotional abuse increases in households with intimate partner violence, and these factors are also correlated with the development of a conduct disorder in childhood, and to a personality disorder in adulthood, pointing to long-term difficulties in managing impulsivity and aggression, and in forming stable intimate relationships. The insecurity of early attachment relationships appears to be crucial in shaping later ones, often leading to a deep need for others to offer protection and care that parents were unable to, combined with difficulty in identifying dangerous partners, and a sense of helplessness when a relationship turns violent. At an unconscious level, such violence is perceived as 'deserved', linking the victims inextricably with their abused parents; those who abuse others are unconsciously identified with the aggressive parent.

How are violent patterns of relationships transmitted from parents to children?

Various theoretical models of human development describe the pathways by which children will come to accept and/or imitate behaviour they witness in their parents' treatment of one another and towards themselves. That is, it is not only the psychoanalytic paradigm that suggests that early exposure to the fact of parental violence, rage, sadism or sexual abuse will adversely impact children who witness it, but that social learning theory, developmental psychology and behavioural schools of thought also predict and demonstrate this finding. There are a myriad causal explanations for this major public-health issue, and in this section I will summarize the main paradigms and the empirical evidence that supports them.

Social learning theory

Intimate partner violence often is associated with abuse of other household members, particularly children. Research indicates that violence is a learned behaviour, and witnessing violence in the home as a child is a strong risk factor for involvement in abusive relationships as an adult. In addition, experiencing abuse as a child has been associated with other risk factors such as depression, substance abuse, poor school performance, and high-risk sexual activity.

Attachment theory: transmission of traumatic bonding

John Bowlby (1969) used the term 'attachment' to describe the affective bond that develops between an infant and a primary caregiver. He described how an 'attachment behavioural system' was one of four behavioural systems that are innate and evolutionarily function to ensure survival of the species. The quality of attachment evolves over time as the infant interacts with his/her caregivers. The type of attachment, or attachment status of the infant towards the caregiver, is partly determined by the interaction between the two, and partly by the state of mind of the caregiver. This state of mind in the caregiver is, in turn, affected by her own relationships to attachment figures, and internal working models of these, giving weight to the sense in which there is a significant intergenerational transmission of attachment patterns.

> In his groundbreaking three volumes on attachment and loss (Bowlby, 1969, 1973, 1980), Bowlby wrote that attachment bonds have four defining features: proximity maintenance (wanting to be physically close to the attachment figure), separation distress, safe haven (retreating to caregiver when sensing danger or feeling anxious), and secure base (exploration of the world, knowing that the attachment figure will protect the infant from danger). Attachment relationships evolve over the first two years of life and beyond, but most importantly these early attachment relationships overlap with a time of significant neurological development of the brain.
>
> (Sonkin, 2005)

Bowlby (1977) defined attachment as a bond between an individual and 'some other differentiated and preferred individual who is conceived as stronger/and or wiser' (1977: 203) and showed how separation, or perceived threats of separation, from this central attachment figure produced intense and powerful emotional responses. He demonstrated how actions triggered by separation from the primary carer in early life are attempts to maintain proximity to her. Anger displays – including shouting, crying and hitting out – may be attempts to communicate to a mother that the infant needs her and protests at her leaving. The protest phase that infants demonstrate when their mother leaves is the stage in which anger is most clearly manifested. Dutton (2007) proposes that it is this aspect of protest that can be seen in the physical abuse that violent men inflict when their female partners either leave them or threaten to leave them. In his sensitive description of the development of violence in intimate relationships, he states:

> Proportional to this sense of the other as having absolute and unrestricted power over the infant, threats or separations to their secure attachment should produce emotional responses that are extremely strong – responses such as terror, grief, and rage. In males these fundamental and primitive emotions are initially connected to a woman. Because that woman holds life and death power over the male infant, powerful emotional tracks are laid.
>
> (2007: 152)

Recent research (Dube *et al.*, 2002; Music, 2011) demonstrates that childhood experiences – including physical abuse, exposure to intimate partner violence, and the neglect that often accompanies it – increase the risk of becoming victimized in adulthood. There is also clear evidence suggesting that the association between attachment and couple violence can be explained by the dysfunctional communication patterns that are linked with insecure attachment, and that create an environment in which couple violence is more likely to occur. A recent prospective study of intimate partner violence in the Netherlands linked avoidant attachment patterns in the victim, and high levels of anger, with violent responses in their partners (Kuijpers, van der Knaap and Winkel, 2012). The link between exposure to violence and insecure attachment is seen as crucial in the individual's development, as is the central role of the family system as a force determining the behaviour and interactional style of its members.

The literature on attachment disorders (O'Connor and Zeanah, 2003) highlights the extent to which patterns of attachment between primary caregivers and their children affect children's psychological development and can be seen in the way they go on to parent their own children. Insecure attachments, with a mother or carer who is unpredictable and often emotionally unavailable, lead to a sense of confusion and unhappiness in children, who do not grow up with a sense of inner security, or the feeling that their own strong emotions (such as anger and fear) can be managed safely by an adult. Hornor (2008: 34) writes:

> Reactive attachment disorder (RAD) is one possible psychological consequence of child abuse and neglect for very young children, younger than 5 years of age. RAD is described as markedly disturbed and developmentally inappropriate social relatedness usually beginning before age 5 years. These behavioural manifestations are the direct result of and come after pathogenic care.

Clearly, women who are subjected to violence and abuse are more likely to have psychological difficulties in attending to the needs of their children and indeed themselves than those without such disruptive and intrusive experiences, and so the risk of impaired attachments increases; this insecurity for the children is compounded by the distress and fear of witnessing interpersonal violence.

Biological models: traumatic injuries and impairments

Data from the neurosciences show that childhood stress can affect numerous brain structures and functions, providing convincing biological foundations for the epidemiological findings. Recent neurological research demonstrates the adverse consequences of assault on the foetus, and the long-term consequences of neurological damage on infants. As Kaufman (2012) explains in his article 'Violence against women is an issue for men too', intimate partner violence takes a terrible toll on children who are exposed to it:

> Contemporary research by neuroscientists shows us that the 750,000 children who witness such violence each year in the UK have marked and measurable deficits in the development of their brains, particularly when the abuse they witness (or directly suffer) is ongoing and when it happens when they are very young.
>
> (*The Guardian*, March 2012)

Gerhardt (2004) describes the direct impact of deprivation, trauma and abuse on the brain of the developing infant, citing a rich body of empirical data. It is now well established that the early years are vital for brain development and that severe neglect can lead to atrophy in parts of the brain, including severe difficulties in managing emotions, maintaining intimacy, empathizing with others, and engaging in ordinary social interactions (Music, 2011). This is demonstrated in cases of extremely neglected and deprived children in Romanian orphanages, where brain activity in the areas associated with language was greatly diminished, and even more significantly, the areas associated with emotional understanding and expressiveness were seriously lacking in life or activity (Chugani *et al.*, 2001). Such is the power of early deprivation on the developing brain. Likewise, trauma also impacts directly on brain functioning. Neuroscientist and psychiatrist Perry showed how trauma directly affects the physiological functioning of children so that they become hyper-vigilant and anxious, seeming never to relax (Perry, 2000); these responses reflect a highly activated sympathetic nervous system.

Alternative responses to stress and trauma involve the activation of the parasympathetic nervous system, in which the body slows down and 'freezes'. Music (2011: 93) explains: 'The parts of the brain which specialise in logical thought can often shut down when faced with trauma, while primitive survival mechanisms take over. This can give rise to the phenomenon of dissociation, in which people can seem to be cut off from their own experience.' This can lead to a failure to respond to unpleasant stimuli emotionally or even physically, as the feeling of being cut off persists, creating a kind of numbness in the face of pain or danger. As described earlier in this chapter, both responses, hyper-vigilance and dissociation, can be seen in children who are exposed to the stress of intimate partner violence, and, in the process, are also neglected.

Psychoanalytic understanding: identification with the aggressor and repetition compulsion

Earlier in this chapter, I described the ways in which children, unable to process certain traumatic experiences, such as the sight of their parents physically fighting, often protect themselves against the full psychological impact of this, sometimes by repressing the sights and sounds through a kind of psychological and physical withdrawal, or by finding some internal retreat or sanctuary.

There may be a strong wish to protect the injured parent, whose helplessness is unbearable, and one such psychic mechanism is to identify fully with them, taking on this role themselves, or even trying to fight the aggressor and protect their hurt parent. Another, equally compelling, solution is to adopt the defence of 'identification with the aggressor' (Freud, 1936) and justify the abuse against the injured party; to find comfort, satisfaction and excitement in taking on the powerful role of the violent parent.

The gender of the child may contribute to their choice of the parent with whom to identify, so that male children growing up witnessing their fathers' violence may feel unconsciously that this way of relating to others represents potency and creates respect. On the other hand, for girls, identification with their mothers may lead to unconscious equations of intimacy with emotional and physical tyranny, and an increased likelihood that they will find themselves entrenched in abusive relationships in their adulthood. If children of either sex have been neglected and physically abused as part of their upbringing, they are at increased risk of victimization in their own intimate partnerships, indicative of the 'repetition compulsion' (that is, the desire to repeat certain familiar patterns of relationships, with the unconscious aim of finding a different solution to a constant psychological problem through re-working it).

In her discussion of the traumatic bonds that develop in these situations, Welldon (2012), using the term 'malignant bonding', describes how early exposure to domestic violence impacts on the child's mind, and leads to a repeated pattern of perverse relationships in later life. The trouble starts with this 'malignant' pattern of attachment in early life, which is then repeatedly re-enacted in adolescence and adulthood.

Clinical illustration: Vanessa: a living reminder

Vanessa was 23 when she became pregnant for the fifth time. I saw her for assessment of her parenting, specifically focusing on her capacity to protect her four-month-old son, and herself, from violence by her partner. Her two older children had been removed from her care after a previous partner had physically injured them. The local authority had expressed concern that she was working in prostitution, and that her most recent partners, including the father of her baby, had actually been pimps.

Vanessa had terminated two previous pregnancies because her partner at the time was violent and her situation was well known to social services: she had been in local authority care herself in childhood for periods of time, and then had short, disrupted placements with her mother, who never gave up the hope of being able to parent her safely. Vanessa had cerebral palsy which seriously affected her mobility and her speech.[1] She had required specialist foster placements that could accommodate her needs, and had struggled to make herself understood at school. While her mother was pregnant with her, her father had frequently assaulted her. On one occasion, he had thrown her down the stairs, for which she required hospitalization. Vanessa had repeatedly been told about his violence and how her mother had subsequently left her father, but had never wondered – or so she said – whether this assault, and the others could somehow be connected to her brain damage; perhaps through contributing to her mother's premature labour.

Despite her great difficulty with mobility and speech, she was a highly attractive woman who had always had boyfriends, who were often violent and involved in dealing drugs. There was a real possibility that they subjected her to sexual coercion and threats, and her physical and psychological vulnerability made this both more abhorrent and, sadly, more likely.

Her presentation was of a highly attractive and confident young woman, wearing fashionable, fitted clothes, despite the crutches she used to assist her walking. She used make-up well, emphasizing her delicate features. Her style had an edgy quality, including a nose piercing, and she appeared proud to be desirable to men. She described her disability with a degree of stoicism that impressed me, particularly in the light of her history of childhood trauma. She appeared to feel empowered by her capacity to attract men, and her exploitation at the hands of young men acting as pimps did not appear to be evident to her, as she felt she was very much in control. She had been the third daughter of her mother, and her older sisters had been placed in care at ages three and five, when her mother was pregnant with Vanessa. Her mother had worked as a prostitute; Vanessa seemed to repeat this pattern, although she did not consider herself a sex worker. As described above, she engaged in sexual activities with men, arranged by her boyfriend, but had a sense that she was consenting to this. In fact, it later transpired that she had not felt she had a choice in this. Her own mother had assured social services that she was leaving this life behind her and was also going to separate from her violent partner, as she had learned (from the horror of losing her daughters into care) that living with domestic violence was unacceptable, and would cost her custody of her children. Sadly, she could not break away from this partner, and it was shortly after this that he assaulted her, precipitating the labour and possibly contributing to her eventual diagnosis of cerebral palsy.

Her disability was something she lived with, and she did not seem to dwell on the idea of the life she could have had. She did not appear to question the origins of her condition or blame her mother (who had failed to protect her), or her father (whose rage was uncontained).

In interview, it became apparent that she sought out men she considered to be protective, strong and capable; those who could command respect on the streets. However, these partners proved to be abusive and violent towards her, sometimes using her forcibly for sex. One man had tried to pimp her to his friends, emphasizing the 'exotic nature' of her crutches and impaired mobility, as if he were appealing to a fetish market. Vanessa was both aware of this exploitation and harsh treatment, in a painful way, and also reluctant to examine it, suggesting that using her disability in this way, as a sexual lure, would place her in a powerful position. She received disability living allowance (DLA) and this was something else that her partners controlled. Her worth was measured both in terms of her sexual attractiveness and the money that her formal diagnosis of disability enabled her to claim. She was treated very much as a commodity, to be traded in.

This case was highly complex, not just because of Vanessa's particular vulnerabilities and strengths. There were also issues related to her son Stephen's ethnicity, as he was mixed race, as she was, but his father Junior was white. His father saw Stephen's darker skin as evidence of Vanessa's disloyalty and proof that he 'wasn't mine'; although Vanessa was herself mixed race, he was convinced that if he were his father, the baby should be white, lighter skinned than his mother. While her love for her son was evident, her loyalty to his father, the last in the long line of violent and abusive partners, was almost unshakeable. She hid important facts about him from the local authority, but these were revealed by subsequent police checks and included a history of Class A drug possession and dealing, an assault against a minor (which made him a Schedule 1 offender), and two charges of GBH, one of which was against a woman.

Vanessa gradually admitted that she had betrayed her vow to protect her son against violence when she had allowed her partner Junior to care for him, and she was aware that he had been drinking and smoking dope while looking after the baby. She had seen that Stephen had a bruise on his arm, as if he had been held in a tight armlock. She had questioned Junior, who denied that he had used force when he had handled the crying baby, but did say it had 'wound him up'. He said he had left him in the cot and he must have hit his arm against the bars. Vanessa told me she accepted his explanation and couldn't bear to deny him the chance to take care of her son. Despite this, she said she knew he had a violent past, having been in care himself as a result of his mother beating him, and that she was risking Stephen's welfare by trusting him. She could see that she was exposing Stephen to the kind of abuse she had seen her mother suffer at the hands of various partners. She seemed to understand that she was taking a risk, but felt unable to change her decision, even when faced with the possibility of losing Stephen into care if she could not either end the relationship with Junior, or prevent Junior from looking after him by himself.

How is it possible to understand Vanessa's lack of curiosity about her origins, and difficulty in learning from her own experiences, despite her intellectual capacities? At one level, she seemed to be in denial about the extent to which her severely impaired mobility left her defenceless in the face of physical assault. At another, she also minimized her emotional and psychological frailty (or, rather, the sense of being unable to move, to run away in her mind to seek protection or help from an inner resource). She depended heavily on her partner to help her to make decisions or to feel that she had a place in the world. She felt that she would falter and stumble when on her own, but actually had resources she could use, such as her intelligence and artistic ability, as well as a real capacity for warmth and empathy.

Although she lost Stephen to social services, as she refused to separate from Junior, she was able to return to a College of Further Education, where she began an art A-Level that allowed her to feel she had a voice, and a vision, that could be communicated to others. She also enjoyed the one-to-one contact with Stephen's social worker, and was referred to a colleague on the Physical Disability team, with whom she formed a good relationship and was able to confide in about Junior's ongoing abuse.

I have since learned that she did leave Junior, some three years later, and was hoping to go to university to do a degree in fine art. It seemed to me that there was a psychic sanctuary buried within Vanessa that had allowed her to find this strength within herself, and that it linked to her sense of safety and love from her grandparents. This attachment experience appeared to have given her some sense of belonging and security, despite the absence of a reliable and protective presence in her mother. Nonetheless, her vulnerability in adult relationships made her prey to violent and sadistic men, who exploited her gentle and dependent nature. At times, her limited mobility had also been used against her, and made her both more fearful of the men who threatened her, and less confident about her own capabilities. Through art, she was able to find both a 'voice' and the capacity to create, using her mind and her body, that helped her to express herself and gain confidence. She attended local art classes regularly and appeared to have been able to form some good relationships with teachers there, again indicating her capacity to relate well to others in a safe environment.

Clinical illustration: The significance of Vanessa's early relationship with her mother

Vanessa experienced her mother as absent and distracted for much of her early life, and it seemed that she was often taken to her grandparents' house, where she gained a sense of being cared for and loved. Her mother was clearly unhappy and preoccupied with her younger children (Vanessa's younger brothers, who did not go into care and were physically abused by her partner) and was also frightened for her own safety. Her daughters had been adopted and she had lost contact with them. She made several attempts to leave him, but found his threats about what he would do to her and the children too frightening to ignore, and also felt that she would not be able to manage to look after three young children on her own. Like so many violent partners, he had isolated her from her small circle of friends, and this had increased her dependence on him. She also felt that he needed and depended on her, and this was, in many ways, true. Despite her history of not being able to care for Vanessa's older sisters safely, she persuaded the local authority that she was no longer being abused by a partner, and so the violence and threats were completely hidden.

Clinical illustration: discussion

Women who have disturbed early relationships with mothers and other caregivers are at an increased risk of developing other difficulties in emotional regulation and relationships, finding the demands of intimacy intolerable. They are in a high-risk group for developing difficulties within intimate relationships and are sometimes classified as having borderline personality disorder (BPD), on the basis of traits such as impulsivity, self-harm, eating disorders and a tremendous fear of closeness, alternating with terror of abandonment. When they have their own babies, they face significant difficulties in seeing their children as separate from them, providing consistent and reliable care and protecting them from repeated experiences of neglect and abuse, which tragically mirror their own. This is often in stark contrast to their conscious wishes to spare their children the deprivation and abuse of their own early lives, reflecting the power of unconscious forces and non-verbal early experiences. Like Vanessa's sisters, her own children were also placed into care at an early age, and like her own mother, she was emotionally, sexually and physically abused by men. Unlike her mother, she was able to escape this.

Being in touch with the sense of fragility, vulnerability and isolation that characterize early life feels unbearable, and so frantic attempts are made to avoid this, both through the creation of highly dependent relationships with men who may appear to offer strength and protection, and through getting into states of mind where these feelings can be pushed away – perhaps through drugs or alcohol, or a high degree of excitement. The need to escape from painful memories has an addictive quality, sometimes leading to actual addictions, and to enmeshment in an abusive, but distracting, relationship.

In psychodynamic terms, this represents a manic defence against underlying depression and fear of being alone, empty and depressed. For Vanessa, being involved in sexually exciting relationships offered her a great sense of relief, self-affirmation and pleasure, but she seemed to have a blind spot when it came to perceiving her partners as dangerous or threatening (and, at one level, did not seem to mind taking a risk with her own or her baby's safety). It was as though the attention and dramatic intensity of the volatile relationship gave her a much-needed distraction from the feeling of emptiness she often had, particularly when on her own. She had struggled to complete academic work and had always felt that, no matter how hard she tried, her mother was not able fully to attend to her, or to engage with her, as though she were 'all there'. She felt constantly pushed away by her, and that men had always come first for her.

Welldon (1988) attributes the development of promiscuity to this deep need to have an inner sense of maternal care; when this is absent, women turn to a kind of desperate quest to find the sense of being loved and attended to through sexual promiscuity. This is an interesting inversion of the traditional view that promiscuity reflects a manic search for a phallus, to replace the father's; as, instead, it is the internalized sense of the mother's love that is being sought. Young women who have had traumatic early lives, including disruptions in care, are also more likely to face other difficulties, including leaving school early, without qualifications and having an unplanned pregnancy.[2] Pines (1993) describes the power of the unconscious fantasy in pregnancy that becoming a mother will also provide a woman with a sense of being filled up and alive; at some level, she is seeking the maternal care of which she was deprived in early life. The birth of an actual baby is then experienced as a tremendous disappointment.

Vanessa's disability also placed her in a higher risk category for experiencing sexual assault, in part because of her relative vulnerability in relation to physically defending herself. At the same time, it was actually her emotional fragility, and search for belonging and acceptance, that led her to search for partners who appeared to offer protection and care. This psychological vulnerability led her to repeatedly enter destructive relationships, but this could be addressed in therapy. Focusing on her physical disability was unhelpful and did not reflect her primary concerns and needs; therapeutic work focused on her inner state rather than her physical state, although she was able to explore links between the two, including the importance she placed on being found physically desirable and beautiful, when part of her felt useless.

Conclusion: the destructive force of violence on young minds

The consequences of exposure to domestic violence on children's development therefore cannot be overestimated. As outlined above, the intense array of emotions that it evokes in young children and adolescents includes fear, confusion, anger, helplessness and rage. When the father is the perpetrator of violence, the child (male or female) may be in identification with the mother and feel ashamed, guilty, scared and helpless, or flip into a state of potent excitement, in identification with the father, alongside a terrifying sense of destructive recklessness.[3] At times, when the violence is sadistic, including torture and emotional abuse, the sight of the parent being humiliated and helpless makes the child feel absolutely wretched and without any sense of security in his or her world. The capacity to make sense of this horrifying treatment, inflicted by one parent on another, is simply lacking, and the child may instead blame either herself or the abused parent, so that the world retains some sense of justice.

Feeling torn between mother and father is deeply stressful, and a child may feel it is her task to keep them happy, and will take sides in the hope that the most distressed parent, or the one threatening to leave, will be appeased. No matter how frightening the scene of the fight or argument, the thought of one parent abandoning the other, or leaving them, is often the worst thing imaginable to a child: being witness to this becomes, in the child's mind, akin to having to prevent it, to protect the parents and create some kind of peace. This is a pressure way beyond his or her capacity, and some children may get involved in the crossfire, actually physically intervening to protect the threatened adult, while others will hide, wishing themselves invisible and waiting in dread for the battle to end.

Despite their awareness of the children's presence, the embattled adults will often disregard them, as they are so caught up in the dramatic intensity of their own emotions. Perhaps even more disturbing is that, for some, the presence of witnesses or an audience can escalate their aggression, as they enjoy the impact of their own destructive power. The frightened children, threatened with abandonment by their aggrieved parent, have become receptacles for the aggressor's unwanted feelings of rejection and humiliation. They are his 'poison containers'; their neediness and vulnerability assure him that he is powerful and respected, it is the children who now feel helpless and alone. This illusion of power and love is one that he wants to hold on to; underneath, he is afraid of being left, neglected or rejected. But illusions do not last forever, and as soon as the false belief in his power recedes and he perceives another slight or humiliation, there is a real risk that he will begin the cycle of violence again. His aggression offers only temporary release from the sense of shame and fear that drives him.

It is important to note that protective factors can mitigate the detrimental effects of exposure to intimate partner violence, such as the quality of relationship with the non-abusive parent (or another significant attachment figure) as well as the particular inner resources of the child. Indeed, the question of whether the abused parent takes measures to protect her children, and has the emotional capacity to hold them in mind, despite the violence she is subjected to, is crucial. Her ability to protect, despite harm and threats to her own safety, and the presence of other secure, reliable and safe attachment figures, have far-reaching consequences for children exposed to violence. The abused partner may often be isolated herself, but if there is a strong and supportive network that can reach out to her, and attend to her needs and those of the children, she may be able to leave an abusive, isolative partner. This is a complex task, as she is often enmeshed in the relationship, may deny its danger, and be ambivalent about ending it.

In this chapter, I have explored how witnessing and experiencing intimate partner violence impacts on children and creates an unbearable scenario in the mind that is acted out both in disturbed and aggressive behaviour (whether towards the self or towards others) at the time, and also leads to an increased likelihood of an 'action replay' of destructive relationships in later life.

In Chapter 1, I described Lucy and Shane, who were caught up in what seemed an endless cycle of violence and reconciliation. When relating her childhood experience of her own father being imprisoned, violence between her parents, separations and reconciliations between them, and suffering from disruptions in her care and schooling, Lucy said: 'It is almost like history repeating itself.' Despite her desperate, genuine wish for a different life for her children, she found herself repeating the familiar and destructive patterns from her own early life, even though there were details of her childhood that she could not consciously remember. This type of acting out can be understood as an attempt at mastery of the trauma: an action replay.

4 Beauty and the beast

Perversion within the family system

No Pleasure without Pain; (before 1576)

What life were love, if love were free from pain?
But oh that pain with pleasure matched should meet!
Why did the course of nature so ordain
That sugared sour must sauce the bitter sweet?
                                    Sir Walter Raleigh

There are some couples whose attraction seems to be made in hell. The reasons for their attraction are unconscious and perverse, and their bond seems based on a shared need to engage in abusive practices, both against one another and themselves. At times, this perverse activity extends to their children, who may be viewed largely as objects to be used for their own gratification.

For some, the relationship has been imposed too early in the life of one of the partners for her to be able to make an informed choice about it, and it has developed into a malignant attachment – this is clearly the case in incestuous relationships, where a child or adolescent has been forced or seduced into a sexual relationship with a parent or sibling.

In this chapter, I will look at various strategies adopted by individuals to cope with anticipated loss and exposure to danger, including clinging to a partner, no matter how abusive, and the retreat to a perverse state of mind, in which the wished-for object can be controlled and manipulated. I explore the development of perverse relationships, and the unconscious forces that maintain them.

Definition of perversion

In contemporary terms, the development of perversion is the history of aggression that becomes sexualized. That is, the aim of perversion is control and power over another, and so aggressive impulses become incorporated in sexual activity. I have called this chapter 'Beauty and the beast' to exemplify the sense in which another person is treated as the bad 'other' who is inhuman, objectified, in the service of the subject's gratification.

Polymorphous perversion was first described by Freud (1916) as the expression of infantile sexuality that has not yet settled on its final object, or object choice; it is directed to a range of objects and reflects an undeveloped sexuality. Clearly, the aim of infantile sexuality is not reproductive intercourse: polymorphous perverse sexuality continues from infancy through to about the age of five, progressing through three distinct developmental stages: the oral, anal and phallic stages. Children's later development enables them to direct sexual drives in more socially accepted ways, culminating in adult heterosexual behaviour focused on the genitals and reproduction. According to Freud, during this stage of undifferentiated impulse for sexual pleasure, it is normal to experience both bisexual and incestuous urges. Contemporary psychoanalysts would no longer see heterosexuality as the ultimate goal of sexual development as, importantly, homosexuality is no longer considered to be a perversion.

The most obvious example of destructive perversion is sadism, in which aggressive impulses are enacted against another person, with enjoyment in cruelty and maltreatment. This form of perversion can be used defensively to enable someone who feels vulnerable to escape from awareness of unpleasant feelings of being helpless and humiliated. The other person will be hurt, sometimes to the point of real injury.

Many of the men and women I assess and treat in forensic services have histories of profound maltreatment and abuse in childhood, in which their ordinary needs for comfort and care were either ignored or met with contempt and brutality. Their sense of need is so profound and its consequences so disastrous that they develop a wide repertoire of defences against their own vulnerability, including violence, indifference and sadism. They turn their anger at their previous maltreatment back on themselves and subject their own bodies to acts of violence and ignore basic needs for self-care. Such self-inflicted violence can afford a perverse pleasure and sense of mastery as the body takes on the role of victim, subjected to acts of cruelty.

I will, in this chapter, explore how couples can be wedded in sadomasochistic practice and destructive relationships with addictive aspects. I consider the sense in which a retreat to perversions ('perverse safe havens') offers a defence against intimacy and relates to childhood trauma; the internal couple is a damaged and damaging one. The relationship between perversion and early trauma, including the addictive use of internet pornography, and elaborate sadomasochistic fantasies, has been explored by Wood (2013) and Kahr (2007) who describe how these apparent solutions to underlying difficulties actually prevent intimacy.

In discussing sadism and the roots of cruelty, I also identify the links between animal cruelty and exposure to domestic violence in childhood. I consider how cruelty to animals is a form of sadism, as there is almost always awareness of the pain and harm that is inflicted, and how this reflects the child's attempt to master trauma, and project pain into another creature more vulnerable than himself. Additionally, I discuss how animal cruelty and threats towards pets can also be part of an abuser's repertoire of tyranny and brutality in relation to his partner and family. This under-researched aspect of interpersonal violence reveals the sense in which helplessness, pain and threats of death are aspects of daily life within toxic partnerships. The abuse of animals reveals the aggressor's identification with the 'beast' within himself. I argue that evidence of animal cruelty in families should also be taken very seriously in terms of risk to children and vulnerable adults.

Perversion as the erotic form of hatred

Perverse behaviour allows people to project their own experience of childhood victimization onto someone else, whether a partner, a stranger or a child entrusted to their care. Such re-enactments may not take place at a conscious level, and they have important psychological functions.

In a psychoanalytic sense, 'perversion' is a term used not pejoratively but descriptively, referring to a particular kind of erotic activity that does not have as its aim genital sexuality, thereby avoiding the intimacy involved in full sexual intercourse. Analysts differ in their understanding of the defining characteristics of perversion. Stoller (1975: 4) describes it as an erotic form of hatred:

> Perversion, the erotic form of hatred, is a fantasy, usually acted out but occasionally restricted to a daydream (either self-produced or packaged by others, that is, pornography). It is a habitual, preferred aberration necessary for one's full satisfaction, primarily motivated by hostility. By 'hostility' I mean a state in which one wishes to harm an object; that differentiates it from 'aggression', which often implies only forcefulness.
>
> This hostility in perversions takes form in a fantasy of revenge hidden in the actions that make up the perversion and serves to convert childhood trauma to adult triumph. To create the greatest excitement, the perversion must also portray itself as an act of risk-taking.

Key characteristics of perversion include risk-taking, deceit, objectification of the victim, secrecy and ritualized behaviour. Perversions also appear to engulf the person who enacts them, providing the central meaning to their existence. They offer tremendous gratification. Stoller's notion of the 'hidden fantasy of revenge' is central to understanding the symbolic meaning of the perversion, and the sense in which it is a repetition of an earlier trauma 'converted to adult triumph' as the victim now becomes the perpetrator. This offers tremendous relief to the adult, but only temporarily. The euphoria soon fades, and the need to rehearse, and then repeat, the action returns.

People who attend for treatment of sexual perversions often appear wholly pre-occupied with them, as though there were nothing else of meaning or value in their lives. This indicates the extent to which perversions can mask an underlying emptiness and sense of flatness, or depression. For some, keeping the perverse behaviour secret, and employing elaborate strategies to preserve its existence, becomes a governing principle of life. Even when not enacted, their fantasies are their main source of comfort and control, keeping a pervasive sense of loneliness and emptiness at bay.

In couples where sadomasochism is practised, there can be apparent consent by one partner to the other's dominance (which may be physical or psychological), which actually masks an underlying sense of fear or intimidation. This dynamic was clearly seen in a couple I assessed for psychotherapy, and whom I will now discuss.

Clinical illustration: Apparent consent in a sadomasochistic relationship

John was the perpetrator of repeated acts of violence against his partner, Louisa, and numerous others, including strangers. His maternal uncle had sexually abused him since his early childhood and he now associated certain sexual acts, including oral sex, with force and violence. At the same time as he wanted to distance himself from traumatic memories of his own abuse, he could not escape the association between coercion and sexual excitement. He described how he and Louisa engaged in consensual sadomasochism, involving role-play and his domination and sadism towards her. Their daughter was sometimes present in the house when they engaged in violent encounters, and although he claimed that she was unaware of the violence characterizing their sex life, she disclosed that she had overheard some of it and had been worried about her mother's evident bruising. Her mother, Louisa, had a history of abuse in her own past and had difficulty in asserting herself. John maintained that she was a fully consensual participant.

This couple came into therapy because Louisa had become deeply distressed and frightened when the violence eventually got out of hand. She felt brutalized and unheard when she had told John 'no', and also discovered that her daughter had begun self-harming. At a certain point, she had made the link between the use of controlled aggression in their sex life, and the self-directed violence that their child was engaging in.

Louisa sought her own therapy, where she disclosed that she had been using these masochistic role-plays and painful sex practices as a form of self-harm, in a way she had not regretted until recently, when she felt that it was brutalizing her and that it also mirrored her daughter's wounds. She could see, as reflected in her child, that these bruises and cuts revealed a psychic difficulty that she needed to address, and that continuing to engage in the violence was not a solution. In fact, she felt that the ongoing sadomasochism was perpetuating a serious problem. At the same time, she felt loyal to John and guilty that she was now disengaging from their customary sexual relations.

While Louisa found the therapy helpful, and began to voice her increasing sense of discomfort and displeasure, John became destabilized, revealing the extent to which he was dependent on the perversion to maintain a sense of self-worth. He was deeply disturbed by the change in his relationship with Louisa, finding it almost impossible to function without this constant, exciting release of his aggression, and the sense of power and control it afforded him. He began to rely heavily on hard drugs and alcohol, appearing increasingly neglected and chaotic. Although he had initially engaged well in the therapy, and understood how his sense of distrust in his family of origin affected his capacity to relate to his partner as an equal, Louisa's newfound confidence in refusing sadistic practices profoundly frightened him. He became convinced that she would leave him and that she did not understand the 'playful' nature of his violence, making him furious and filled with an unwelcome sense of guilt that he could not bear. He then retreated from the therapeutic work, reverting to substances and alcohol to numb himself.

Some months after the relationship broke down, and he had returned to heavy use of illegal substances, he was arrested and sentenced for a serious assault on an elderly woman. He had attempted to burgle her house and then inflicted a severe series of injuries on her, though she did not resist his intrusion or try to stop him from taking her goods. The woman was simply present, vulnerable and a suitable victim for his sense of entitlement, rage and sadism. He denied any sexual arousal during the assault, but it is possible to consider his attack on her to be a substitute for his 'consensual' sadism with his sexual partner, who had ultimately rejected him. In this sense, this unknown, vulnerable stranger 'stood for' the woman who had humiliated him and in his wholly distorted and unfocused thinking, she had invited this attack. The court, unsurprisingly, gave him an extended prison sentence, taking into account his breach of probation orders, history of drug-related violent offending, and inability to engage reliably in therapeutic work.

Like military personnel who find their violence contained within the highly structured institution of the army, John was much better able to function within a custodial setting. Here, he was without freedom, without responsibility and without access to vulnerable females with whom he could enact his darkest and least-contained fantasies.

I learned from his probation officer that John was relieved when he was sentenced to a lengthy period in custody and had behaved compliantly and cooperatively with all aspects of prison regime. The point at which he had felt most 'available' in the therapy was when he had been relating to me the details of his abuse in his early life, and his anger and hurt about this, but this moment of therapeutic intimacy was short lived as he described not being able to manage the feelings it had awakened, and claimed that he had then found himself behaving more violently with his partner over the next week.

It became clear that the violence in his sexual relationship was protective in terms of his sense of being distant from memories of his own victimization, which he now projected onto his partner, who had herself been abused. It also served as a container for his aggression, defining and focusing his rage through a sexual channel. When this was no longer available, he began to act out violently in non-sexual ways, with strangers. Rather than face the meaning and origins of his violent impulses and destructive behaviour and learn to think about and contain it in the here and now, he chose to return to the 'dangerous safe haven' of drug abuse and violence and, ultimately, the strict external controls of the prison.

Louisa also seemed to be recreating an earlier pattern of self-destruction and humiliation. When she saw that her own daughter was developing overt self-harming behaviour she could no longer convince herself that she was occupying the realm of a safe fantasy world. This awareness was helpful both for her daughter and for Louisa herself, allowing them to discuss their fears, and to create distance from John, who was becoming less stable, and inflicting greater levels of injuries on her. Shortly before he was imprisoned, she found the courage to leave him, and the false security of their relationship.

The development of perversion

Attachment model: insecure attachment and intimate partner abuse

Attachment theory explains why the most apparently dysfunctional relationships may be hardest to break. I note its significance throughout this book. The destructive and distorted bonds between couples are perhaps most vividly illustrated in sadomasochistic relationships, whose sadism may eventually become uncontained and directed against others, including children in the family. For some, these relationships have become hells they wish to leave, but are unable to, as they are so frightened of the abuser; but, for others, there is a more active participation in the destructiveness that defines the relationship, and that is directed towards others.

Attachment theory was first developed by John Bowlby (1969) to explain why humans and other animals have particular, strong, bonds with others, and how, under certain conditions, these attachment systems can be affected adversely, with significant consequences for the individuals. He proposed that there was an innate motivational system to generate proximity to significant others that could be activated at times when separation was threatened. The kinds of activities that are found in such an attachment behavioural system include crying, clinging, protesting and seeking contact, and can clearly be seen in infants – both human and primates – at the point of separation. This has tremendous implications for children who are exposed to unreliable, abusive or absent caregivers, and for the nature of their later development and relationships with significant others.

Attachment theory has formed a central role in the understanding of how early relationships are instrumental in creating a blueprint for adult behaviour, and has been extended into sophisticated psycho-dynamically orientated therapeutic models including mentalization-based treatment (Bateman and Fonagy, 2004, 2010, 2012). It has particular relevance for understanding the toxic, symbiotic attachments that can be found in some violent partnerships and for helping violent individuals learn to reflect on and contain their impulses.

The attachment model can inform the psychoanalytic accounts, and vice versa, rather than the paradigms standing in opposition to each other. As early attachment patterns develop, the individual psyche incorporates particular types of object relationships that can be unconsciously instrumental in shaping choice: of partner, of parenting style, and of ways of relating to one's own dependence and vulnerability.

While the bonds of abusive relationships appear, on the face of it, to be the most destructive, in fact they may be the strongest. Bartholomew, Henderson and Dutton (2001) note in their study of attachment patterns in couples, over a two-year period:

> What became obvious, when the interviewers later compared notes, was that the most dysfunctional relationships were also the most stable . . . we became impressed by how particular forms of insecurity appeared to put individuals at risk of becoming involved in, and having difficulty leaving, problematic and even abusive relationships.

The authors then researched attachment and domestic abuse over a seven-year period and found similar patterns of stability, pointing to the tenacity of these bonds.

A psychoanalytic view of the development of sadomasochism

Grossman (1991) proposes three possible mechanisms responsible for the development of sadomasochistic practices:

1. As the child learns to express and regulate aggression, he develops psychic defences that contribute to the formation of his ego and superego.[1] It follows that a conflict related to aggression may distort this development and lead to repetitive aggressive behaviour.
2. Pain and painful affects are 'sources' of aggression. This raises complex issues about the relationship between aggression and drives.
3. The most relevant hypothesis for us, here, is the relationship between severe trauma and fantasy, in that such trauma can interfere with the development of the capacity to fantasize. Such fantasy can be transformative and thus diminish the impact of the traumatic experience.

Fantasy formation is an important and complex function that both contributes to and is dependent on ego integration. Severe trauma impairs the capacity for fantasy (Fish-Murray *et al.*, 1987), leading to a failure to transform the traumatic experience through mental activity. Instead, repetitive behaviour and intrusive imagery that repeat or attempt to undo the traumatic experience are possible consequences. . . . In addition, or alternatively, inhibitions, avoidances, and withdrawal may be attempts to avoid painful, repeated occurrences of a traumatic state.

(Grossman, 1991: 23)

If sadomasochism can best be understood as a solution to a relational difficulty of how to manage aggression in oneself and in intimate attachments, it is possible to understand how unconscious attempts to elicit harm to oneself serve an important psychological purpose. According to Grossman's conceptualization, sadomasochism is produced as a result of problems in the development and management of aggression in relation to psychosexual attachments and the development of psychic structures.

It was found that children who had been exposed to either physical or sexual abuse in early life, or those who were born prematurely and had been subjected to painful, if necessary, procedures, were found to evoke punitive responses in later life, and could be said to unconsciously provoke abuse. This statement is not a moral judgement and should not be taken to condone maltreatment towards those who suffered in early life, but adds further weight to the notion that such abuse is fundamentally damaging, in ways that extend beyond the flesh, into the psyche of such traumatized individuals. Grossman goes on to say that:

> In all of these cases, the traumatised children had also become, in some fashion, provokers of attacks on themselves and attackers of others. Some longitudinal studies correlating trauma in childhood with aggressive behaviour were also presented. The cases were dramatic and at times startling in their documentation of the fact that from early infancy on, there is a capacity to respond to traumatic treatment with destructive and self-destructive behaviour.
>
> (Grossman, 1991: 26)

He describes how the painful stimuli in childhood, and traumatic experiences with carers, can be turned into sources of pleasure as well as 'unpleasure', in an attempt to create some form of psychic equilibrium. As he develops, the individual establishes his adult identity as one that can manage and control his environment, in contrast to his earlier helplessness and vulnerability. The seeds of later sadomasochism are sown in early object relations. The constellations he describes are traumatic, and all demonstrate attempts to attach aggressive feelings to libidinal impulses and experiences, to defuse the horror and helplessness of earlier experiences.

> Pain and painful affect evoke aggression towards those people who are perceived as the perpetrators. To preserve the relationship, the expression of aggressive impulses directed against other people who are more powerful, gratifying or dangerous, threatening, and in control must be modified in some way. In some cases, sexual activity is utilised, as are other pleasurable experiences. Sometimes, the sexual activity itself may be a part of an enforced relationship, and its pleasurable quality may be ambiguous. In childhood, as well as in the traumatic situations of later life, pleasure–unpleasure fantasies become another vehicle for the management and channelling of aggression, leading to some familiar forms of sadomasochistic fantasies.
>
> (Grossman, 1991: 31)

This view is consistent with Stoller's (1975) and Glasser's (1979) conception of perversion as the sexualized form of aggression, containing within it unacceptable feelings of rage and hatred in disguised, eroticized form.

Violence as a psychic retreat: perverse safe havens

The use of violent and sexual perversions offers a fantasized solution to the terrors of intimacy. It creates a psychic retreat, as Steiner (1993) first defined, in which the person can feel secure, away from contact with frightening others, and in control. It functions as an internal pathological organization that defends against intimacy and enables its inhabitants to feel secure in the confines of their own minds, and well elaborated fantasies. I use the term 'perverse safe haven', first coined by an insightful and tormented man, Craig (discussed in further detail in Chapter 8), who was caught up in violent impulses he could neither fathom nor control. He agreed with my interpretation that these violent and sadistic sexual fantasies offered him a false sense of liveliness and escape. They offered a form of sanctuary where he felt safe.

The distinction between fantasies and action is crucial here, as Welldon (2002: 7) notes:

> When considering sexual sadism, it is important to notice the difference made between sadistic *fantasies* and sadistic *actions*. Perversions are defined predominantly as actions, rather than fantasies. In other words, anyone is 'allowed' to indulge into sexual fantasies of all sorts without the 'danger' of being categorized as a pervert.

Craig used his fantasies of sadistic violence and sexual violation to fend off feelings of depression, helplessness and emptiness. Just as the haven gave him a false sense of security and retreat, it also offered him a false liveliness, a manic defence against depression. According to Welldon (2008), perversion is a manic defence designed to protect against the deathliness of depression, involving ever-increasing attempts at escape. In this state, he was in omnipotent control, not helpless and scared, as he so often had been in childhood, witness to his father beating his mother and his siblings, and unable to find containment in the mind of his mentally ill mother. His underlying sense of shame motivated his sadistic fantasies; through these he could recover a sense of power and relieve his sense of humiliation and fear.

Implicit contracts in sadomasochistic relationships

Partners in sadomasochistic relationships make an implicit contract that one will be dominant, and another submissive, and that pain inflicted by one partner on another will be agreed to. There is an assumption of mutual consent. A psychoanalytic understanding of perversion is that it is a solution to the problem of intimacy, with its threats of obliteration for those individuals with a fragile sense of themselves, and an experience of overpowering or perverse mothering.

Glasser (1979) proposed the notion of the core complex, a constellation of defences that ensures that the individual will regulate levels of intimacy by establishing rigid controls over another, thus preventing either engulfment or abandonment, both of which are psychic terrors feared in equal measure. The person who has been treated as an object by their primary caretaker (often the mother) struggles in his adult sexuality to maintain a balance between preserving his own boundaries and a wish for fusion, which has an implicit threat of engulfment. The wish for a merger with an ideal object lends itself to the fear of being swallowed up and lost, and so the compromise is to develop strict control over the object, or other person, enabling the individual to feel safe in his desire without either being engulfed or abandoned. Sadomasochism is one such perverse solution to these terrors.

Vulnerable groups

There are particular groups who are especially vulnerable to abuse and exploitation, and whose need for care and affection makes them prey to others who seek to control, intimidate and harm them. While many of the men and women discussed in this book so far have histories that create vulnerability in terms of disorganized attachment and low self-esteem that sow the seeds of violent relationships, there are particular individual characteristics that further exacerbate risk. Some people with learning disabilities, for example, and severe mental health difficulties, as well as people with physical disabilities, may be especially reliant on their partners, or less able to access services that could assist them. There are predatory and antisocial individuals who consciously target these vulnerable groups and exploit them financially, as well as emotionally. This can take the form of verbal and physical threats and actual violence, as well as the use of strict and illegal controls over finances and their partner's movements. This is akin to the kind of exploitation and control that pimps can exert over women and men they 'run' in sex work. The case of Vanessa, in Chapter 3, is an illustration of how a woman with a physical disability seemed to be drawn to violent men, who apparently offered protection and care, and then, when involved with them, was both psychically and physically impaired in terms of leaving the relationship. Her physical vulnerability placed her at particular risk, as well as having some impact on her conception of herself and her own sexuality.

Father–daughter incest and damaged offspring

I include incestuous relationships in this discussion, as I consider incest to be a form of psychic violence against the person, even in those cases where it has not involved physical aggression. I argue that the couple that is created through this situation is a 'toxic' one, in that there is little opportunity for growth and development for the victims of incest so long as they remain in this restrictive, distorting and perverse relationship.

I have worked with survivors of incestuous relationships on ameliorating the impact of their abuse, particularly in terms of their deep fear of intimacy. The fundamental abuse of trust and vulnerability has lifelong consequences. The impact of parental incest on a child is profound and can leave victims with a distorted sense of their own complicity or culpability, as they feel they could – and should – have stopped this relationship. The guilt that arises from any pleasure in the relationship due to the sense of having been chosen, and the gifts and special attention that can accompany the incest, is profound. This guilt is deeply painful to address. Additionally, to the extent that all children may have unconscious wishes to be the partner of their opposite-sex parent, when this becomes a reality, it leaves children in a desperate state of confusion and anxiety, as they may believe that they have somehow willed this relationship into existence.

It is essential for the ordinary and healthy growth of children that Oedipal wishes are not enacted, that the parental couple remains intact and that the child is enabled to develop a sense of the crucial distinction between fantasy and reality. Children need to be able to engage in innocent fantasies of marrying their father or mother without actually finding themselves in sexual contact with this parent. The sexual impulses that underlie such fantasies need to be kept in the realm of the imaginary if development is to progress normally. When the incest taboo has been violated, it not only leaves children unable to trust their own fantasy life and the power of their own wishes, but the sense of betrayal of the same-sex parent is highly disturbing, leaving children with conflicting feelings of shame, triumph, anger and sadness, as they have taken the place of their non-abusive parent. This can feed into their wish for punishment. They may also feel anger at this parent's failure to protect them from incest or even, in some cases, for 'turning a blind eye' to the abuse.

In cases of sibling incest, essential boundaries are also crossed, and parents or caregivers may be blamed for their failure to protect the children in the household. Such couplings occur in situations of neglect, trauma, or where high levels of sexual abuse exist in the household and where children are sometimes encouraged or forced into sexual activity with one another. Although such relationships can sometimes be romanticized (see Ian McEwan's (1978) *The Cement Garden*), they are destructive and confusing.

The offspring of incestuous relationships, if there is a pregnancy, can catalyse discovery of the sexual relationship and can serve as physical evidence of the damage that such couplings create, as these children often have congenital difficulties. The children also provide incontrovertible evidence of the incest, as their DNA reveals the true status of parents, as the clinical material below illustrates.

Clinical illustration: Claudia: incest and incestuous offspring

Claudia was 24 when she was referred to me for help with recurrent depression and complicated, unresolved grief reaction following the loss of her two children, her four-year-old son Marley and ten-month-old daughter Joy, into care, and their subsequent adoption.

On first meeting, she appeared lively, attractive and insightful, but had recently made a serious suicide attempt. She had been reunited with her birth father at the age of 19. Claudia described how she had sought out her father to ask him to help look after her younger brother, Elliott. She had had no contact with her father between the ages of two and 19, but had wanted to find him in order to request that he be assessed as a carer for Elliott, who was 12 and had special needs. She was just 19 when she made this request. Her mother was a heavy drug-user, and was clearly unable to look after him. At the time, Claudia was in a relationship with a known drug-user, and her own lifestyle was considered to be unsafe for Elliott, though she often looked after him.

While lodging with her father, she entered into an incestuous relationship with him that resulted in the births of her children. Genetic tests confirmed that both children had a rare life-threatening genetic illness, which meant they could not produce critical hormones and that they required medication of hydrocortisone daily. Through genetic sampling of the DNA of both children, it was discovered that they had the same disorder. This was an extremely rare strain of the mutation and, as a result, expert opinion was obtained indicating that it was impossible for the birth parents not to be related, and that it was considerably more likely that their father was either the same individual or that both fathers were related to each other and to Claudia herself.

Further DNA evidence confirmed that Claudia's own father was, in fact, the biological father of both children. The health visitor was concerned about the care Claudia had given Marley and Joy, who appeared dirty and unkempt and were admitted to hospital for failure to thrive in infancy, both times apparently as a result of the condition, which was undiagnosed at that point. Social services became involved in the case after these admissions: Claudia conceded that once Joy's condition had been diagnosed she did not administer medication to her for a four-month period as advised. At no point did she seek medical advice. Marley had suffered non-accidental injuries while in the care of his putative father. Claudia did not engage with the local authority, but moved the children to stay with their maternal aunt and uncle, who eventually agreed to foster them.

There were serious family concerns: that she was vulnerable to forming inappropriate relationships with abusive partners; that her mother misused drugs; and that during Claudia's pregnancy with Marley, she allowed her mother and her mother's partner (who used crack cocaine and heroin) to stay with her. Her mother had been a drug user and allowed people using hard drugs, including heroin and crack cocaine, to do so in their house until she, at the age of 12, had requested that the police come and raid the house as she wanted her mother to stop taking drugs. A female police officer had tried to get her mother into a detoxification programme, but after a brief period of engagement, her mother had stopped attending this.

Claudia herself had a long history of drug and alcohol misuse and eating disorders. She had long maintained that her son Marley had been conceived when she was raped by her boyfriend at the time. Social services had been aware of her as a child at risk, and became involved in her pregnancies, as she was considered to be highly vulnerable to abusive relationships. The central concern was that she would be unable to protect either herself or her children from physical harm.

At the initial meeting for assessment, I asked Claudia about her father. Her mood seemed to fluctuate dramatically when discussing this, and she went from being quite giggly to becoming significantly more guarded and looked dark. She described her father as being 'a knob' and said that at first he had been 'a carer' to the children. She went on to explain that they had pleaded guilty for having an incestuous relationship that had produced her children. Shockingly to me, she had been charged for the crime of incest as she was over 18 at the time of their sexual relationship. She had conceded to plead guilty to this rather than go through with any other form of criminal proceedings against her father.

When I asked about her decision to seek out her biological father, Claudia said that if she had known then what she knows now, she would 'not have bothered'. There was a clear repetition of her own childhood, in which her mother had not been able to protect her: she had been sexually abused by her mother's partner – her stepfather (who was now dead) – from the age of five. Claudia described activities that appeared to be of a more widespread paedophilic activity in the household, including tapes of children engaged in sexual activity, close association between her stepfather and other men with paedophilia tendencies, and various forms of sexual abuse, although she stated that this was not in the form of penetrative intercourse. She had grown up in an abusive and neglectful household, in which the children were exploited regularly, or left for long periods of time to fend for themselves

Poignantly, Claudia was able to reflect on her childhood as being one of great neglect, as well as emotional, physical and sexual abuse, during which she had not felt she had any safe or secure attachment figure to turn to for protection and comfort. She had told a school friend about the abuse, and this friend had then told her mother who informed social services. She was taken into foster care, but ran away repeatedly to return home; she said she was too worried about the welfare of her younger brother, who was still at home, to stay away. Her childhood was highly disruptive and traumatic and the local authority's brief intervention had not been effective.

While Claudia was serious when relating these facts, and conveyed a sense of anger and distress, she also made it clear that she did not want to think too much about the emotional impact these experiences had on her, and tended to dismiss various members of her family by saying 'She's just a knob' or 'He's a knob', in a defensive way. Claudia has a history of violent offences, and during the interview repeatedly described 'pasting' other people or 'going mental', revealing that her main outlet for emotional expression was aggression.

During this initial assessment interview, it became clear that Claudia's traumatization was so severe that she could not make the links between her experience and its impact on her current and future life, because it was too overwhelming for her to process. She had dissociated from the trauma as a way of protecting herself from emotional overload. Her history had been characterized by such severe abuse and neglect that it was difficult for her to know what a non-abusive style of parenting and/or relating could be like.

Claudia put me in mind of a quick-moving, lively young animal, darting through the building and, even, in our meetings, moving into and out of focus as if hiding. Her manner was so lively and engaged that it seemed to seduce me out of pursuing her underlying terror and hurt. When, at our second session, her mask slipped, she felt much less flighty and elusive, and more of a substantial presence in the room.

It was clear that throughout her early life she had retained a vulnerability and sweetness, underneath a feral exterior, and older adults often felt protective of her. This was still evident in the meeting with me, and she was very appealing, with an air of innocence and fragility that evoked caring responses. A family friend had wanted to privately adopt her and had looked after her for a year when Claudia was aged 15–16. Claudia described her as one of the people who had tried to help her and who had even made her an appointment at a local young person's centre that would offer her support and help. However, Claudia said she didn't like this centre and knew that this foster-carer 'couldn't cope', saying 'She kicked me out the day before my sixteenth birthday'. Further exploration revealed that she had, unconsciously, set up this rejection, perhaps as a way of controlling the abandonment she anticipated, by bringing a group of drunk and aggressive older teenagers into the home without the foster-carer's permission.

A consistent theme in Claudia's account of her early life was her desire to protect and care for her siblings, including her brother Elliott. On one occasion, she describes how one of her mother's partner's children had kicked Elliott, and so she 'went mental, I hit back at her because she hurt Elliott'. It seemed that aggression, which she described mainly in terms of protecting other people, was one of her main ways of asserting herself and obtaining some justice in a world that had treated her and her siblings harshly. She was ruthless in her defence of her sisters and brothers, using any means necessary to protect them. Claudia described how her biological father had constantly controlled her behaviour and threatened to beat her half-brother Lewis with a belt if she didn't do what he said. This was a weapon against her that she couldn't bear and, thus, was a powerful tactic. Although she was not able to protect her own body, she was devoted to her brother and couldn't stand to see him beaten.

She described how subservient her role in her father's household was; after moving in with him at 19, she was treated as a servant to him and carer for his children with his new partner. She was made to look after her three half-siblings, given very little freedom and threatened, both physically and verbally, if she wanted to venture out on her own. Once, when she had wanted to go out rather than babysit for her three half-siblings, her father had slammed her head into the wall. Although she had called the police for help, when they arrived at the door she had not answered, fearing the consequences of pressing charges against the man she so needed, and feared. The children had witnessed this and were terrified, as their father's rages were fierce and unpredictable.

As Dutton (2007) describes, two possible responses to aggression are to either become angry oneself, or to withdraw; to go into a kind of escape/withdrawal mode, especially if the violence is seen as uncontrollable. In his frightening display of violence, her father revealed his need to control her behaviour to the extent that she was not allowed out. His rage could be understood as a response to an attachment disruption, when she expressed the simple wish to go outside the home, to see others. He viewed this as a betrayal, and became fiercely possessive and jealous of her in a typical pattern displayed by violent men. Claudia, like Elizabeth Fritzl described in Chapter 1, was doubly 'owned' by her father: as his daughter and as his sexual partner. He felt he had the 'right' to possess her sexually, emotionally and bodily. Furthermore, she then related to her own body, and the bodies of her damaged babies, as objects, possessed by others, rather than subjective creatures in their own right.

There was a paradox evident in her presentation: she was so hurt that she blocked off awareness of her abuse, and its damage, appearing psychically protected from it through a high level of denial. She spoke of her tremendous sense of attraction to her father when she first reconnected with him, and the sense that he fully understood and cared for her. She had consciously lied about their relationship and passed over opportunities to reveal the truth and end their partnership, despite his cruelty and despite his ongoing relationship with his own partner.

Claudia's relationship with him could be seen as a form of 'Stockholm syndrome' in which she had idealized and fallen in love with her own abuser, the father who virtually held her hostage. In one way, she seemed to be too traumatized to know that she had undergone severe abuse and betrayal. This was most evident when discussing her relationship with her father, where her limited understanding of the seriousness of the implications of an incestuous relationship, and the consequences for Marley and Joy, was striking. Despite her usual concern and protectiveness, she seemed unaware of the harm they had already suffered. She had normalized events and experiences that were highly unusual and disturbing. When she had to face the pain of what she had done to her children, through her sexual relationship with her own father, she seemed to cope through a form of denial and dissociation. Her children had been removed from her care, and while she missed them terribly, she could understand why this decision had been made. It was clear that she had not been able to relate to them as fully separate individuals, with needs and vulnerabilities of their own.

Due to her personal strengths and some aspects of her early attachment that had, remarkably, remained intact, Claudia was able to engage in the psychotherapeutic work I offered her. She had the desire, intelligence and insight to reflect on her own unconscious processes, including the sense in which she had convinced herself she had sought her father out to take on more care and responsibility for her younger brother (also his natural child), but actually longed for contact herself. This contact soon turned sexual, and she described the intense attraction between them. She was fundamentally confused about the difference between sexual and affectionate feelings between parents and their children. She had sexual relations with him in the presence of his partner, with whom he still cohabited, who was the mother of his other children. Claudia had lived with him as both a daughter and sexual partner, and their behaviour was not secretive. It seemed that her own early experience of extreme abuse was continuing to be enacted with her father, not only in terms of incest, but also in relation to exhibitionism and a compulsive aspect. It was not clear to what extent she was coerced into this behaviour, as her father was so controlling and violent, and to what degree it was freely chosen. She felt that at some level she wanted to be caught, punished and prevented from continuing this relationship. Despite the tremendous sense of guilt she described for having conceived damaged and ill babies with her own father, she gradually began to realize that she had been exploited and intimidated by him. She saw that she had been disabled by the severe abuse and sexual perversion to which she had been subjected in early life. Not only was she able to accept her own responsibility and agency in her actions, but she was also able to mourn the loss of her children, and her own wishes for a reconciliation with a loving father (the idealized father in her mind, in contrast to the exploitative and predatory man who had violently abused her), without becoming suicidal.

She was able to return to education and develop her considerable intellectual resources as a young person, rather than an adult partner to her own parent, or a teenage mother. She was able to keep her distance from her mother and father, while continuing to maintain a relationship with two of her siblings, both of whom seemed able to have formed reasonable relationships with partners. Although she felt despairing at times, and found it hard to manage the weight of some of her worst memories, she was able to use the sessions and the containment of her educational course to enable her to resist suicidal thoughts and fantasies.

We worked together for over two years, during the course of which she formed a relationship with a man who, though he was ten years her senior, did not seem to be in any way violent, sexually perverse or sadistic. Although she sometimes felt hopeless, suicidal and overwhelmed, she was able to put these feelings into words in the sessions and continued to reliably visit her two disabled children, and to show them real warmth.

Clinical illustration: discussion

The kind of 'domestic holocaust' that Claudia experienced is one that Welldon (2012) describes, where couples caught up in malignant bonding use tapes and recordings of their abused children as homemade pornography.

The impact of growing up with drug users as parents is significant. Foster (2013) and Youell (2013) describe this beautifully in terms of how these children are unable to use their mothers as requisite containers for their toxic affects. This container/contained relationship is reversed, with the child attempting to act as parent, and eventually becoming overwhelmed by the impossibility of this task. In Claudia's case, her exploitation by multiple adults was deeply traumatic and she seemed to cope through dissociation. Foster (2013) describes the kind of object-relating in the children of female drug addicts in terms of secondary deprivation, with the response of the care system and therapeutic services representing yet a third deprivation as the mother, and children, are once again rejected and 'unheld'.

Despite the horror of her childhood abuses and her incestuous relationship with her father in early adulthood, Claudia was able to recover healthy aspects of herself that seemed to preserve her life force.

It was difficult to believe that someone so grossly abused could be resilient. Indeed, she had been charged with a criminal offence for engaging in incest, and also lost two children into care, but she nonetheless had some inner strengths and resources that sustained her. Her attachment to a maternal aunt, who lived in a nearby city, and had not participated in any abusive activities, was strong. She had turned to her at times of crisis, although she had not confided in her when she sought out her biological father, knowing she would disapprove. This may have been one of the most significant relationships in her life; it seemed that this positive experience of a caring and reliable adult gave her some sense of hope in the external world, and in her own capacity to give and receive care.

Animal cruelty, intimate partner violence and sadism

The strong association between childhood disturbance, particularly conduct disorder, arson and cruelty to animals, has been documented in the psychiatric literature; these characteristics are also risk factors for the development of psychopathic or antisocial personality disorder in adulthood. The sadistic use of animals parallels the sadistic use of human beings.

The need to understand the role violence may play in animal cruelty in childhood has been emphasized by reports that animal cruelty is a serious risk-marker for mental health problems. The *Diagnostic and Statistical Manual of Mental Disorders Fourth Edition* (DSM-IV) (revised) cites animal cruelty as one of the earliest and most severe symptoms of conduct disorder (American Psychiatric Association, 2012). Many studies have also found an alarming connection between animal cruelty by children, and violence in adolescence and adulthood (Merez-Perez, Heide and Silverman, 2001; Slavkin, 2001; Verlinden, 1999). This is even more important when such treatment is outside socially sanctioned treatment of animals; for example, cruelty to pets, such as cats and dogs, has been retrospectively linked to criminal violence for both male and female prison populations (Felthous and Yudowitz, 1977) and criminal behaviour in general (Ascione, Kaufmann and Brooks, 2000). It is worth noting, however, that in this study, the majority of exposed children were not cruel to animals, and it may be that it is the most disturbed and vulnerable children who act out in this way.

Animal cruelty by children is correlated with exposure to domestic violence. In her Canadian study of the children of 47 mothers with two children and histories of domestic violence, compared to 47 mothers with two children with no history of domestic violence, Currie (2006) found that children exposed to domestic violence were significantly more likely to have been cruel to animals than children not exposed to violence. Furthermore, children who had been exposed to domestic violence between their parents and who were cruel to animals, were more likely to feel jealous, unloved and fear animals compared to children who were similarly exposed to intimate partner violence, but who were not cruel to animals. These children viewed their environment as more threatening and unpredictable than other exposed children, and reacted to animals as though they were threats. In analytic terms, one can see this act of cruelty as reflecting what Anna Freud termed 'identification with the aggressor'. It seems that these children were taking out their desire for revenge on these animals, rather than communicating their feelings of helplessness through other means. In another sense, the children were re-enacting with the animals what they had seen between their parents (analogous to the Edlington children described in Chapter 1).

Clinical illustration: Jodie

At the age of four, after suffering a serious non-accidental injury to her arm, and a series of other less serious injuries, Jodie was taken into care and placed in a loving foster home. Her two older siblings were also taken into care, but they were placed together; she was considered too vulnerable and developmentally delayed to be placed with them, as they had both been seriously sexually abused and displayed highly disturbed behaviour, including aggression and disinhibited sexual play. It was thought that Jodie had also been sexually abused, as a baby, but as she still had very little speech it was difficult to determine the truth of this. At this placement, she secretly inserted pens in the anus of the family dog. The bleeding caused him pain and required veterinary intervention. Eventually, the dog was put down; his death contributed to the acutely traumatic quality of the situation and Jodie never confessed to her behaviour. It seemed likely that Jodie's sense of shame and embarrassment stopped her from confessing.

What appeared more concerning is not that she may have re-enacted her own experiences of penetration by a more powerful person than her, using a vulnerable animal, but that she did not respond to the animal's cries and evidence of pain. Again, this would have mirrored her own experience of abuse, where her own pain and distress would have been ignored, and her body used for the gratification of others. Nonetheless, her preoccupation with the dog indicates that she was primarily concerned with asserting a degree of power and control over a helpless creature, when she felt quite helpless herself. In some ways, she clearly identified with this wounded animal. Her sexual behaviour in childhood appeared to have a compulsive quality, not only in relation to the dog, but also in terms of reported masturbation to the extent that she made herself bleed; this appeared to me to indicate that her sexual behaviour was a sign of real disturbance in her and had come to assume a central role in offering her a sense of comfort and control. It was clearly a problematic area (in terms of her being able to behave in socially appropriate ways) and indicated her early abusive sexualization.

I also considered it possible that she may have been jealous of the dog, which captured her foster-carer's affections, but she was not able to articulate and explore these possibilities in interview, either appearing to want to deny the whole issue, or genuinely failing to remember the details. I note that her foster-mother, remarkably, appeared to have understood and forgiven the animal abuse, despite her understandable distress, and to have a genuine love for Jodie.

Research indicates that a history of animal cruelty in childhood is significantly associated with antisocial personality disorder, antisocial personality traits, and polysubstance abuse in adulthood.

The literature clearly indicates an association between exposure to intimate partner violence and childhood disturbances, including wilful cruelty to animals, which can be indicative of a sadistic state of mind, or a failure to empathize with the suffering of others. In intimate partner violence, such cruelty to pets, and other companion animals, can play a part in the sadistic and controlling treatment by one partner to another. Threatening or actually hurting a beloved animal can be a weapon used to terrorize the abused partner, and may also traumatize children who witness this.

In several cases of intimate partner violence, I have learned of beloved dogs, cats, rabbits and other pets being kicked, killed, drowned or shot, often in front of the pleading partner and/or children. The symbolic force of this act is evident, as the aggressor demonstrates not only that he has the power to kill or torture these animals, but also that he could turn that destructive force onto others. The children and partner feel helpless and despairing as they are made to witness this. If the animal is harmed or even killed, they are left not only bereft of their pets, but also guilty of not being able to protect them. The aggressor in these circumstances will not necessarily be in a rage, but can be cool and calculated as he exacts sadistic revenge on those he feels have wronged him. In cases of extreme sexual perversion, partners and children are also made to act as animals or to perform sexually with animals. It is difficult to imagine the depravity of such perversion and the tremendous damage that is done to adult and child victims through forced participation in such activity.

Through over 24 years of work in forensic clinical settings, I have encountered the use and abuse of animals in the brutal treatment of children and adults, with long-lasting consequences. The countertransference to hearing about such events and experiences is powerful and can leave me feeling literally knocked out, and sick to my stomach. It is difficult not to identify with the battered child or maltreated animal oneself. The tales of cruelty evoke feelings of abject helplessness and a strong wish to escape. It is possible that the childhood histories of so many forensic patients remain unknown to the staff who work with them on a daily basis, because they contain narratives of horrific cruelty and sadism; the unconscious wish of those who work with them is to remain unaware of these details. Their difficulty in hearing about such events and processing them is only a tiny fraction of the pain that these patients have experienced. It is easier to view these individuals as simply perpetrators and forensic patients than as the traumatized children they were, frequently exposed to scenes of cruelty and sadism.

The level of damage that exposure to this cruelty can do is difficult to estimate, but, given that many of the clients have come from situations of deprivation and neglect, the role that their pets played in their lives as attachment objects is often underestimated. They recall that being made to witness pets being hurt by their parents or step-parents was a terrible experience that reflected their own helpless pain and mute anger. They were not allowed to feel secure in their love for their pets, just as their own attachment to their parents or caregivers was also fragile and insecure. At some level, they feel that the animal represents them. Their own ordinary affection and childish needs could not be tolerated. It is clear that their own vulnerability and dependence were not ordinary aspects of their childhood that could be respected and protected, but were signs of weakness that offered opportunities for exploitation and abuse.

Even where the non-abusive parent wishes to protect the animal, but fails to, the child is still damaged. She is exposed to the fact of one adult's brutality, and another's impotence. This can mirror just how the child feels when she is unable to prevent her mother from being hurt by their father, or vice versa. Her anger at the non-abusive parent can be intense and can leave her feeling guilty and confused.

To deal with these unacceptable feelings of anger at a weak and helpless parent, or a clearly brutal and abusive one, the child turns their rage back on themselves and accepts the view that she is bad, and therefore to blame for this harm. She feels it is her fault that the pet has been hurt; either because she failed to protect the pet or because she behaved badly and deserved punishment, which was then meted out on a beloved pet. This is similar to abusive partners who hurt children as a way of punishing their partners, as this has a force and horror that is arguably worse than direct abuse.

The primitive nature of this brutality, and the sadism it implies, is indicative of the level of functioning employed by the violent partner, which is in the realm of id rather than ego or superego functioning. The id, as the seat of unconscious sexual and aggressive impulses, is in charge in this act of brutality. The usual mediation by the conscious part of the self (ego) with its internalized set of social and moral rules (superego) has been suspended. I consider this type of savage violence that accompanies a mindless state to reflect an animalistic level of functioning – without empathy, compassion or humanity.

The patient I describe in Chapter 8, Craig, is a man with a long history of neglect and abuse in childhood, including exposure to extreme violence by his father towards his mother. He had tried to intervene to stop his father beating her, but had got hurt instead. His only stable relationships were between his younger siblings and himself, as he took on the protective parental role for them during long periods of neglect while his mother was incarcerated in a psychiatric hospital and his father worked away from home. He lived in fear of abandonment but had little capacity to tolerate emotional intimacy, keeping his family under strict control to ensure that they didn't leave him, but finding it impossible to relate to them in an affectionate way unless he was high on drugs.

Craig habitually retreated into a perverse safe haven of sadistic sexual fantasies. When his anger burst forth, often in the context of heavy alcohol use, he would use dog leads, chains and belts on his partner, subjecting her to shocking scenes of brutality and humiliation, and even threatening her life. His children were aware of this, and on at least two occasions his wife left him, along with them, only to return in response to his suicide threats. His wife was threatened and hurt by the instruments he used for his aggressive dog. This dog seemed to embody Craig's inner sense of confusion and conflict – a creature that was alternatively neglected, maltreated, and then shown love and affection. He could also be seen as a guard dog, stopping the family from leaving him. This mirrored his own conflicted, untrustworthy and volatile sense of himself and relationships with others. His treatment of the dog revealed his early object relations: how he had been treated and how he subsequently treated others. The dog was left alone for hours each day in the yard, and clearly also served as a guard dog, perhaps to keep the family closely protected, or, alternatively, preventing them from leaving him. Craig had some capacity for concern and care, although this was heavily distorted and inconsistent, again reflecting his earlier experiences of inconsistent parenting. He had some affection for his helpless mother, though he also hated her because she was unavailable to him, instead preoccupied by her own frightening internal state.

Dehumanization of others: animals as a metaphor

Feminists have argued that the use of slang terms for women including 'dog' and 'bitch' also speaks to the dehumanization of women, and that violence follows gender lines that transcend biological sex. That is, intimate partner violence is gendered such that all violence is male, and the recipient of this abuse is female, regardless of their biological sex (Mackinnon, 1987). Studies have looked at the experiences of battered women, abused children and their pets, in relation to abuse by their violent partners, and found that abuse of their pets (or threats to do so) were a common part of the repertoire of techniques used to exert terror and control in the household. This is now considered one of the markers for an abusive relationship, and a sign of the degree of control and brutality that defines 'intimate terrorism' (Johnson, 1995, 2006). Symbolically, this violence is an attack on vulnerability, and represents the domination of helpless creatures for the gratification of the abuser; this is an act of sadism and points to the abuser's own terror of helplessness and weakness in himself, as well as his capacity to take pleasure in the suffering of others.

Recent studies have identified cruelty to animals not only as a risk factor for later violence, but also as indicative of child abuse.

Finally, it is possible that considering the treatment of animals within households would aid risk assessments in child protection enquiries. A recent study of child protection investigations in Canada suggests that observation of the conditions of household pets, and routine questions about the treatment of animals, can be a useful guide to the presence of family disturbance: 'The results suggest that child protection workers (CPWs) should consider routinely asking children and caregivers questions about animal cruelty and observe the behaviour and living conditions of family pets when conducting risk assessments' (Girardi and Pozzulo, 2012). Through sensitive and thorough exploration of the treatment of all creatures within a household, human or animal, it is possible to glean a rich sense of the degree of brutality and sadism that operates within the home.

In this chapter, I have explored how perverse relationships develop between partners, and how they are maintained, sometimes through unconscious 'contracts' that operate within couples. I have also outlined how early experiences of incest and physical violation can distort an individual's sense of herself and her capacity to form secure attachments to others, to the extent that sadomasochistic or incestuous relationships appear to be acceptable, or even desirable. In two of the clinical illustrations presented, I described how there is a 'breaking point', where the person engaged in the more helpless, masochistic role attempts to escape from the destructive partnership, finally recognizing that the level of harm is too much to bear. Treatment for people involved in perverse relationships is complex, but can offer an opportunity for reflection, and the development of another kind of relating, in which their own subjectivity is respected and supported.

5   Murder in the family

Murder occurs concretely in most cases when it has been committed many times previously in daydreams, nightmares and sometimes in unconscious fantasy. Before the deed, conscious and unconscious efforts, such as psychosis and sado-masochism, are designed and devoted to keeping the murder encapsulation from action.

(Doctor, 2013)

Parents who kill

It is a shocking fact that the group most at risk of homicide in the United States and United Kingdom are children under the age of one year old.[1] The criminological data supporting this chilling finding do not even account for the murders that are most difficult to detect – neonaticides or infanticides – as these may never even come to light. Infanticide is a crime that refers to the killing of an infant by his mother within the first year of life. For some mothers, this type of killing is the outcome of a secret, hidden pregnancy and birth, in a situation where bringing a baby into the world will lead to shame and rejection. Here, the very first dyad, the mother–baby unit, is a toxic one, with fatal results. I will explore infanticide and neonaticide in this chapter, and then explore other forms of filicide, the killing of children by their parents, including those committed by, and within couples. Doctor (2013) describes how such killings can be seen as the products of fantasy that have, until that moment, been resisted.

How common are child murders?

Yarwood (2004) looked at cases of child homicides from six countries: England, Wales, Scotland, Canada, the USA and Australia. He found that:

[Over] the 12-year period 1992 to 2002/03, an average of 78 children per year aged under 16 years were victims of homicide in England and Wales representing an average of 11.5 per cent per year of all homicides. The numbers of child homicides per year ranged from 64 to 99, corresponding to 7.8 per cent to 13.7 per cent of all homicides respectively.

These totals did not include cot deaths (SIDS; sudden infant death syndrome) unless homicide had been suspected. It has, however, been suggested that up to one in ten of such deaths could actually be cases of murder or neglect (Foundation for the Study of Infant Deaths, 2004)[2] or so-called covert homicides. A study of sudden unexpected deaths in infancy found that 4.6 per cent of the total sudden deaths of infants investigated were thought to be due to non-accidental injury. In the infants whose deaths were classified as sudden infant death syndrome, maltreatment – through acts of commission or omission – was thought to be a contributory factor in a further 4.8 per cent of the deaths, pointing to the potential within families for causing fatal harm to the most vulnerable (Fleming *et al.*, 2004).

Research has established that the global rate of child homicide is 1.92 for girl victims and 2.93 for boy victims in the age group 0–17 years, per 100,000 inhabitants. Although considered rare, researchers believe this may be the most under-reported form of homicide. Kauppi *et al.* (2010: 229) conducted a major retrospective study to illustrate the differences in maternal and paternal filicides in Finland during a 25-year period:

> In the sample of 200 filicides [neonaticides (n = 56), filicide-suicides (n = 75), other filicides (n = 69)], the incidence was 5.09 deaths per 100,000 live births: 59 percent of filicides were committed by mothers, 39 percent by fathers, and 2 percent by stepfathers. The mean age of the maternal victims (1.6 y) was significantly lower than that of the paternal victims (5.6 y).

The rate of five homicides per 100,000 inhabitants, is substantially higher than official statistics; this points to the covert nature of filicide. Indeed, neonaticide (murder of a newborn within 24 hours of birth) may be one of the least reported crimes, often taking place following a concealed pregnancy, and committed by a young woman whose family would not tolerate the shame of her unwed childbirth. This will be explored further in this chapter.

A recent review of retrospective studies of maternal filicide and neonaticide conducted by Hatters Friedman *et al.* (2005) in 39 industrialized countries, identified that among children under age 5 years who were murdered in the last quarter of the twentieth century, 61 per cent were killed by their own parents, 30 per cent were killed by their mothers, and 31 per cent by their fathers. They found that the characteristics of perpetrators varied greatly depending upon the sample studied; for example, if the sample of women came from the criminal justice system or a psychiatric population. Neonaticide was often committed by young, poor, unmarried women with little or no pre-natal care. Given the rising incidence of filicide, the authors stress the need to identify risk factors for this tragic crime. Clusters of significant risk factors for filicide include: demographic factors, social milieu, psychiatric history, victim characteristics, specific situational factors, prior family conflict and violence, and a history of contact with social service agencies.

Yarwood (2004) identifies the following key features of child homicides:

- most children killed are under the age of five or six;
- infants under one year old are at highest risk of homicide;

- boys are generally at slightly more risk than girls;
- child homicide victims account for 8–14 per cent of all homicide victims;
- a parent is the principal suspect/perpetrator in 50–70 per cent of all child homicides;
- fathers are responsible for about two-thirds of child homicides and mothers approximately one-third;
- biological fathers are responsible for approximately 55 per cent of murders of their own offspring and biological mothers about 45 per cent;
- mothers are responsible for the majority of infant deaths (infanticides);
- children under one year old are especially vulnerable to physical assault.

Yarwood notes the role played by mental illness in child deaths, as a significant proportion of parents who kill their children do so in the context of psychosis, including being under the delusion that they are behaving altruistically. A substantial number of filicides occur following parental separation. The fathers are predominantly the perpetrators of these filicides and a significant number of them then commit suicide. Of those who do not kill themselves after the homicides, a significant proportion will require psychiatric services.

Lethal violence

The seriousness of domestic violence cannot be underestimated. In a significant number of cases, the perpetrator actually kills their partner. This can follow a long period of tyranny in which the woman was terrified she would be killed. Her partner will often have used threats of death to terrify and control her, evoking the words of T.S. Eliot in *The Wasteland*: 'I will show you fear in a handful of dust'. In a minority of cases, the 'battered woman' kills her violent partner, but the vast majority of perpetrators are men, who assault and murder their female partners. In this chapter, I will discuss these homicides; I have elsewhere described the motivations of battered women who kill (Motz, 2008).

According to the Supplemental Homicide Records (SHR; NJC, 2000; cited in Roehl *et al.*, 2005), at least 30 per cent of American women who are killed are murdered by an intimate partner or ex-partner – a higher percentage than that of women murdered by a stranger. It is further suggested that this is an underestimate of actual rates due to misclassifications, and that the actual percentage of homicides of women by their partners or former partners in the USA is more like 40–50 per cent (Campbell *et al.*, 2003a, 2003b). Furthermore, these deaths may have been prevented if serious attention had been paid to warning signs of disturbance in the couple, or wider family system, as demonstrated by contact with social services:

> In cases of intimate partner homicide, the victim or perpetrator or both have usually had contact with criminal justice, victim assistance, and/or health agencies (Campbell *et al.*, 2000). The agencies will hold a fatality review and ask themselves, 'Could we have known? What were the signs?' The public and press will ask, 'Why wasn't more done to protect her?'

In hindsight, there usually was a sign. Often, there was a failure to read that sign or to act on it. Sometimes it is difficult to convince the victim that the risk was serious enough to warrant drastic and penalizing alterations to her lifestyle to stay alive.[3]

(Roehl, O'Sullivan, Webster and Campbell, 2005: 2)

Homicide followed by suicide

Although a relatively rare event, intimate partner homicide followed by suicide is an act of violence that often occurs within a family context and is predominantly perpetrated by men. A recent review of 44 cases in the United States found that a substantial proportion of the victims (13.7 per cent) were the children of the perpetrator. Overall, most victims (74.6 per cent) were female, and most perpetrators were male (91.9 per cent). The authors found that a recent history of legal problems (25.3 per cent), or financial problems (9.3 per cent) was common among the perpetrators Their results support earlier research identifying the importance of intimate partner violence (IPV) and situational stressors on homicide/suicide. Their findings indicated that efforts to provide assistance to families in crisis and enhance the safety of IPV victims were needed to reduce risk for homicide/suicide (Bossarte, Simon and Barker, 2006).

In the vast majority of cases, there is one perpetrator and one victim; the perpetrator is male and older than the victim, who is female and was subject to domestic violence within the partnership, and who was either a current partner, or separated or divorced from the perpetrator. Perpetrators often have a history of drug and alcohol abuse, and a history of mental illness or depression is common. Motivations for these crimes can include sexual jealousy, fear of abandonment and depression. Among male perpetrators, nearly one-third of those who killed their intimate partner (n=438) also ended their own lives, while only 1.7 per cent of those who killed a non-intimate (n=3459) also killed themselves. The findings of this study were consistent with the findings of previous research looking at the characteristics of the perpetrators and victims of homicide followed by suicide.[4]

[I]n another case, a man was evaluated for suicidal intent by a psychiatrist on call from an emergency department. Although well trained in traditional suicide risk, this mental health professional failed to assess for and take into account the salience of domestic violence in the man's marriage, his recent separation [from his wife], as well as his destruction of her property and his access to guns. The psychiatrist decided that the man was not immediately suicidal and let him go. Within hours of his release, the man killed his wife and then himself. Their eight-year-old son heard the shots and found the bodies.

(Roehl *et al.* 2005: 2)

The level of trauma that this little boy experienced cannot be overestimated, as he lost not one, but both parents, and had already been subjected to first-hand experience of domestic violence between his parents. In these tragic cases, children are victims, even when they are not killed or physically abused themselves. Harris-Hendriks *et al.* (2000) describe the tremendous impact of intimate homicide where father kills mother:

> Many of the children had suffered multiple losses; they lost not only their mother, but their father, other relations, home, possessions, school, friends and community. They had to live with their shame as being the children of a killer and with their guilt that they had not been able to prevent the killing. In many cases they had been witness to the killing and some had been left alone with the dead body of their mother all night. . . . Occasionally their own lives may have been in danger, especially if they had witnessed the killing. . . . Traumatized and bereaved, they have then had to adjust to life with a new family who might be strangers to them or, even if related, not well known. Relatives might themselves be grief-stricken or ashamed of the part their kin played in the death and therefore not fully available to care for them in their need.
>
> (Harris-Hendriks, 2000: 3–4)

The notion that suicidal intention is the flip side of the homicidal impulse (Hyatt Williams, 1998) is all too clear in this, and other, tragic cases. The perpetrator has killed off any hope, or sense of a life worth preserving, as well as the person whom he wanted to keep close to him: the partner or child whose presence he required. There is now no escape from his sense of hopelessness. These acts indicate desperate states of mind and omnipotent fantasies of total control, to the point where the moment of dying is chosen.

The research conducted, using the data from the National Violent Death Reporting System (NVDRS) in the United States, indicates that, although rare, this crime is nonetheless one that has profound consequences for families; that women are more at risk than men, and that preventative measures can save lives. This data from multiple states taken from the NVDRS indicates in 2003 and 2004 that overall, most victims (74.6 per cent) were female and most perpetrators were male (91.9 per cent) and that a significant proportion of the victims (13.7 per cent) were children of the perpetrators (Bossarte *et al.*, 2006).

The authors conclude that:

- Homicide followed by suicide (homicide/suicide) is a relatively rare event, defined here as one person killing one or more others and then taking his/her own life within 24 hours.
- Most perpetrators of homicide/suicide events were male (92 per cent); most victims were the perpetrator's current or former intimate partner (58 per cent).

These results suggest the appropriateness of targeted prevention efforts for victims and perpetrators of intimate partner violence, as well as the need to maintain awareness of increased homicide/suicide risk following situational stressors.

Infanticide

Infanticide is a crime that fundamentally challenges our deeply held views on the sanctity of motherhood. A typical case of infanticide is one where a young woman, often from a socially deprived background, cannot risk telling her family or friends about her pregnancy, delivers the baby on her own, often in her own home, and then drowns the baby within the first few hours of life. The shame of the unwanted pregnancy is her primary motivation, rather than delusional beliefs.

Other, psychotically driven, cases of infanticide occur within the first year of life, when the mother develops delusional beliefs about her baby, and may even kill her child out of 'altruistic' motives (that is, to save the baby from imagined persecution). I explore the tragic phenomenon of infanticide in detail elsewhere (Motz, 2001, 2008) where I describe some of the unconscious motives that can be discerned in this crime, as well as socioeconomic and cultural factors that contribute to its likelihood.

In the most typical case of infanticide, the mother is young and single, with the father often off the scene or unaware of the pregnancy altogether. In some cases, infanticide is associated with hysterical denial of pregnancy, indicating that the fact of having a baby growing inside one is impossible to think about or consciously acknowledge. The birth of the actual baby can come as a horrifying shock to these young mothers, who may choose to kill the child rather than risk exposure of their shameful, unwanted baby. Their state of mind during the killing, and for much of the pregnancy, is a dissociated one, and their intention is clearly not to cause suffering, although it is arguable that they are nonetheless culpable for their actions.

The 1938 Infanticide Act in the United Kingdom is predicated on the notion that the hormonal influences on mental reasoning that occur in pregnancy and following childbirth, are of sufficient magnitude to enable the killing of a newborn child to be considered an act of mental and biological instability for which the perpetrator cannot be held responsible.

In Greek mythology, Medea was wife to Jason, who betrayed her for the king's daughter Glauce. Medea took her revenge by sending Glauce a dress and golden coronet, covered in poison. This resulted in the deaths of the princess and her father, the king Creon, who was burned to death when he went to save her. According to the tragic poet Euripides, Medea continued her revenge, murdering her two children by Jason. This is a mythical illustration of vengeance and murder by a narcissistic and cruel mother who can only view her children as a part of her, so that she cannot allow the possibility of their separate existence. She takes the worst vengeance possible on their father by killing their children.

Revenge through murder of children is the cruellest punishment that can be inflicted on the other parent; threatening to kill the children is one of the most powerful threats used to make a partner stay in a bad relationship. Women as well as men are capable of killing their own children in order to punish partners whom they feel have wronged them. The perpetrator often turns the murder weapon on themselves, demonstrating their wish to die with their children and not to be held to account for their murder.

In some cases, it appears that the loss of the relationship either precipitated or catalysed depression, making homicide/suicide appear to be the only solution. The main motive in those cases appears to be hopelessness and despair, rather than a straightforward wish for revenge, although it is well established in psychoanalytic theory (Hyatt Williams, 1998) that the suicidal impulse also contains within it a homicidal one.

In cases of attempted suicide, alongside murders, where the mother appears to have loved the children and attempted to 'take them with her', rather than wanting their deaths to be a form of vengeance, it is clear that she has not been able to conceive of their separate and discrete existence, continuing beyond her own life. The mother's profound inability to know where her body ends and her children's begin leads to these tragic consequences.

One such case occurred in May 2013 in Lowestoft, Suffolk, in the UK, when Fiona Anderson, a young mother, killed herself and her three children after her partner had left her. She was heavily pregnant, and the couple had recently split up. Ms Anderson had suffered with depression for years. At the time of the offence, she was reported to be depressed and feeling isolated; it would seem that she acted out of sheer desperation; at the same time as she clearly felt tormented and betrayed, it is possible that she wanted to hurt her ex-partner (Craig McLelland, the children's father) in the cruellest way possible. Tragically, she had not received the support she urgently needed. The night before she killed her children and then herself, she had posted on her Facebook page 'My babies will come with me'. She had also visited her ex-partner on the morning of her death to give him keys to her flat, and was alleged to have stabbed him in the arm a few days before. The link between homicidal and suicidal urges is evident here.

Despite the fact that children are most at risk of violence, including death, within their own families, 'stranger danger' seems far easier for the public imagination to bear – it is much more palatable to locate sources of evil outside the home, in faceless 'others', than to look at the stark reality of violence, sometimes fatal, that takes place in the domestic realm.

It is also simpler to place blame entirely on one perpetrator. However, like honour-based killings, it is often the case that, if one partner actively kills a child, the other colludes with him (or her) by looking away. The accomplice parent may have been aware of their partner's murderous feelings, abusive behaviour and dangerous potential, but turned a blind eye, or even colluded in the cover-up, perhaps providing an alibi or helping to hide the body of the victim – her own child.

Clinical illustration: Brutality begets brutality

In the following situation, the mother June, a highly vulnerable woman with a history of severe trauma, formed a relationship with someone she had met in her care home when she was 15 and he was 17. At the age of 10, she had gone into local-authority care after being found to have suffered significant harm at the hands of her own mother and stepfather, who had left her alone for long periods of time, mainly to indulge their own drug-taking and alcoholic binges. She had been subjected to physical violence as well as gross neglect by her carers, and had been sexually abused by a friend of her mother's, Pete – a heavy drug-user who would stay at the house for long periods of time. He had been June's only source of companionship when her mother and stepfather were using drugs, and would sometimes protect her when her parents were assaulting her.

What started as a friendship between them, soon developed into a sexual relationship, where June was exploited and physically hurt, sometimes being comforted, sometimes ignored, after violent sex. In her confusion, she identified this form of attention with love and care. Eventually, when June was 11, the sexual violation became too much, as Pete wanted to involve other men. She disclosed what was happening to one of her few friends, who informed the police and social services. This had a good result, in that she was believed and taken into local-authority care, and then a specialist foster placement. She formed a close relationship with a mature woman who specialized in fostering abused children. This was one of the few periods of stability in June's life to date, and lasted three years.

Tragically, when she was 14, the foster-carer became ill and was no longer able to foster June. June was devastated and blamed herself for the illness; she falsely believed, that she had been too hard to bear, that her toxicity had poisoned her foster-carer. They kept in contact, and this offered her some sense of hope, but was also tantalizing, as she felt such intense and loving feelings for this woman and wanted so much to be with her, yet couldn't. She then had a brief period of time back with her mother, who had now left her stepfather – but found her mother depressed and alcoholic, unable to offer her any sense of stability or care. Having now had an experience of loving and reliable care, she found the contrast between her foster-mother and biological mother unbearable, and requested to return to local-authority care, eventually moving to the children's home where she met her future partner Tony.

Tony's early life had been, if anything, more deprived and traumatic than June's. He was the youngest child of six, all of whom had been taken into local-authority care after his father had killed his mother in a jealous rage. He had been two at the time of her death, and in the room when the murder took place. He was placed in a series of foster homes along with two of his siblings, but had been a withdrawn, disturbed and anxious child who would isolate himself, in contrast to his older sisters who had been emotionally more stable after their mother's death. His father was serving a lengthy prison sentence and the only source of reliable support for Tony was his maternal grandmother, but she was clearly devastated by her daughter's death and in poor health herself, thus unable to offer any of the children a home.

In the context of shared childhood trauma and highly disrupted adolescence, the two found each other. June said they felt like soulmates, who could understand one another and relate to each other's history of deprivation and need. They clung to one another and decided to live together once June was able to leave care. She became pregnant almost immediately and decided to keep the child, although she was only 16 years old.

During the first trimester of June's pregnancy, Tony began to leave her for longer periods of time, going out drinking with friends and, she suspected, flirting with other girls. She would accuse him of infidelity and started to check his phone. Her own interest in sex had dramatically declined during her pregnancy, and Tony said he was frustrated and felt rejected. After one such argument, he began to beat her. She had taken his mobile phone and was checking it for suspicious texts; he grabbed it back from her and his arm hit her face, then he began to beat her harder, strangling her and kicking her. The sense of pain he felt as she was physically and psychologically preoccupied with another (her growing foetus), and his own guilt about seeking other sexual encounters (which she discovered), was unmanageable, resulting in his violent explosion. The unborn baby was attacked, June was hurt: the cycle of sadomasochistic brutality that was now to characterize their relationship had begun.

After one particularly violent assault, June was admitted to hospital with severe abdominal pain and a threatened miscarriage. She was covered in bruises, and had a cut along her stomach. At first she said Tony had cut her stomach with a glass, but then retracted this statement and said she had self-harmed, feeling so desperate and filled with anger that she needed to discharge her feelings.

The baby, Leila, was eventually born prematurely, with cerebral palsy, raising questions about the possibility of intrauterine assault causing brain damage. June became acutely depressed, and as her depression worsened, she allowed Tony (now drinking heavily) to take greater responsibility for her. Her dream of breastfeeding Leila had proved impossible, and she felt a failure at everything, including motherhood. She was filled with guilt and self-hatred upon learning of her baby's diagnosis of cerebral palsy, and convinced that the infant would die. She was not eating or sleeping, and the health visitor had arranged for her to see her GP with a view to commencing antidepressant medication and referral for counselling, as her mood was so low. This appointment was not kept because, when Leila was 10 weeks old, June went to see one of her friends in an attempt to snap out of her depression. She was gone for a few hours, and returned feeling slightly more cheerful, though still anxious, particularly on the way home. When she arrived, she found Tony in a frantic state, saying Leila had fallen out of her Moses basket when he had put her down. She saw that the baby was floppy and listless, and had blood coming out of her nose, with her eyes shut, making whimpering noises. They called an ambulance. Leila was taken to hospital, where she was seen immediately, and it became evident that she had suffered a subdural haematoma – a severe brain bleed – most probably caused by shaking or a severe blow to the head. Within a few hours of admission, she was pronounced dead. Eventually, Tony admitted that he had lost control and shaken her, as she would not stop crying; he pleaded guilty to manslaughter and was sentenced to five years in prison.

The couple separated some weeks later, and June resumed contact with her foster-mother, who had recovered from an acute phase of her illness. She had read about the story in the papers, as it made the local news, and sought June out, eventually offering her a home. As she was a born-again Christian, they became heavily involved in the church, and June prayed daily for salvation, believing that her own sinfulness had caused Leila's death, her foster-mother's illness and her own suffering, including Tony's beatings. She prayed for forgiveness for going out on the night Leila had died, and felt that her only hope lay in a life of self-sacrifice and righteousness.

It was clear that June took on a profound sense of responsibility for the violence that was inflicted on both her and her daughter, and that her childhood experiences taught her to accept brutality as normal, or even deserved. She had no early experience of a 'containing' mother who could help her to process painful feelings, and no sense of how to be alone with her own feelings. It was inevitable, in some ways, that early motherhood destabilized her and proved impossible to cope with. She had, at times, also felt angry and helpless when faced with her needy, demanding and damaged infant. Her aggressive feelings towards this helpless baby were impossible for her to face and she turned inwards, her hatred turning in on herself as she became increasingly depressed. The birth of her child, with her needs and fragility, was an overwhelming and terrifying event, evoking feelings of helplessness and rage. Her own unheard cries were echoed in the baby's cries.

Even in pregnancy, June wanted to punish herself, later admitting to me that she had self-harmed, wounding the stomach within which life grew. As well as offering her a contact with a trusted attachment figure, her return to her foster-mother's house allowed her a legitimate form of containment and care, within the highly structured and firm boundaries of a dominant Christian faith. This enabled her to feel safe in managing her intense feelings, and looking to an external authority to guide her and protect her from the chaos and brutality of an abusive sexual partner.

The power of her destructive early life, her own abuse experiences and her vulnerability to repeated patterns was evident through her choice of partner and, for her, hope and help were found through a form of spiritual purification and reunification with a secure attachment figure.

Although June was not consciously murderous towards her baby, there was a part of her that was so helpless, and desperate, that at times she wanted to end her own life. She saw Leila as an extension of her, a damaged and unwanted creature who could not be properly loved or cared for. She was not able to ensure her safety, much as she could not ensure her own. Tony appeared to have lost control impulsively, rather than deliberately setting out to kill the baby; but his characteristic violence and lack of empathy, coupled with his unresolved grief about his own mother's murder, left him with an underlying feeling of rage and fury that he would unleash against those he saw as helpless. His guilt at not being able to save his mother, and his hatred of his father for killing her, left him with an unbearable sense of helplessness and fear. He projected this feeling onto those around him. When he could not stop Leila from crying, he lost control altogether and finally stopped her forever; his inability to manage his feelings, and his own experience of being traumatized and abused, appear to have been reawakened by the baby's cries. He also, in that moment, unconsciously identified with his own father, who had killed.

Treatment issues in working with mothers who have killed or harmed children

The literature on filicide, or the killing of children by their parents, indicates some gender differences, and that the majority of such deaths are inflicted by mothers, generally with different motivations than fathers. A recent review of 200 such filicides in Finland over a 25-year period, found that women who killed were far more likely to be suffering from psychosis or depression than were the men, and that their children were younger at the time of death. This has important implications for treatment of female perpetrators. In contrast, male perpetrators were more likely to be diagnosed with a personality disorder, to be jealous of their partners and violent towards them, to abuse alcohol and to have witnessed domestic violence between their parents. More mothers had killed for altruistic motives than had fathers, and maternal filicides were more often associated with later suicides.[5] In a ten-year study of filicide in Austria and Finland, the authors found that:

> fathers who commit filicide may represent at least two subgroups, the one not unlike the common homicide offender; the other, the overloaded, working and suicidal father. Mothers may include several types of offenders, one of which is the neonaticide offender.
>
> (Putkonen *et al.*, 2009, 2011)

This is consistent with Websdale's (2010) distinction between the livid coercive killer, and those respectable citizens who kill in a state of 'humiliated fury', often with underlying depression. These men then kill themselves.

The question of treatment for women who have either committed these crimes, or enabled them, is discussed below. The issue of avoiding a re-enactment of toxic coupling in the treatment is central. It is easy to fall into a punitive or protective relationship with the patient in therapy, who can evoke strong feelings of anger or a powerful wish to rescue. This can be understood as an unconscious projection by the patient of wishes to be either punished in accordance with her own guilt feelings, particularly awakened if she has left or 'abandoned' her violent partner, or to be rescued and transformed. The latter is the unconscious wish to be reborn and to receive the protective and loving care of which they were deprived in early life, and that appeared to be met through the violent relationship that has now broken down.

Both powerful wishes can be projected directly and may resonate with the therapist's own unconscious needs and fantasies. The power of projective identification with these aspects of the patient and her history is intense, and offers a rich source of communicative data. The therapist may, at times, become identified with the controlling, punishing partner, who scolds the other for her perceived weakness and reluctance to leave destructive situations; she may feel frustrated and angry, using interpretations as a form of violence. At other moments, she may be in danger of enacting the role of the fantasized saviour, who offers endless succour and care. Acting into these wishes is ultimately unhelpful and will not allow the patient to find her own sense of containment and self-efficacy and to express and own the rage she feels. Rosenfeld (1987) describes the powerful force of such countertransference responses as resulting from the therapist's wish to perform 'a corrective emotional experience'. This must be resisted if the patient is truly to be helped to articulate and process what has previously been unbearable.

The link between homicidal and suicidal urges (Hyatt Williams, 1998; Motz, 2001, 2008) is particularly strong in individuals who have fragile conceptions of self, and narcissistic ways of relating to others. Their children are viewed as objects, reflecting aspects of themselves, including hated parts that they disavow. In the case of murderous couples, there is an unconscious contract between the two that enables acts of profound cruelty, deception and betrayal. This creates the conditions for child abuse and murder, as well as the killing of other third parties who pose a threat to the couple, or whose torture and death provide a form of excitement.

This powerful link between homicidal and suicidal feelings is essential for the therapist to bear in mind, as, when insight increases, so too does the wish to punish oneself. This insight can also be seen when a female accomplice to killing reclaims her projected aggression, and acknowledges her own murderousness. Once she is no longer able to locate these unacceptable and frightening states of her mind in her partner, her psychic equilibrium is jeopardized and suicidal feelings may then surface with catastrophic intensity. Just as a mother who has actually killed her own child, albeit in a psychotic state, may become seriously destabilized as the psychosis recedes and she recovers insight, so too can a woman who has configured herself as a passive, tragic victim in the murder become deeply depressed as she recognizes her own active part in the crime. She has also killed off hope, as represented by her child, and this can lead to profound helplessness and depression (G. Adshead, personal communication; discussion at a seminar of the International Association for Forensic Psychotherapy 'Evil:

Philosophical, Pyschotherapeutic and Legal Perspectives', held in Oxford in June, 2013).

This process of insight is evident when child abusers, who have acted as part of a couple or a gang, begin to recognize the extent of their own individual culpability and cruelty. Through psychotherapy, they can begin to acknowledge their own responsibility and finally give a thought to the damage they have inflicted – neither of which will have occurred during their immersion in the abusive activity and in the partnership that fed on such sadism. Shengold (2000) describes the impact of child abuse as a form of 'soul murder', and provides rich clinical and mythical material to illustrate this. He reveals how the psychological damage in victims is manifested in later life. While not inflicting actual physical death, the legacy of severe emotional, psychological and sexual abuse is so intense and pernicious that the psyche can be considered in some ways to be 'dead'. These kinds of violations are dramatic examples of 'soul murders', where the very heart of an individual has been so damaged through abuse and neglect that her capacity for life and for joy is killed off. Only the most sensitive and intensive psychotherapeutic interventions can address this damage.

Malignant bonding

Welldon (2012) describes situations in which children are deliberately killed by a couple as examples of 'malignant bonding'. A couple unites in their desire for cruel re-enactments, sometimes for sexual excitement, in which children are used as objects to be tortured and violated for the pleasure of adults. She explains how in some cases the children's suffering is recorded, for the purpose of homemade pornography. The sadomasochism involved in such sexual torture can be seen as a form of rehearsal for the actual killing; the murder has happened time and time again in fantasy, before it is enacted in real life. The children are kept alive in order to be used in sadistic, horrific ways; they are wholly depersonalized and viewed only as means for gratifying the couple's perverse desires.

For some who engage in these acts of cruelty and degradation, their role as abuser affords an escape from earlier experiences as victim; in this way they can 'master trauma' (Stoller, 1975) and project unbearable feelings of shame, pain and humiliation onto others. In this way, they rid themselves of unacceptable feelings. Stoller refers to this type of perversion as 'the erotic form of hatred', in that aggression and cruelty are sexualized. They are enacting the role of their own abuser in order to (temporarily) free themselves from their sense of helplessness, and in this way, reveal the psychic defence of 'identification with the aggressor' (Freud, 1936). Others who engage in sexual torture and murder of children may not have themselves experienced such abuse, but either become inured to its brutality, or become aroused by the sense of power and control it affords. Within such perverse couplings, children are used only as objects, and not seen as subjective creatures whose vulnerability needs to be protected, and whose autonomy respected.

In some cases, couples actively kill together, acting as accomplices in murder. The peculiar ingredients that create such a toxic couple can be understood as an unconscious fit between two highly disturbed personalities who, through their partnership, feel validated and enabled to commit horrific crimes. They act as moral arbiter for one another, creating a unique code of ethics that condones violence and murder. When their psychopathologies meet in particular ways, these partners enhance and exacerbate one another's callous disregard for the welfare of others; outside this partnership, neither individual would commit the crime of violence. The perverse world this couple creates is one where children are viewed as disposable objects, things to be used and abused for their gratification. They are treated as 'poison containers' (deMause, 1990) into which the adults pour unwanted feelings and hatred.

In these toxic couples, the partners have shared violent fantasies that they act on together, excited by the participation of the other. I have encountered this kind of perversion and cruelty in cases where sexual sadism is operational and the mother has been used as a 'decoy' to elicit the trust of others, who then allow the couple to have access to their children. At times, their own children are also abused in this way for the gratification of the adults. Such cases include the highly publicized one of Rosemary and Fred West, in which both parents actively participated in sexually perverse and sadistic acts. The impact of this case on the children involved, and others, has been powerfully revealed in Carole Hayman's excellent film *No-one Escapes*.

In other partnerships, like the case described below, one partner is apparently the weaker and more easily led, who has disavowed her own aggression into her violent partner, and passively 'goes along with' the violence, rather than actively participating in it. This is a different dynamic from the 'folie à deux' of suspending empathy, compassion and care for vulnerable children entrusted to one's care in favour of inflicting brutality; the kind of malignant bonding referred to by Welldon (2012) and mentioned above. Nonetheless, the consequences of long-term neglect can also be fatal, and the degree of suffering intense and prolonged.

Clinical illustration: Jay: denial and disavowal of violence

Jay was charged with cruelty and neglect after her partner Noah beat her six-month-old daughter Amber to death; he was not the baby's father. Jay had become pregnant by an older partner when she was 16. Within a month of her pregnancy, this partner had disappeared from her life, and she had no further contact with him. Amber had been born prematurely and her survival was in doubt from the beginning of her short life. While Jay was out, working on a night shift in a hosiery factory, her partner had violently assaulted the baby, whose crying he had been unable to stop. He had beaten her viciously, first shaking her, and then using his fists and other objects to silence her. This had followed Jay's discovery a few days earlier that bruises had appeared on Amber's face and arms after she had been left alone in Noah's care.

Jay's attraction to this violent man seemed connected with her own experience of abuse over many years, leaving her mute and lifeless at times. Noah was a drug user, and had a history of burglary, violence and other criminal activity, including shoplifting and stealing and driving cars for 'joy riding'. Jay found that being with him gave her a sense of enlivenment that she found compelling. She enjoyed being taken along with him when he committed burglaries, and said she even found the police encounters gave her 'a buzz', particularly when the police cars had their sirens on and chased the couple as they drove away from crime scenes. He also introduced her to crack cocaine, to which she soon became addicted.

He had met her when she was six weeks pregnant – some two weeks after the baby's father had left the scene – moving in with her within three weeks. Noah first assaulted Jay in the second trimester of her pregnancy by kicking her hard in the abdomen; he was frustrated by her lack of interest in sex and called her a 'slag and a bitch'. His physical attack was directed at the mother–baby dyad, as he deliberately targeted her stomach.

Noah was violent and controlling, isolating Jay from her friends and family and subjecting her to painful and humiliating treatment. He control-led her finances and spent the money on his own drinking, gambling and internet pornography, depriving her of any kind of independent life. She had told other professionals at various times about the violence to which he subjected her, which could be severe. Although she had called them out on two occasions, she felt that the police were often rather dismissive, and this contributed to her sense of helplessness and powerlessness. She had told her mother that her partner isolated her, but never told her about any of the violent incidents. Finally, Jay disclosed the violence she was experiencing to the health visitor when her daughter was 12 weeks old, after he had hit her across the leg with a dog lead the previous day. When I met her, she told me that she had eventually given the dog to a friend, explaining that because Noah would kick the dog when the dog tried to protect her, she had 'to get rid of the dog'. Jay quietly stated 'Everything he said, I did, but he would still get violent and beat me up'. She was clearly damaged physically and psychologically from involvement in this relationship. After the first assault, Noah beat Jay a few times a week, generally when he was high on drugs. Although Jay appeared to understand the potential harm that these assaults could cause the baby, she remained adamant that she wanted to remain in the relationship. This was an example of her inability to act on some awareness of danger. It was as if she was in a state of total inertia.

Despite noticing the baby's bruising after leaving her with Noah a few days before the fatal assault, she continued to leave her with him to go to work. Jay had confronted Noah with her fears about him causing the bruising, but he had denied them, begging her to give him a chance to prove himself. She was desperate for him not to leave her, and felt scared and ashamed of what she had seen; Jay kept her mother from seeing the baby, in case she grew worried about the injuries. When her mother visited, hoping to spend time with her granddaughter, Jay wouldn't let her in the house, saying that Amber had a cold and so couldn't be taken out of her cot. Jay clearly knew that Amber had been assaulted and was at risk. Her shame and fear led to her sacrificing her baby's safety, and ultimately her life.

After Amber's death, she pleaded guilty to the charge of wilful neglect that was brought against her. Although she had initially been charged with cruelty to a child, this was later dropped. In his summing up, the judge expressed the view that she had suffered enough through the death of her child, and that her main crime was to allow her violent partner to have unlimited and unsupervised access to a highly vulnerable infant, rather than to have wilfully committed acts of ill-treatment herself. He added that her care of the baby had been inadequate, and the infant had failed to thrive.

Jay was now pregnant with a second child, by a different partner, some 18 months after her daughter's death, and wanted to assure social services that she had matured sufficiently to protect and nurture this new child. I was asked to assess this.

My encounter with her was painful. She remained largely unresponsive throughout two assessment sessions and gave only the briefest of answers to questions. I was left with the strong impression that she was somehow deadened, and had been emotionally petrified since early life. She was frozen, unreachable and almost mute.

Clinical illustration: history

Jay's mother had been unpredictable and neglectful; apparently depressed. She had used alcohol to excess. Jay did not know her biological father, who had left before she was born, and her stepfather had been violent and abusive to her mother as well as to her. Jay was being sexually abused by her stepfather and felt sure her mother must know about this. She remembered trying to spell it out, but feeling 'blanked' by her, and dismissed. At the age of 11, she had finally come to the attention of the local authority, after a teacher at school had noticed her unkempt, depressed appearance, and her disinhibited sexualized behaviour. Jay had trusted this teacher enough to confide in her about the abuse, and she was removed from home, as her mother refused to believe the truth of Jay's allegations. She could not accept that her violent partner would do this to her daughter, and did not want him to leave the family home, preferring Jay to leave. This failure of protective mothering was later repeated in Jay's own choices and decision-making.

Jay had returned home at 13 after her stepfather left the family home, but felt rejected, sad and unsafe. It was possible that her mother had been trying to protect her by having her removed from the abusive home environment. When she came home, her mother had a new, non-abusive boyfriend. She and her mother established a more harmonious existence until Jay was 15, when she began to take drugs and have sexual relations with older adolescent boys.

Clinical illustration: Jay's first pregnancy

One of Jay's deepest wishes was to have a daughter herself; when we explored what she had hoped for, it became clear that unconsciously she had wished for a little girl with whom she could merge in a blissful state of union, as she imagined other mothers enjoyed with their daughters. She longed to feel fulfilled and loved and had, during her pregnancy, experienced this sense, despite the violence inflicted on her. The birth of her daughter, Amber, had shattered this for her and she felt even emptier than before. Dinora Pines (1993) describes the huge contrast that some young mothers experience between their fantasies of motherhood, and the harsh reality of the actual baby, who has so many needs: to be taken care of, fed and loved:

> There is a marked distinction between the wish to become pregnant and the wish to bring a live child into the world and become a mother. For primitive anxieties and conflicts arising from a woman's lifelong task of separation/individuation from her own mother may be unexpectedly revealed by the emotional experience of first pregnancy and motherhood.
> (Pines, 1993: 98)

From the beginning, Jay found Amber difficult to settle and feed, and felt increasingly unhappy and alienated, sometimes imagining that Amber was not a real, human baby, but an alien creature.

Clinical illustration: Jay's presentation

Despite Jay's evident vulnerability, it was hard to reach her emotionally in the assessment interviews, and my usual sense of wanting to take care of, or rescue, the desperate child within was absent in my countertransference to her. I came to understand, after close reflection, that this mirrored her own profound difficulty in taking care of another person, that her frozen state and apparent dissociation both protected and removed her from the world. All caretaking – of herself or an infant – had stopped before it had begun.

It was as if Jay's own rage had gone underground, and that, rather than express her aggressive impulses, which she feared might completely overwhelm her, she found herself locked into a familiar relationship, where her apparent protector had continually abused and hurt her, even threatening her with death. She had one close confidante, who had advised her to leave this man, but she felt that she needed Noah above anyone else.

The questions were: Why she had chosen this particular partner? Why she had remained with him? How much had she abdicated all control of her own body and mind, and colluded unconsciously in her baby's murder? Her decision to go to work, over a night-shift, and leave Noah in charge of the baby made little sense. One of my central concerns was whether she had any capacity to address these fundamental questions – could any of this be made conscious?

The risk of addressing her disavowal of aggression was significant, as it clearly protected her from an unbearable burden of guilt. Her conception of herself as helpless in the face of her partner's demands was psychologically protective for her, and her own culpability in allowing him to 'take care' of her daughter could be pushed out of mind. This shielded her from crippling guilt about Amber's death. The dilemma was that confronting her sense of herself as a victim could result in the onset of severe depression, but not doing so would leave her 'stuck'.

In order for her to be able to care of a child, it was imperative that Jay could see how her own unarticulated rage had contributed to her choice of partner, her passivity in the face of an unplanned pregnancy, and her emotionally petrified state. Her unconscious response to her daughter's fragility and prematurity had been to distance herself, rather than face up to the helplessness that she saw so concretely and painfully reflected in her infant. Her new partner had no history of violence, and had a supportive family. In this relationship, Jay was not able to project her own aggressive impulses into him, and so needed to bear them within herself and find a voice for her anger. The question of her capacity to parent a helpless child was a complicated and unhappy one. Even if those around her trusted her, it was not clear that she could trust herself.

I considered whether it would ever be possible to consign the care of a child to a woman who was, in an important (if unconscious) way complicit in the death of her first child. She had made repeated suicide attempts herself, after her daughter's death, making the most serious attempt when she awaited sentencing, showing how fragile she was, and how hard it was for her to contain her feelings of grief and guilt. She repeatedly said that she felt that she had already died, that she too had been killed when her daughter had been, seeing herself in her battered daughter.

Jay was not able to successfully undertake the requisite therapeutic work, despite placement in a therapeutic residential centre with the new baby (a boy) and his father. She remained unavailable to the child, and seemed in thrall to her new partner, who encouraged her to flout the rules of the unit and stay out past the curfew drinking with him. While he had no history of violence, there were other concerns that emerged, including alcohol and gambling addictions. Although her ex-partner was serving a prison sentence for Amber's death, she remained in contact with him by letter, despite the deep concerns this raised for the child protection agencies.

Sadly, despite her best intentions to parent her second child successfully, her level of disturbance and dependence was too great to allow her to attend to the baby's needs.

(Motz, 2012 in Aiyegbusi and Kelly)

Clinical illustration: discussion

Jay had no experience of containment in her early life, and had not learned to feel safe in her own skin. She had no maternal object into whom she could reliably project her own angry, hungry and scared feelings, as her mother was herself preoccupied, depressed and neglectful. The impact of domestic violence on Jay's mother seemed profound, as she turned to alcohol and appeared unavailable to her frightened daughter.

Jay seemed to be looking for the love and affection her mother had been unable to show her, but several of her partners were also violent towards her. Because of her early exposure to violence between her parents, Jay tacitly accepted this as the norm, and unconsciously sought it out as a familiar pattern. To do otherwise would be to risk the unbearable state of feeling that she was not suffering as her mother had done, and this guilt was intolerable. Her earlier pattern of attachment was repeated in her choice of partner: the confused state – where the person she depended on was also the person who abused her – was a familiar one. In attachment terms, this was an example of a traumatic bond, and reflected her disorganized attachment to a person who was both her carer and her tormenter.

Jay blamed herself for the violent actions of others. She was haunted by not being able to protect her mother. Her mother had often told her she wished she hadn't been born, as if she believed she would have been able to leave her partner if she had been childless. Additionally, Jay felt guilty and ashamed of the sexual abuse, as if it were her fault. The terrible burden of guilt, both conscious and unconscious, led Jay to seek out forms of suffering and punishment, and also to identify with her own mother as the subject of violence.

The earlier failure within Jay's psychological development was her inability to acknowledge and manage her own destructive and aggressive impulses, which were instead disowned and projected into her violent partner. He carried this violence for her, and she could disavow it, remaining forever the passive victim. This psychic splitting had been essential for her survival in early life, when she did not trust herself to express rage at either the stepfather who abused her or the mother who turned away. Indeed, even in discussion with me she only expressed anger at her stepfather, retaining an idealized view of her mother as helpless and innocent, despite the cruelty she had allowed Jay to suffer.

The question of Jay's depression, and her unacknowledged rage, was central. She needed to be shown how much she identified with the damaged and dying baby. Perhaps part of the fantasy in relation to her first-born baby was that if she was hurt, even killed, that part of her that was so damaged could also be killed off.

At the same time, she was unaware of this. This wish could be understood as an unconscious one, and can also be seen in the psychological state known as 'learned helplessness', where a mother perceives herself as incapable of taking protective action – for herself or her child. She felt psychically fused with the helpless infant and couldn't bear this, facing the choice of either violently turning away from this hated part of herself, allowing it to be killed, or killing herself directly. Although she didn't actively hurt her child, she felt powerless to protect her, and in this sense enabled her violent partner to inflict injury on her baby.

Without intensive treatment to build up her ability to face the horror of what she had allowed to happen, the risk of Jay repeating the pattern remained high. She would continue to be drawn to violent partners, and to see any future babies as part of herself, deserving poor treatment and impossible to protect. This did not mean that she didn't also love the baby who had died, nor that she would not love future babies, but that a part of her that had not been allowed to develop and grow would also not be able to relate to a baby as a separate, vulnerable and needy creature, whom she must protect as an adult.

The extent of Jay's traumatic presentation was so severe that she reminded me of children whose early sexual abuse stupefies them, leaving them disconnected intellectually to the point that they appear to be cognitively impaired. Valerie Sinason first described this in 1986, describing mental handicap as secondary to trauma.

Jay's situation illustrates how early exposure to domestic violence affects children's development. One of the consequences can be a sense of passivity and helplessness in the mother; this interferes with her care of the child, sometimes with lethal consequences. When Jay was prosecuted for wilful neglect of the child, having seen the bruises on her face a few days before the final assault, the prosecution suggested that if she had told someone what she had seen, the murder could have been prevented, concluding: 'In a nutshell, she chose her relationship over the child'.

Jay seemed to embody this damage, both as the mother who is unable to attend to the needs of her child, and as the daughter who was neglected and hurt, and found herself repeating the pattern of her own early life. In the end, however, she was left without the child she hoped could save her, and faced the harshness of her reality alone. Her masochistic relationships could be understood as a form of self-harm. In order to break this pattern, she urgently needed to have psychological, emotional and practical help, enabling her to gain a different sense of herself and a new way of relating to others. However, her terror of facing the deep levels of pain that she had buried inside herself made such help seem persecutory, and she chose to push it away.

In some cases where a child or children die, the relationship between the couple is an abusive one, and both can turn their aggression onto the children. In 2000, eight year old Victoria Climbié (originally from the Ivory Coast) was killed by her aunt Marie Therese Kouao, and her boyfriend Carl John Manning, after being systematically tortured by the couple over an extended period of time. The inquiry resulted in a 400-page report by Lord Laming (2003) outlining the failings of the child protection agencies involved in this tragic case, but also how the abuse intensified after Kouao became involved with Manning. He describes the brutal and sadistic abuse the couple inflicted on her:

> Given that her hands were kept bound with masking tape, she was forced to eat by pushing her face towards the food, like a dog. As well as being forced to spend much of her time in inhuman conditions, Victoria was also beaten on a regular basis by both Kouao and Manning. According to Manning, Kouao used to strike Victoria on a daily basis, sometimes using a variety of weapons.
> (Laming, 2003: 35)

The shared cruelty of the couple was evident in the descriptions Laming provides in his passionate and outraged report. He reports on the findings of the post-mortem examination by Dr Carey (for further discussion, see also Motz, 2008):

> All non-accidental injuries to children are awful and difficult for everybody to deal with, but in terms of the nature and extent of the injury, and the almost systematic nature of the inflicted injury, I certainly regard this as the worst I have ever dealt with, and it just about the worst I have ever heard of. At the post-mortem examination, Dr Carey recorded evidence of no fewer than 128 separate injuries to Victoria's body, saying "there really is not anywhere that is spared . . . there is scarring all over the body".
> (Laming, 2003: 12)

In another highly publicized case, described below, an apparently vulnerable mother was allegedly complicit in allowing her husband to set fire to their shared home, with their six children sleeping in it.

Couples who kill: the Philpott case

The shocking case of Mick and Mairead Philpott resulted in their conviction on 2 April 2013 for the manslaughter of their six children, after starting a fire in their own home in Derby, ostensibly with the aim of blaming it on Mr Philpott's mistress, Lisa Willis, and mother to four children with him. She had recently left the household, where she had been living with these children and her child from a previous relationship, the couple and their six children. Although this was an unconventional 'couple', Lisa Willis was tyrannized in the familiar pattern adopted by intimate terrorists and had already suffered from emotional and physical abuse at Philpott's hands. He was reportedly furious that she had left him, taking their children with her.

In this complex and bizarre case, a third man was also involved: 46-year-old Paul Mosley, who was also found guilty of manslaughter by the jury at Nottingham Crown Court following an eight-week trial. While Mick Philpott had a criminal past with a propensity for extreme jealousy and violence, it is unclear what motivated Mairead to collude with him in this grotesque killing. After the three were found guilty of manslaughter, the facts about Mr Philpott's violent history were revealed:

> In 1978, Philpott launched a savage attack on his then girlfriend, 17-year-old Kim Hill, then turned the knife on her mother. He was convicted of attempted murder and grievous bodily harm (GBH) with intent, and locked up for seven years.
>
> (Bentley and Dolan, *Daily Mail*, 2 April 2013)

In his latest trial, the jurors were not informed about Mick Philpott's previous convictions. He had apparently planned the attack on Kim Hill after receiving a letter from her saying she wanted to end the relationship. Aged 21 at the time, and serving in the Army, he had gone absent without leave to seek her out and assault her. Several years later, he had also pinned down another girlfriend and held a knife to her throat. Unsurprisingly, it emerged that Mick Philpott was a tyrant; a man who regulated every movement of his current wife and former girlfriends, intimidating them with violence and threats, and even instructing his sons to beat one former partner. The use of children in intimate partner violence is a characteristic of 'intimate terrorism'. Lisa Willis testified at his trial and gave evidence confirming Philpott's regular use of violence and brutality to subdue, intimidate and terrify. Like Mairead, she was a woman with a traumatic background; she had met Philpott at age 16 when already a mother, and orphaned. Mairead Philpott had previously been in an abusive relationship, and both women were sexually and physically tyrannized by Philpott.

Mairead Philpott appears to have been more passive in this fatal plan. She may well have believed that his plan – to save the children before they died – would work, but she is now left bereft, as all her children were killed in their sleep. It is possible that she, too, was intimidated and controlled by him, to the point that she lost her own sense of agency or compassion.

Conclusion

This chapter has explored aspects of murder in the family, including partners who kill one another and parents who kill, both individually and as a couple. The facts of extreme couple violence against children, the dangers to children under the age of one, and pregnancy violence, point to the urgent question of perinatal assessment and care of the parents as well as the unborn child. This will play an essential role in the identification of high-risk parents as well as pregnant women who are most likely to be seriously harmed, along with their unborn babies. The seeds of murderous violence can be sown early on.

6   Shelter from the storm
Home, homelessness and violence

Where we start from: mother and the sense of home

In this chapter, I describe how men and women with severe attachment difficulties in early life often struggle to internalize a sense of sanctuary or 'home'.
They are at risk of repeating disturbed relationships in their adult life and seeking security from their partners, even when they become violent and abusive.
Their desperate need for security and 'home' reflects their search for 'a safe
base'. Tragically, the search for home – actual and symbolic – can maintain their
attachment to dangerous partners.

As the lines below from T. S. Eliot describe, home is where we start from; early
life experiences shape us and are encapsulated inside us:

> *East Coker*
>
> Home is where one starts from. As we grow older
> The world becomes stranger, the pattern more complicated
> Of dead and living. Not the intense movement
> Isolated, with no before and after
> But a lifetime burning in every moment.
>   T. S. Eliot, *Four Quartets* 1940

I will discuss the link between disruption and disturbance in early life, later homelessness, and the increased risk of violent relationships, with reference to the
seminal work of John Bowlby (1969) and attachment models of development.
I outline empirical data that identifies the increased risk that homeless people face
of experiencing violence, and highlight the increased vulnerability of homeless
females to suffering violence within intimate relationships. Furthermore, women
who experience interpersonal violence are also more likely to become homeless
as a result of this abuse, when they eventually leave the relationship. As women
who are homeless are more likely to have suffered abuse in early life, they are
unfortunately also at increased risk of re-victimization through later abuse (Coid
et al., 2001, 2003). I explore what it means symbolically, psychologically and
physically to have no home and no sense of place in society.

There is a strong link between childhood neglect and trauma and home-lessness. In this chapter, I will explore the development of cycles of violence, homelessness and re-traumatization. One consequence of the absence of secure attachment experiences in early life is increased aggression. The child may not develop the capacity for reflection and emotional regulation that is a pre-requisite for secure attachment in adulthood, creating further difficulties in their relationships. The development of empathy is related to secure attachment. Insecurely attached children characteristically react to others with indifference or aggression, sometimes using intimidation to try to achieve their goals; they will be less empathetic to the feelings of others. This has clear implications for their capacity to understand the mental states of others, their own choice of partner, and parenting style.

The link between antisocial personality disorder, aggression and insecure attachment has been demonstrated and explored in terms of a developmental failure to 'mentalize' in the work of Bateman and Fonagy (2001, 2004) and more recently by Bateman and Fonagy (2012) and Yakeley (2012). All human beings are born with aggressive impulses, and early socialization and attachment experiences are the building blocks for managing these: 'Among the important evolutionary purposes of attachment is the socialisation of natural aggression' (Dutton, 2007). Conversely, without secure attachment, aggressive impulses may remain unchecked.

The homeless female body

While men are also often the victims of homelessness, I largely focus in this chapter on the experience of homeless women, who are much more frequently the victims of sexual as well as other violence by their partners.

I explore legal concepts of the body as property, the symbolic meaning of home, the social problems of homelessness and its role in the establishment of violent relationships. In Chapter 7, I extend this discussion of the female body as a possession to explore cases of violence and murder in forced marriages.

The notions of home and homelessness are particularly significant in the experience of women who are violently abused in toxic relationships from which they then flee. For some women, freedom means leaving their home, while for others, such as those escaping forced marriages, it can result in losing not only a stable home but also a place in their community. In such cases, homelessness, both psychological and social, has major consequences: some of these women are left outside mainstream society, cast aside by intimate family, and potentially at heightened risk of further assault and abuse. For others, leaving the home that imprisoned them can be the start of a better life.

Homelessness is clearly a complex phenomenon, with many causes, including substance and alcohol abuse, family breakdown, exile from another country and criminality. It can also be caused by intimate partner violence that drives women out of their homes, and by families disowning girls deemed to have dishonoured them by not agreeing to marriages arranged for them (see Chapter 7).

It is important to consider not only the complex interplay between social and cultural forces and individual psychological factors, but also the sense in which a violent couple should be understood against the backdrop of the wider societal system. The homeless and those who disappear into forced marriages are cast out of the mainstream, and, in turn, their 'invisibility' and outsider status leaves them more vulnerable to abuse and assault, with fewer avenues of protection. Young people in care are similarly vulnerable, having fallen outside the family systems designed to protect and nurture them, seeking affection and attention elsewhere. Although the care system is intended to offer surrogate protection, nurturing and monitoring, sadly, this is not always possible. The recent, highly publicized, cases of young girls in care being sexually exploited by gangs of men in Oxford, Rochdale and Derby for their own financial, psychological and sexual gratification, are stark proof of this. In Oxford, seven men were convicted of charges including rape, arranging prostitution and trafficking vulnerable young people, most of whom were in local-authority care:

> These men picked their victims well: children between the ages of 11 and 15 who had grown up with no nurturing, very little love and even less protection; girls who would not be listened to or missed when they ran away from children's homes or played truant from school; girls easily groomed into believing they were being shown affection.
> 'I have no choice; I just want to be loved. I've never been loved and this shows me love', one of the girls told a friend.
>   (Laville and Topping, *The Guardian*, 14 May 2013)

The toxic couplings created by forced marriages, and the violent partnerships that women on the street are much more likely to form than 'housed' women, are products of unconscious and conscious societal beliefs that these women are no more than objects, possessions to be treated without respect or dignity; they are denigrated, hurt and violated. Both men and women who are homeless are more likely than others to have been treated abusively and/or neglected in childhood.

The female body as property

The idea of the female body as the possession of another person has its roots in distorted applications of biblical edicts, from the Old Testament to the Koran, and can be used to justify the subjugation of one human being for the benefit of another. These objectified others have become possessions, a form of goods to be exchanged between privileged members of society – often men – and do not have value as subjective individuals (see Mill, 1869). This dehumanizing dynamic is enacted between the couple, with the master and his property – the servant – who may have entered the contract with apparent free will, unaware of the domination to which she has implicitly agreed. In cases of forced marriages, this subjugation is clearly socially sanctioned, at least by the immediate community, if not by wider society.

Developing a sense of home from the inside out

As Winnicott (1960) describes in his accounts of early life, the original symbiosis between mother and baby is the beginning of our psychic development; this is where we start from. It is the sensitive interplay between mother (or other primary caregiver) and baby that enables the infant to develop a sense of itself; this includes the growing awareness of having an inner and outer being, a body with boundaries, and a mind with thoughts and feelings. In this way, a mind becomes 'housed' or contained.

These early relationships establish templates for later life and, as earlier chapters describe, secure attachment to a sensitive, reliable caregiver in early life is a vitally important precursor for healthy psychosocial development and future relationships. Those who have not had this crucial experience are far more likely to form violent partnerships than individuals who have had a secure start in life.

As well as its physical reality, there is an important psychic meaning to home: for someone to have an inner sense of a sanctuary, they need to have experienced a maternal capacity for containment. From this early experience of being held in the mind and arms of another – being both physically and psychologically held by her – the individual develops their own capacity to contain and detoxify powerful affects.

After birth, an infant cannot differentiate between what is outside and what is inside their own body, and desperately requires to be held by her mother in order to have a sense of being contained and integrated. For this to happen successfully, the mother has to provide a reliable, consistent and responsive environment for the baby (Winnicott, 1960). This process is essential in the development of a sense of being an embodied self, with boundaries, and with the capacity to self-regulate. It is as if the developing baby learns to do for itself what the mother first does for her. This is akin to Bion's (1962) notion of containment by the mother of the infant, and is crucial for the development of thinking, of a sense of being held together and not just a being in a state of 'nameless dread' in which no sense can be made of terrifying forces of hunger, rage and fear. It is the mother's task to provide the psychological and physical containment that enables the infant's needs to be met and feelings to be recognized. These toxic affects are borne by the mother and then returned to the infant in a form that can be digested, for example, through soothing words and affectionate gestures. This process is the foundation for all later thinking, symbolization and self-regulation.

Different paradigms allude to this capacity; it can be understood as the capacity to mentalize (Bateman and Fonagy, 2004) developing from a mother's reflective functioning. This relates directly to what Bion (1962) describes as the mother's capacity to convert beta elements, raw affective states, into what he calls alpha elements, that are the building blocks for thinking and symbolization.

Bateman and Fonagy (2001, 2004) have further developed a theory of mentalization that is predicated on a similar developmental process: in order to manage intense states of arousal and convert raw data into the basic building-blocks of thought, a child needs to have had the prior experience of another person doing this for them, reflecting back their feelings and mental states and also giving them words with which to define and communicate them. It is the mother's vital function of mirroring the infants' feelings that allows babies to identify, experience and integrate powerful states of mind and bodily sensation and, ultimately, to develop a sense of themselves as the container within which they exist. The child then learns she has a mind housed within a body, with feelings and thoughts that can relate to other minds and other bodies. Without this fundamental experience of 'reflective functioning' and secure attachment, it is difficult for developing infants to be clear about where they stop and someone else begins; their experience of integration and of their own boundaries is fragmented and confused.

Consequences of disturbed early experience for later relationships

As described in Chapter 3, early attachment experiences impact significantly on later relationships. Bateman and Fonagy (2004) trace the origins of borderline personality disorder (BPD) to disturbed attachment experiences; whenever the arousal system is activated in later life, the individual is at risk of becoming very disturbed and acting impulsively. This is evident, for example, when violence is triggered at the point of perceived abandonment.

From earliest infancy, skin and its sensations are central to the emotional experience of a baby, who is held against his mother's breast, nursed, caressed, tickled and bathed. For some babies, the experience of being dressed and undressed is itself an attacking, disintegrating event and, for almost all, comfort is derived from skin-to-skin contact with their mother, and the experience of being put down, away from her, is distressing, causing them to cry. The psychological evidence for the significance of skin-to-skin contact in early bonding is robust,[1] and the analytic literature asserts the primacy of early experience in providing the foundations for the construction of an integrated self.

It is evident that, from infancy, the sense of integration starts from the outside in, and from the relationship with the primary carer: this physical and emotional containment enables the baby to develop psychic containment and a sense of self. The primacy of the skin is clear. It provides the first sense of the ego, the holding structure that integrates experience. From this primary experience, the mind can develop and grow. Men and women who have had had disrupted early experiences of attachment, without a primary caregiver performing a reflective function that enables them to know about their own mind as seen in another's, are at risk of feeling unintegrated, unreal and without any firm foundation in later life. They can often experience themselves as highly vulnerable to the wishes, desires and projected fears of others. This can be a frightening experience of disintegration and depersonalization typifying the phenomenology of borderline psychopathology.

Lucy, described in the first chapter, demonstrated this type of experience in relation to Shane, who projected into her his own sense of total vulnerability and helplessness. She tried to retain a sense of her own identity but found it very hard to do so, in the context of his projection onto her of his blueprint of an abandoning and uncaring woman. Similarly, she felt terrified of abandonment by him and sought to preserve the relationship at all costs. As a response to the violence and chaos of the relationship, she became depressed, felt alienated from others and used alcohol and self-harm at various points in her attempt to release the tension and to regain a sense of reality, that is, to reduce her feelings of dissociation and unreality. When she engaged in a programme for women who were abused by partners, she felt far more able to see how much the feelings she had taken on of being humiliated and pathetic, were actually projections of the way that Shane felt about himself. This helped her to feel less ashamed of her role in the relationship and the risks to which she had exposed her children in order to preserve it. She understood how and why she had repeatedly turned to Shane to offer her sanctuary, and that this was futile. She eventually began to regain self-respect.

When someone feels insecure internally, they may feel compelled to seek containment and a sense of security through contact with another, upon whom they rely literally and symbolically to hold them together.

Swinburne (2000) describes the developmental process that leads to a sense of internal containment. He outlines the consequences of its disruption or failure for the development of an inner sense of home – which he calls the 'home in the mind' – and how this leads to tremendous dependence on others to provide this:

> [I]t is the presence of a boundaried internal space which is central to any individual's capacity to retain a sense of home within the mind. . . . If we apply this theory to the idea of home, we see that while the individual who is able to develop internal space with a containing object will then be able to function at the symbolic level, and will therefore be able to experience home in the non-psychotic sense – what we might call the home in the mind – the individual who fails to install a containing object and develop a sense of internal space will have no option but to project his feelings into containers which exist outside of his own psyche.
>
> (Swinburne, 2000: 224)

In the following clinical illustration, I describe Lori, a 22-year-old woman who was essentially rootless, homeless and lacking an internal sense of safety and external protection.

Clinical illustration: Lori: no place to go

I assessed Lori for her suitability for psychotherapeutic intervention in the context of her history of trauma.

As described in Chapter 2, violence often begins during pregnancy: Lori's mother, a prostitute, was often beaten during her pregnancy, suggesting that, even before conscious memory, Lori's experience of her mother's womb was of an unsettled, disturbed environment. Up until the age of two, she had been left in the care of her mother, who was an alcoholic. At times, she was loving and affectionate to Lori and her sister, but would then leave them alone for extended periods. Lori remembered being left to take care of her six-month-old sister, in a bare room, with no food to eat and nothing to drink, for hours on end. She recalled how when her mother returned, she would often be drunk and distressed, but would sometimes bring fast food for them to share. There was no sense of order or security and being fed was unpredictable and chaotic. She was often left hungry, alone and scared.

By the time she was assessed by child protection agencies at the age of three, Lori was noted to be small for her age and clearly malnourished. Up to then, she had escaped the attention of the local authority despite her gross neglect and level of deprivation that included malnutrition. Her father had left her mother before she was born, and the extended family lived in another part of the country and were only infrequently in contact with Lori's mother. As a toddler, she had been taken to hospital by a worried neighbour on more than one occasion, and this had finally attracted the attention of social services, who put her and her sibling on the at-risk register, and eventually placed both into foster care. At the time she was taken into care, when she was nearly three, she had suffered a broken leg. Although the medical investigation of her injuries did not point to deliberate cruelty or physical assault, it was evident that she had suffered gross neglect and 'failure to thrive'; her broken leg was found to be accidental, caused by her lack of supervision, and resulting in a dangerous fall from a low wall she had been climbing. Indeed, the degree of her neglect and the reports of long periods of time wandering the streets on her own were clear signs of her mother's inability to care for or protect her. Imagining this very young child wandering the streets, wholly unsupervised, was both chilling and prophetic. It foreshadowed her bleak future and repeated homelessness. This image also conveyed the sense of her restless searching for care, which continued up to the present day.

After being taken into care, Lori had no contact with either her mother or sister; she was thin, underdeveloped and with severely delayed language skills. Her mother could clearly not keep her 'in mind', and struggled to meet her basic physical needs, let alone her emotional ones. It is difficult, at times, to conceptualize the harmfulness of neglect, but its consequences are profound.

Her presentation in assessment evoked an image of the neglected and lost child she had been some 20 years ago, as she seemed disorientated, bewildered and wounded, sitting in the consulting room with me. Despite her years, she appeared to me a small girl, who evoked a wish to take care of her, to run her a bath, give her fresh clothing and a hot meal. The sense of deprivation she conveyed was difficult to bear, and she looked frail and thin. She still seemed to be somewhat insubstantial, in a literal and figurative sense: it was hard to feel I had 'got hold' of what she wanted to communicate, and I noticed that she would drift into and out of contact with me. She kept all her outer clothing on, despite the heat in the room, and left me wondering whether she was shy of revealing her excessive thinness, self-harm scars, or any outline of her body. It seemed she felt so exposed and anxious just meeting me that she needed to use her coat as protection. I wondered whether she retained these layers of clothing to give her a sense of being safe in her skin, and held.

Lori described having been 'passed from pillar to post' all her life, experiencing multiple foster placements and, finally, an unhappy adoption when she was eight. Her central childhood experience was one where she was unwanted, lost and 'kicked out' of placements, both children's homes and foster homes. She had found it impossible to settle anywhere, and had bed wet and soiled until early adolescence, leaving a mess wherever she went. She had disturbed eating patterns, and remembered being described as a 'fussy eater'. She was a girl who remained dangerously thin.

This symptom of soiling was an important expression of something inside that felt uncontainable to her, and could, quite literally, not be borne. She had no inner sense of being able to process and filter through experiences, and separate out nutrition from toxic waste. It was as though her capacity to contain anxiety and manage her own impulses was so damaged that it was expressed through this physical leakage.

In infancy, she had been so neglected that she had learned to ignore hunger pangs, and managed to fend for herself during her mother's frequent and prolonged absences. She had not been able to learn about what her body needed through a sensitive caregiver mirroring back to her both her mental and physical states; her difficulty in knowing how and where to defecate seemed to reflect this, and also demonstrated a high level of emotional stress and anxiety. Although this was a physical problem, it also signified a psychic and developmental difficulty – she did not know how to digest, process and excrete material she took in, and how to use nutrients that were essential for life and growth. She felt, at some level, that she should not occupy any space in the world and that she did not deserve nutrition. She seemed stuck in time as a malnourished infant.

Lori's early deprivation and neglect had left her with an impoverished sense of her boundaries, both internal and external, as well as real difficulty in taking in and integrating good experience, as shown in her basic intolerance of good food, or care; it was as though she could hold nothing good inside her and could not use her mind or body to appreciate care, food or a home. These goods had been offered too little, too late, for this already damaged child, and she was left in a more or less constant state of refusal. She could not integrate her own destructive feelings, and so she evacuated them, projecting them into those abusive and cruel partners and parents who, in turn, enacted them, often against her. Her adoptive father had beaten her on several occasions. Lori seemed repeatedly to become a receptacle for other people's violence, and also to project all her aggressive impulses into those around her. Her past led to her repeating destructive dynamics in her closest relationships.

As well as revealing her developmental difficulties, her soiling and wetting exacerbated her sense of being messy and unwanted, impacting adversely on her environment and on her foster-parents' attachment to her. It created shame and rejection for her as it was met with anger by her foster-parents, following several unsuccessful attempts by her to hide soiled underwear and sheets. Sadly, these well-meaning foster-parents were themselves deprived of the opportunity to express their confusion and despair about her double incontinence. They did not have a mental space or 'home' to work through their feelings and try to make sense of what the soiling meant to Lori, and how it could be understood. Instead, they were left with the dirty evidence of her distress and faced with her repeated deception and anger towards them. Their other children felt distressed by the smell and dirt that accompanied Lori, and could not bear to be near her.

At eight years old, she moved into the care of a religious couple, who later adopted her. They appeared to tolerate her incontinence, though she was given the task of cleaning her own bed linen. Their rules were strict and clear, and at first Lori felt settled and happy. However, they had a biological son with a learning disability, who was two years older than Lori and, as he entered adolescence, Lori claimed he was aggressive and sexually predatory towards her, though she was not believed when she complained about him. A binge drinker, her adoptive father was sometimes violent – both towards her and towards her adoptive mother. She learned at the age of nine that her mother had been a prostitute through overhearing a conversation between her adoptive mother and a friend. She had not retained contact with her half-sister, and often felt she wanted to find her, and her biological mother, as she felt alienated from her adoptive family.

As she developed into full adolescence, she found her adoptive family's rules too much to abide, and felt that they were restricting her. Despite her pervasive sense of sadness, she found some enjoyment through being with friends, drinking and using recreational drugs. She was sexually active at 13, and hid this from her adoptive parents, fearing that she would be sent away. Ultimately, she was asked to leave the family home, at the age of 16, and she said they did this on 'the day the money ran out'. This was one of many evictions from home, which left her feeling rejected, detached from her adoptive family, estranged from her biological mother, and at the mercy of friends, acquaintances and landlords. Her only good memories of this strict home involved the pets she had been able to care for; especially the two dogs. She dreamed of taking one with her to protect her. On leaving, she was at high risk of being targeted by predatory males, and felt desperate for another home, lodging with various acquaintances until finally being taken in by an elderly neighbour. He was the person to whom she felt closest.

When I met her, Lori's violent ex-partner Troy had recently been jailed for his vicious assault on her and for several offences of theft. During our four meetings, it was clear that she was still preoccupied with him but she had accepted that she had to choose between him and her own safety and, for now, had parted company with him, staying with an older friend. She and Troy had met in the homeless shelter and she had thought he had 'nice eyes, nice smile and a funny personality'. At first, she felt they were 'kindred spirits', bonding as she had with others in children's homes in early childhood, feeling in touch with his sense of isolation and unhappiness.

Approximately six to seven months into the relationship, Troy began to hurt her – she said he 'chucked her down' and constantly hit her, also beating up her puppy. She gave a graphic and vivid description of how, on one occasion, he had kicked, punched and smashed the dog's head against the wall until 'she was swollen and deformed – looked like an alien'; she attributed some of his violence to his excessive drinking. I thought her description of the monstrous transformation of her beloved pet was also how she saw Troy when he changed, in front of her eyes, from the man she loved into a furious beast – an alien.

In her search for a home, and a partner whom she could love and trust, someone she had craved all her life, she had turned to him, as protector and carer or, as she put it, 'a father figure'. She had become so used to abuse in her early life that it was, at times, difficult for her to see how cruelly he treated her, although she saw herself as being much like her dog, which he teased, tortured and mutilated. She knew that if the dog were spared this treatment she would 'be in for it', as if they were interchangeable creatures in her partner's mind; both were weak objects against whom he could vent his anger.

Tragically, Lori seemed to tolerate extreme levels of violence towards her, and towards creatures in her care, feeling wholly unable to prevent this and very frightened about what would happen to her if she did assert herself. This was vividly illustrated in her description of how badly her puppy was beaten, and how she would cower behind her, to which she would respond 'Why you doing that for? Mummy ain't going to do nowt', indicating her sense of helplessness. She felt unable to protect either herself or a vulnerable animal that was her responsibility. The solution she had found was to give her dog away, losing all contact with her but at least ensuring the dog was out of danger.

She had some sense of guilt and remorse, but still did not feel she could go and see the dog, saying it would bring back painful memories. She said she had been afraid that if the dog weren't beaten, she would be. It was clear that she both identified with this battered animal, and sacrificed her, allowing the dog to be abused in place of her.

Lori understood the dynamics of her relationship with Troy, saying 'To him, I wasn't his girlfriend, I was a part of his property' and had obtained a restraining order against him. She was still terrified of him and worried that he would pursue her when released from prison, saying 'I know he will come looking for me'. At the same time as this was a dreadful prospect for her, I had the sense that it was also something of a relief, in that she felt at least one person noticed and minded if she were not present. In general, she felt invisible, homeless and fundamentally unwanted.

Lori's history of trauma, abuse, rejection and intense depression, coupled with her learning difficulties, left her vulnerable to exploitation and abuse. She had little self-esteem, high levels of dependency and a profound fear of being on her own, exacerbated by her experiences of physical and sexual assault. She had suffered severe disruption and confusion in her early life, including her mother's repeated abandonment and neglect of her.

Her vulnerability was apparent to others who seemed to target her; she was sexually assaulted on three occasions by men she knew. This contributed to her sense of depression, fear, unworthiness and reliance on others to be with her to serve as protection against a world that proved to be dangerous and unpredictable to her. She looked to her partners as symbols of home, apparently offering care, structure, warmth and constancy. She powerfully communicated to them: 'Without you there is no place for me to go.'

Like so many of the young women I have seen, some of whom are literally homeless, and most of whom have had inadequate experiences of care in infancy, Lori had no inner sense of 'home' in the mind, where she could feel contained and held. She did not have a place where she belonged and could feel safe, either psychically or physically. Her false sanctuary was often found in the arms of violent men, who offered her imprisonment rather than safety, control rather than guidance, and punishment rather than care.

Clinical illustration: discussion: insecure attachment and homelessness

Lori had not experienced a reflective mind to hold *her* in mind, nor loving arms to hold and soothe her, but was left to fathom out the world and manage as best she could her savage hunger pains and fears of abandonment, when left alone with her baby sister for hours. One can only imagine how her sister's cries made her feel when she too was left unattended, and what helpless and disturbing sensations overwhelmed her. She had a recurrent sense in adulthood that she was falling apart. Her early neglect was repeated in the present, and her sleep was dominated by nightmares of falling: dropping into an endless void. She then sought the comfort of a partner to stop her feeling so uncontained. Her dog, too, had been a source of protection and companionship, but sadly she had been badly injured by her violent boyfriend, who had wanted to destroy anything and anyone else in her life. The use of animals in domestic violence was explored in Chapter 4, and is also resonant here; attacking her dog was a sadistic aspect of Troy's treatment of Lori.

In psychoanalytic terms, she had no sense of a good containing object to introject or take inside her, and no way of developing an inner sense of sanctuary, living in a persecutory world; Lori could only evacuate her terrors onto the world around her, in which she then felt unsafe, left in a limbo state where danger existed both inside and outside of her. In this way, she did not develop what Swinburne calls a 'home in the mind'.

Swinburne (2000) discusses the profound failure to contain faeces in his clinical illustration of a man 'who turned himself inside out', linking this physical and psychological difficulty to an inability to use nurturance and take in something good, because of the primacy of uncontained destructive feelings. This predominance of destructive feelings results from the failure in the maternal capacity for containment in early infancy that could have led to the integration of hateful and envious emotions, allowing the developing infant to integrate her impulses. Where this hasn't happened, the infant does not learn to distinguish between inside and outside, developing only the weakest sense of self, and evacuates experiences rather than taking them in, or digesting them.

How to address psychic homelessness

One concrete and psychological solution to this type of internal homelessness is residential treatment, along therapeutic community lines. Sadly, these invaluable resources are hugely expensive and increasingly rare. The recent closures of the Arbours Crisis Centre, the Cassel Family Centre and the Henderson Hospital in the UK, testify to the current culture of cost-cutting and quick-fix treatments. I recommended that Lori be engaged in treatment, within a non-residential therapeutic community, that could offer her the containment she desperately needed. Unfortunately, funding could not be obtained for this treatment and she was only offered weekly supportive psychotherapy, with which she engaged unreliably; but I hoped she engaged enough to be able to take in something from the work. In her case, her level of deprivation was so profound as to require intensive psychological 'holding' in the form of daily groups throughout the week, and a place to go.

When violent feelings cannot be contained

Those with no capacity to inhabit an interior space are more likely to become dependent on others, and on their surroundings, to serve as containers for their unmanageable and difficult feelings. They are missing the sense of 'home in the mind' described above, that would allow them to process difficult feelings and reflect on disturbing experiences without needing to simply evacuate them, either through violent action or through thought-blocking. They will increasingly rely on primitive defences, such as projection, to evacuate painful or unwanted feelings and aspects of themselves, and locate them in others. Similarly, they may require firm, even rigid and impermeable, boundaries to enable them to feel safe, as they have no sense of internal borders. Sometimes, these boundaries even extend to the walls of prison cells.

The phenomenology of self-harm reveals an attempt to demarcate a sense of boundary, as opposed to inchoate distress in people who have no early experience of being held physically or psychically. The earliest ego is the body ego, and there is a clear language of the body with a description of the meaning and function of the skin, and being held, in infancy, since the skin and its mutilation is a central feature of violence. Bodily symbols and gestures develop from these crucial early experiences; they pre-date language, but articulate the most fundamental human needs. When these experiences have been traumatic, the infant can be affected in a way that leaves them 'stuck' in a preverbal stage of distress, without the use of words to describe their painful experiences. In adulthood, times of crisis can reawaken these early feelings, whose intensity is then managed through violent action rather than language or reflection.

In search of a homeland

In the course of care proceedings and in forensic services, I repeatedly encounter women who engage in restless movement between homes (which are imprisoning), the streets (which offer no protection), and their unions with destructive men. These partners are seen initially as islands of safety and constancy, but turn out to be violent and abusive, often driven by their own fears of abandonment and early, repeated experience of rejection and neglect. The to and fro is relentless, as the quest for home proves impossible to fulfil.

Their male partners are all too often also caught up in a cycle of violence and a search for an idealized sanctuary; a fantasy of a home that is always safe, welcoming and entirely their own. In an important sense, their partner's body symbolizes the home, the body of the mother that is kept safe and welcoming, only for them. It is easy to see how this quest is destined to fail, as the reality of another human being, with her unpredictable subjectivity, and other people to 'house' (in pregnancy or in motherhood), is too much for the men to bear. Their sense of exile is defended through violent assault. This can also be understood not simply as an expression of rage, but also as an assertion of ownership. For some, it is an unconscious expression of pure distress and terror at perceived abandonment. As described in Chapter 2, some authors classify the types of violence that occur in abusive partnerships as either 'situational couple violence', where both partners periodically lash out physically, or as a far more dominating and comprehensive form of control that has been termed 'intimate terrorism' (Johnson, 1995). The violence that begins in pregnancy would appear far more likely to fall into the latter category, as the pregnancy and future baby represent a force that can't be controlled, and constitute a threat to the violent partner's degree of coercion and control over his partner and her body.

The violence by men towards their pregnant partner, as discussed in Chapter 2, can be seen in this light as an attack on the body that betrays them, offering shelter and love to another, rather than its rightful 'owner' – the man in search of the home he feels he has finally found. Likewise, attacks on property and burglaries can be understood symbolically as assaults on the body of the mother, in which goods are stolen and shelter is violated. The wish for ownership of the woman's body is not simply rooted in a patriarchal society, but has its roots in earliest infancy, in the baby's wish to inhabit a safe, secure and permanent home. Attacks on this 'home' as represented by the mother's body are performed by partners on the bodies of females, and by women themselves as they inflict injury and pain on their own bodies. I have argued elsewhere (Motz, 2008) that these acts of self-harm are also symbolic attacks on the mother's body, as represented in their own.

The contract: shared ownership, consensual slavery

A clashing cymbal, evoking the sound of a cracking whip, a master beating a slave, punctuates Nina Simone's haunting song 'Be My Husband'. Her refrain is that she will do anything to keep this man, her husband (although he betrays and maltreats her), because, as she tells him 'outside you, there is no place to go'. This can be understood not only as a concrete statement of actual dependence on him, but symbolically, as their relationship represents her only home, and sanctuary.

Women who locate their own violence in their partners may initially feel relieved of the burden of their overwhelming feelings of anger, but this soon becomes a persecutory situation as they are eventually enslaved by these violent partners. Just as prison can initially offer inmates a sense of safety and freedom from the chaos and threats of their own overwhelming impulses, the fierce and confining love of a violent partner can, at least initially, offer a false sense of protection. Over time, however, this initial sense of safety can become suffocating and may be replaced by a longing for freedom. Once the terror of being taken over by inner forces without (external) restraint is forgotten, the woman may wish desperately to be on her own but, ironically, the time when she feels most able to dare to leave her violent partner is also the point where she is objectively most at risk of harm, or even death, at his hands.

The search for containment

As described earlier, when there is little sense of an internal sanctuary, primitive states of projection become operational and unwanted feelings are put outside, into these other people and other places. Although this initially feels like a relief, as all the badness is projected into the external world, the result is that the world becomes terrifying. The consequence of this splitting is a sense of paranoid fear of being trapped in a terrifying and persecutory world, full of bad objects. This state of mind reflects the absence of an interior sense of self who can remain intact, withstanding difficulties and psychic assaults. Someone in this state of mind is in the paranoid-schizoid position, in a fragmented and primitive state of anxiety. They don't feel secure in themselves as a container that can integrate both good and bad feelings. This sense of being uncontained in turn creates even greater dependence on others who seem to offer their only means of feeling physically and psychologically held. This can lead to great difficulty in leaving partners, even when they are violent and abusive.

When homes are shared with violent partners, even when a sense of sanctuary has been eroded, the idea of leaving home, paradoxically, is increasingly frightening. There is a desperate wish to hold on to something or someone outside who can hold them together, so that leaving represents a kind of falling apart. People who are insecurely attached can find separation almost impossible, as it feels like a violent wrench rather than a necessary process of individuation.

Ironically, violence in the household is sometimes the reason that women do leave home, when the hope of finding sanctuary (inner home) in their partners is revealed to be unfounded, but those who find themselves homeless are then at increased risk of violence by others. The risk of exposing their children to homelessness can also deter women from leaving violent relationships. For those with economic, social and family resources to protect them, leaving the violent partner does not necessarily mean becoming homeless, although it is still a time of increased risk of serious violence by him. But for most vulnerable women, finding another home may prove impossible. The recent cuts to shelters and refuges for battered women in the UK will further endanger women and children. Rates of victimization in homeless women are high, and this will be explored in the following section.

The experience of violence in homeless women

Victimization and violence are prevalent in the lives of homeless people, often beginning in childhood through the experience of abuse and trauma. The impact of childhood abuse and trauma has been identified as a pathway into homelessness. Furthermore, the psychological impact of childhood abuse and trauma has been linked to victimization and perpetration of violence within homeless populations. Victimization and perpetration of violence has been predominantly studied in homeless adolescents and women (Couldrey, 2010). Homeless women are far more likely to be victims of intimate partner violence than are homeless men; this difference is robust under statistical controls. In their 2005 multi-site study in the USA, Jasinski *et al.* analysed the experience of violence among 800 homeless women living in one of four cities in Florida, and a comparison sample of approximately 100 men. They found that:

> A significant number of women were victimised in their lifetime, and almost one-quarter of the women indicated that violence was one, if not the main, reason they were homeless. In fact, almost one-third of the sample of women indicated they had left a childhood home due to violence. Rates of sexual, physical and stalking victimisation were much higher in this sample compared to the National Violence Against Women Survey, which used the same

measures. For the women in this study, childhood experiences of violence were consistently associated with negative outcomes such as alcohol and drug use, depression, and low self-esteem. Moreover, the results of the multivariate analysis indicated that childhood violence significantly increased the risk for adult victimization net of all other factors in the model. In addition, other risk factors included current alcohol use, being divorced or separated, a greater number of children, number of times homeless, and depression. What this analysis tells us is that homeless women are a vulnerable population with childhood violence at the crux of this vulnerability.

(Jasinski *et al.*, 2005: 1)

The results of their statistical analysis of the lives of 400 homeless women indicated that 'childhood violence significantly increased the risk for adult victimisation, net of all other factors in the model'. It is evident from their study that both minor and severe violence experienced as a child increased the risk of many factors (including homelessness) that were then associated with a greater risk of adult victimization. The need for programmes to combat child maltreatment is urgent. For the women in this study, efforts would be too late; however, homeless shelters may not be equipped to handle the myriad problems that these women may be dealing with. Shelters are not psychologically sophisticated, and are designed to address practical needs, such as healthcare and the immediate issue of housing. However, they may not be equipped to delve deep into the childhood experiences of the women who arrive at their doors. Without psychological intervention, homeless women are in danger of repeating the cycle over and over again, and putting both themselves and their children in grave danger.

The authors of this study raise the crucial question of the potential role of domestic abuse in the cycle of episodic homelessness, suggesting that one pattern is based on women who flee abuse, making themselves homeless. Later on, their partners express remorse and their rage temporarily recedes, sometimes leading to reconciliation, as the women move back in

only to suffer another cycle of abuse–homelessness–remorse–reconciliation at a later date, over and over again. Or, equally possible, women are abused, escape to homelessness, eventually link up with another abusive male partner, only to be abused again.

(2005: 12)

The authors found that approximately one homeless woman in four is homeless largely because of her experiences with violence. Ironically, the search for home leads so many vulnerable women into chaotic, violent and unsustainable situations. In order to stay in these households, they give up their own minds, and feel that they become bodies under siege. Adlam and Scanlon (2005) describe homelessness as a case of 'unhoused minds' and, indeed, women whose search for home has led them into violent partnerships, can become dislocated from their hopes, aspirations and sense of peace.

The couple in search of home

Although women are, more often than men, homeless because of experiencing intimate partner violence, there is clearly a shared dynamic in the relationships that can be understood as a mutual search for a 'psychic' home. The following clinical illustration is of a young mother, Sinead, who lost her four children to care because of the risk of harm to which they were repeatedly exposed, despite her repeated and short-lived attempts to leave her violent partner.

Clinical illustration: Sinead and Quentin

I was asked to assess Sinead to see if she could protect her two children, and herself, as they had all been exposed to severe violence, although she was the only direct victim. She had sustained broken arms, black eyes, a kick in the stomach that caused a miscarriage and, most recently, a strangulation attempt that had left her with severe bruising on her neck and had terrified her. Her partner Quentin had served time in prison as a result of her pressing charges on him in relation to the most recent offence. He was now out of prison and the couple had, for the time being, separated. They had separated several times in the past, and even convinced childcare agencies that their contact was over; but this was not true, and the deceptions unravelled, revealing that they had reunited, and the children were again witnessing severe violence to Sinead and, at times, intervening to protect her, although the oldest one, a boy, was only six years old.

Sinead returned to her violent partner time and again, feeding on the false hope that he would change his behaviour, only to be battered once more. Like Lori, she had first met Quentin in a homeless hostel, attracted to him, in part, because of their shared experience of time spent in care, and the sense of being understood by him – they were outsiders together. She had experienced physical abuse in childhood, as her father was frequently violent towards her, her two siblings and her mother. She had then lived with her maternal grandmother until she died when Sinead was 14, and she had a period of time living with other relatives and friends until, at 16, she moved into a hostel for homeless young people.

Her wish to find a home with him led her to leave her friends, family members whom she had some contact with, and her job – a source of security – to travel with him. He took her to seven different villages and towns in the course of three years, subjecting both Sinead and their two young children to severe disruption and instability in their environment. This relentless search for home was in fact a kind of nomadic quest that left them constantly displaced, and always outsiders – the children never feeling safe or settled, and the parents under tremendous pressure. Moving on became a way of life: a false solution. Quentin was jealous of her apparently flirtatious associations with men, and often accused her of sexual betrayal; he thought that one way of ensuring that these friendships wouldn't develop was to keep the family on the move. In this way, he also succeeded in isolating Sinead from family and friends and stamping his mark on her: she was his alone.

Through this constant upheaval, any sense of home was shattered, and the only constant force in the family was Quentin's relentless degree of control and violence. In turn, Sinead became dependent on alcohol and turned to her children to comfort and protect her. Their frequent moves initially prevented social services from being able to keep track of the family and monitor the children effectively, but on one occasion the youngest girl was injured in a violent scuffle between the parents, and ended up in hospital. The family on the run was now under the radar, and had to stay put, as the local authority became aware of the full extent of the children's exposure to disruption, violence and alcohol misuse. Not only did Sinead lose her home, her partner and her family, but the children also suffered significant losses as they were removed and taken into care. When I interviewed Quentin, it was clear that he felt equally orphaned, abandoned and homeless, neither seeing nor accepting his role in the tragedy.

Talking with Quentin revealed that he was also looking for 'home', trying desperately to establish a sense of security and certainty that he wanted, but using physical and psychological domination over others to achieve this. He had suffered severe emotional and physical abuse during his own childhood at his mother's hands, and this seemed to have greatly affected his development and his capacity to trust women in general. He recalled an occasion when he had been beaten to the point of semi-consciousness because he had spilled orange juice on his mother's sofa, and another time when he was told to strip naked and stand in the corner of the room all night, again because of a relatively minor transgression. He remembered his childhood as being a time of more or less constant fear of his mother's violent temper – which was directed largely towards him – and his father's frequent interventions to protect him. He had been humiliated and shamed by his mother, and had become a target of bullying at school, often being teased for the shabby clothes he wore, called a 'tramp' and told he smelled. Like so many children who are bullied at home, he also became a target for his peers, mocked for his obvious neglect and unable to hide his sense of shame and inadequacy. He was haunted by a sense of humiliation. His rage served to protect him from depression and shame.

Clinical illustration: discussion of violence as a response to perceived abandonment

The contrast between viewing Quentin as an abuser, perpetrating violence on his pregnant partner, and imagining him as a battered child, begging his mother to stop hitting him, and pleading for her forgiveness for the most minor transgressions, could not be greater, and yet both were real and powerful aspects of his psychological make-up. He was both victim and perpetrator, enacting in the present the role of powerful, sadistic and wholly unreasonable tormenter, while still feeling like an unlovable child who would inevitably be left – a victim. Sinead knew this reality; she understood that he was a complex mix of vulnerability and cruelty, and this understanding made it harder for her to simply leave. She loved him and could identify with his sense of shame and confusion. Both Gilligan (1997) and Websdale (2010) describe the significance of shame, humiliation and fear on the development of violence towards intimate partners.

At times when Quentin perceived his partner to be critical of him or to be making threats to leave him, his early experiences of feeling hated and rejected would resurface which, in the context of alcohol abuse, would have destructive consequences. He would unleash his frustration and rage on to the target of his fury, the woman by whom he felt hurt, humiliated and rejected, despite desperate attempts to secure her love and commitment. The more he perceived her to be threatening him with abandonment, the more he became enraged, and behaved destructively, using any available means to secure a sense of his power and control, and alleviate his terror of being left. He was also operating with the kind of primitive psychological defences that were described in relation to Lori, the homeless woman who had no inner sense of home, or containment.

Quentin evacuated his violent feelings and sense of humiliation into Sinead and had no sense of being able to contain or manage these unbearable states of mind, instead becoming overwhelmed by them. His unconscious representations of Sinead were horribly distorted. He saw her as the mirror image of his neglectful mother and experienced her affection and care as mockery and deception; in this sense he was much like Shane, described in Chapter 1, and so many others.

This situation helps us to understand how early experiences tend to be recreated in later life; the power of these associations is enormous. The abuser – in this case, Quentin – is sensitive to any perceived rejection or abandonment; he is looking for evidence that he is unlovable, often finding it impossible to accept it if he is shown love and loyalty. He had an early experience of witnessing parental violence and being beaten by his own mother. He learned that feelings of anger, shame and need are normally expressed through violence. He perceived himself to be helpless and humiliated in relation to Sinead, whom he viewed as virtually omnipotent, responsible for most things that bother or frustrate him.

The compulsive aspect of abusive relationships relates to this unconscious fit where deep-seated emotional needs are met and familiar destructive patterns are enacted. There is a shared dependence and a shared fear of abandonment, though not one that is necessarily articulated. The abusive relationship thus has strongly entrenched destructive dynamics, involving mutual need, making it difficult to escape from or choose to leave.

The desperate wish for a safe, reliable and permanent home and notion of the 'lifetime burning in every minute' is particularly resonant for men like Quentin, and women like Lori. The whole of the past seems to be permanently alive in the present, with a violent force. It is 'burning in every minute' in that, each day, in every encounter, there is a felt experience of all the earlier traumata flooding the present moment, and all the future pain is envisaged there and then. In this way, there is a collapse of thinking and feeling in relation to present events, and so every disappointment, every perceived humiliation and pain encapsulates a life-time of pain and deprivation. In this state of mind, it is impossible to think, reflect or even to stay still; one means of psychic defence is the resort to violent action.

This sense of the collapse of time and space is further described by Campbell (2006) in her description of the dilemma of the homeless person, for whom being inside a house is trapping, yet being outside of one is terrifying, evoking a sense of abandonment. She refers to the 'claustro-agorophobic' dilemma (Rey, 1994) in which the fear of abandonment and the fear of intimacy in relationships are equally strong. This conflict leads to a perpetual sense of restlessness and dissat-isfaction, as relationships are quickly jettisoned and new ones impulsively formed. This dilemma was also evident in the way that Quentin, desperate for a 'home', couldn't settle in any one place and so kept moving. He could not find proof in his partner of the total sense of devotion, reliability and love that he craved and so he would attack her.

Young people who have run away from home because of abuse (whether physical, sexual or emotional) can find themselves in a state of perpetual longing for the home they wanted to have, but have never found. They are also searching for the inner sense of peace and belonging of which they were deprived in early life. Temporary shelters and even the streets may appear to offer some kind of solution to the dilemma of being neither inside nor outside a home, or finding a safe place to be; being on the move can feel like the only sanctuary, as perpetual motion appears to offer an escape from either being trapped or being left behind. Running away also carries with it the wish to be found and brought home, and it is this – often unconscious – wish that is so tragically unfulfilled: 'It is joy to be hidden and disaster not to be found' (Winnicott, 1965).

Home as torture chamber

At the other extreme from homelessness, there are the terrible crimes that are sometimes committed secretly in homes, where women and children are sometimes imprisoned, raped and violated. Few have been more graphically and chillingly reported than the recent case of Josef Fritzl in Austria in 2009, who imprisoned his daughter Elisabeth for over 24 years, keeping her in the cellar of his family home where he regularly raped her, and where she gave birth to seven children – the products of these incestuous rapes. Here, home has been dramatically and sadistically perverted into a torture chamber, from which victims can never escape and the perpetrator is guaranteed a future without abandonment.

Significantly, it appears that Fritzl himself spent long periods alone in child-hood and felt neglected by his mother. In one sense, taking his daughter hostage and imprisoning her was both revenge for this repeated neglect and a means of ensuring that he would never feel like this again; instead, he gave his daughter and their children the terrifying experience of being helpless, trapped and living in more or less constant fear. Elisabeth Fritzl lost one of her children, and the others spent their early years in darkness. The symbolism of her imprisonment in this dungeon, and the physical reality of its confines, is deeply painful to learn about. Her father's sadism and inability to see her or the children as separate, sentient creatures is evident. She said of Fritzl: 'He was very brutal against me. When I did not agree to have sex, then the kids would suffer. We knew he would kick us or be bad to us.' Fritzl also threatened to leave her and her children to rot behind the locked door, and bullied the children when they dared answer back to him. She said: 'He would often say we had no chance down under, in the cellar where it all happened. He said he could close the door whenever he wanted, and then we would see how long we survived.'

Although this is an extreme and exceptional case, in fact, the kind of intimate terrorism and abuse it depicts are found, to a lesser extent, in many other families, behind closed doors. Here, home is a prison; a torture chamber in which women and children are wholly objectified or even killed, and where their captivity at the hands of a sadistic man is not seen, nor prevented, as it goes on underground. This underground torture chamber is a dramatic and apt metaphor, pointing to the secret lives of captive victims in the domestic holocausts that can coexist with respectable, apparently civilized, households. The threats that Fritzl used against Elisabeth and the children and severe punishment for perceived disobedience are familiar weapons that maintain destructive household regimes. The underground cellar that existed literally in the Fritzl household exists psychologically in many ordinary households, in which a violent perpetrator terrorizes his family, finding a sense of affirmation in his total control over them. He turns the home into a prison cell, convincing the others that there is no escape.

Finding a place in the mind of the therapist

In the therapist's countertransference, working with women, and men, who have been held captive in situations of domestic terrorism, it is possible to feel like a hostage, bearing witness to torture and degradation. This can be experienced as a position of helplessness and powerlessness. However, if it can be used to inform the therapist's work, the position of bearing witness and working through the sense of entrapment is deeply significant. To be able to understand, experience and make sense of these traumatic events, and to work out their long-term impact on how future relationships will be formed and perceived, is to offer the former 'hostage' a mirror, and a sense of hope that can mitigate against the force of relentless repetitions.

At other points in the psychotherapy, the therapist can seem to become either an abandoning parent, or the persecutor, the one who appears to imprison the other in an unwanted relationship, and who has to battle against their free will. Again, this represents a valuable opportunity for the person who has been actually imprisoned by a partner, or a caregiver before them, to work through her fears, and counter her usual responses to the sense of entrapment. For this to be possible, the therapist must be attuned to the repetition of imprisoning relationships in the transference and countertransference, and to the need to interpret and articulate this so that the former hostage can find a refuge; a home in the mind that offers shelter from the storm.

7   Without honour

Shame, forced marriage and honour-based violence

Where Shall We Bury Our Shame?

Where shall we bury our shame?
Where, in what desolate place,
Hide the last wreck of a name
Broken and stain'd by disgrace?
         Sir Thomas Moore: lines 1–4

A man's honour lies between the legs of a woman.
                                        (Arabic saying)

This chapter explores the dynamics of forced marriage and honour-based violence. I discuss partnerships in which a vulnerable person is forced to marry someone due to familial and cultural pressures. These are examples of toxic couples, in which brutality and abuse exist between the individuals but, often, there is more than one perpetrator of violence as the wider community is involved.

The crimes committed in the name of 'honour' often involve the wider family system, in addition to the partner of a 'shameful' wife or girlfriend. Such crimes occur within organizations, including strict religious communities, where the fact of shameful secrets may lead to a conspiracy of silence. The group, or collective, cannot tolerate evidence of perceived wrongdoing and so annihilates the threat within – even when this involves violence or, worse, murder. This violence is viewed as a necessary evil; fundamentally, a way of restoring family honour and revenge on those who dishonour it that is justified, if not required. Reflected shame and honour (the shame and honour that can be brought to others by one's own behaviour) is an integral part of the concept of 'izzat', a notion of honour prevalent in cultures in North India and Pakistan, across religions and genders. The notion of justifiable vengeance for its violation is an integral part of this concept.

In extreme cases, the source of shame is literally buried when the woman is killed to prevent her from further dishonouring her family – if she has either refused a forced marriage, or has been seen to shame the family by behaving in ways that are considered to be unacceptable.

This chapter differs from previous chapters in that, while the perpetrator of violence is the intimate partner, in honour-based crimes there are often multiple perpetrators, especially in cases of honour-based killing. The violence extends beyond intimate partners.

As well as discussing the role of shame, forced marriages and honour-based crimes, I provide a clinical illustration of the role of aggression in coercive marriages, as told through the eyes of the male perpetrator. I am aware that it is the voices of the women that are so often silenced, but felt it was also important to consider the impact of coercion on men. This does not detract from the central issue of violence to women, but in fact outlines how coercive dynamics can increase the risk to them by men who vent their frustration, anger and resentment against their wives and other females.

Such domination is not simply practised by men against women. In a fascinating recent paper, Rew, Gangoli and Gill (2013) explore violence between female in-laws in India within middle-class households, particularly that directed from mothers-in-law to daughters-in-law. Like other forms of domestic violence, this cannot be simply attributed to the end goal of receiving dowry funds, or as part of a male oppression of women, but involves nuanced issues of power and control, that requires careful analysis, and attention to the issue of mothers' relationships with, and status derived from, their sons. The role of the extended family in isolating, intimidating and abusing the daughter-in-law is significant.

I have chosen to retain the term 'honour-based violence' as illuminating and meaningful, and to conceptualize forced marriage within the context of cultural and societal norms. However, I accept that it is not a practice that is confined only to certain ethnic groups, and I do consider it to lie on the continuum of gender-based violence. There are areas of commonality with other aspects of domestic violence, including the fact that the risk of violence to women increases at points of exit or attempts to leave the relationship. Like other forms of violence against women, it is predominantly the woman who is the victim of the coercive marriage, and abuse, although men too can be (less often) physically victimized.[1] I suggest that the psychological and social pressures on the men are also oppressive, even if it is more often the case that the females are the targets of violence. The questions of consent and coercion are central to this discussion and also underlie other manifestations of domestic violence.

The law and honour-based violence

A relevant source of information is offered by the Crown Prosecution Service in its guidance beginning with a broad definition of honour-based violence: 'Honour-based violence is a crime or incident which has or may have been committed to protect or defend the honour of the family and/or community'. I consider it helpful to offer further definitions, as provided in the (2012) UK government document 'The right to choose: Multi-agency statutory guidance for dealing with forced marriage':

Forced marriage

26. A forced marriage is a marriage in which one or both spouses do not (or, in the case of some adults with support needs, cannot) consent to the marriage and duress is involved. Duress can include physical, psychological, financial, sexual and emotional pressure.

Honour-based violence

27. The term 'honour crime' or 'honour-based violence' embraces a variety of crimes of violence (mainly but not exclusively against women), including assault, imprisonment and murder where the person is being punished by their family or their community. They are being punished for actually, or allegedly, undermining what the family or community believes to be the correct code of behaviour. In transgressing against this correct code of behaviour, the person shows that they have not been properly controlled to conform by their family and this is to the 'shame' or 'dishonour' of the family.

(Department of Finance and Personnel, 2012: 7)

Welchman and Hossain (2005: 6) state:

The term 'crimes of honour' encompasses a variety of manifestations of violence against women; including murders termed 'honour killings', assault, confinement or imprisonment, and interference with choice in marriage where the publicly articulated justification is attributed to a social order claimed to require the preservation of a concept of honour vested in male family and or conjugal control over women and specifically women's sexual conduct – actual, suspected or potential.

Forced marriages and their infringements on human rights have profound detrimental consequences for both men and women, but are particularly damaging to females, whose body and wishes are sacrificed for the sake of familial honour. It is far more often the woman who is the victim of these acts of honour-based violence, and young women, of reproductive age, are particularly at risk.

It has been argued that the notion of honour-based violence is predicated on the premise that the body of a female is the possession of males in the family. The Metropolitan Police's 'Honour-based violence and the law' information leaflet argues that acts of violence are not exclusive to one culture or religion, but are always connected to the male domination of women:

Honour-based violence (HBV) cuts across all cultures and communities: Turkish, Kurdish, Afghani, South Asian, African, Middle Eastern, South and Eastern European, for example. This is not an exhaustive list. Where a culture is heavily male dominated, HBV may exist.

Cultures in which HBV exists sometimes also practise forced marriage, and do not accept that a woman can have a partner before marriage, or that she can choose her own spouse. Remember that, where there is a forced marriage, there is also likely to be rape.

. . .

Evidence from research and analysis in the Metropolitan Police Service (MPS) shows that, where murders occur, most often wives are murdered by their husbands and daughters by their fathers. Honour-based violence is often a child protection issue.

(Metropolitan Police *Honour Based Violence*
Leaflet, 2008: 1)

Honour-based violence clearly occurs in a wide range of countries and the cases described are not highlighted to identify any one culture or religion as particularly pernicious, but to illustrate the deep tyranny and injustice in such acts of interpersonal violence. There are a range of honour-based acts of violence that demand close scrutiny; in this chapter, I focus on those that occur within the domestic sphere and relate to women who are perceived as dishonouring their religious community.

The scale of the problem in the United Kingdom

It is difficult to quantify this problem, as it so often goes underground, remaining a hidden crime. Home Office figures suggest there are around 12 'honour' killings in the United Kingdom each year, but the total is likely to be far higher. Honour killings can be motivated by a young woman's refusal to go along with a forced marriage.

Forced marriage is not the same as arranged marriage, nor is it in any way a religious practice. Clearly, there are cases of forced marriage other than those taking place within certain religious communities, and the key issue is that of consent. A person who is highly vulnerable, for a variety of reasons, including a learning disability, severe mental health issues or because they are underage and cannot be considered to give consent, could all become victims of a forced marriage.

In the UK, forced marriage often takes place between people under the age of 18: in 2009, 41 per cent of victims reporting to local agencies were under 18, and the percentage of actual victims who are under 18 is likely to be much higher. This fact has important implications: forcing children and young people into marriage has negative impacts on their educational and economic outcomes, as well as their sexual and emotional development (Wind-Cowie *et al.*, 2012). Statistics from the Forced Marriage Unit (FMU) over the year 2012 are similarly alarming, in that the FMU gave advice or support related to a possible forced marriage in 1485 cases and reported as follows:

Where the age was known, 13% involved victims below 15 years, 22% involved victims aged 16–17, 30% involved victims aged 18–21, 19% involved victims aged 22–25, 8% involved victims aged 26–30, 8% involved victims aged 31+. The oldest victim was 71 and the youngest was 2. 82% involved female victims and 18% involved male victims.

The FMU handled cases involving 60 different countries, including Pakistan (47.1%), Bangladesh (11%), India (8%), Afghanistan (2.1%), Somalia (1.2%), Turkey (1.1%), Iraq (1%), Iran (0.9%), Nigeria (0.9%), Sri Lanka (0.9%), Egypt (0.6%), Saudi Arabia (0.6%), Yemen (0.6%), The Gambia (0.5%), Morocco (0.5%), and Ukraine (0.5%). The origin was unknown in 7.7% of cases.

. . .

114 cases involved victims with disabilities. 22 involved victims who identified as lesbian, gay, bisexual or transgender (LGBT).

(Foreign and Commonwealth Office:
Forced Marriage Unit, 2012)

There is an ongoing discussion about whether the definition of forced marriage should be expanded in order to include those marriages where the victim is tricked into giving their consent, either through false information or the withholding of critical information.

There have been several high-profile cases of honour-based killings reported in the UK, Canada and the USA in recent years. In other cases, where death is not the outcome, the victim is subjected to less severe physical abuse and bullying over the long term as 'punishment' for 'bringing dishonour on the family'. This gross distortion of human rights in the name of honour has sanctioned horrific acts that have only recently been acknowledged and explicitly named as crimes in the UK's Forced Marriage (Civil Protection) Act 2007. It is essential to examine these crimes, as they directly contribute to the problem of socially, culturally and religiously sanctioned violence against women.

The collective nature of honour-based killing

In honour-based killings, there are often multiple perpetrators, and the wider society is clearly implicated in this abuse and horror. This has some parallels with Chapter 6, in that homelessness is also a problem perpetuated by wider society, and thus by multiple perpetrators, witnessed by many, and yet largely overlooked as a major social difficulty that should be addressed urgently.

Muslim advocacy organizations argue that honour killings are a misnomer, stigmatizing Muslims (and other specific groups) for what is simply domestic violence, a problem that has little to do with religion. It is also argued that the media coverage of honour-based killings focuses attention on cultural issues, contributing to racial bias, rather than situating this form of violence against women on a continuum of other brutal manifestations of domestic violence, in non-ethnic-minority households, in which women are also killed. The argument is that this is not a problem tied into the culture of one particular ethnic group. However, Phyllis Chesler completed a study of more than 50 instances of North American honour killings, and argues that the evidence suggests otherwise, and that the role of religion is key, implicating the wider values held by the community, which are hugely distorted in these crimes (Chesler, 2009). Closer analysis reveals that these crimes are actually committed within a family or wider group, who together carry out the beliefs enshrined in the community.

Young people leaving home

One of the features of forced marriage is that it requires young women (and sometimes young men, as the clinical illustration shows) to leave their family home and assume the role of a reproductive adult. Leaving home suddenly, without preparation, is not unique to forced marriage, and can be traumatic. A variety of societal and cultural norms require that individuals be evicted from their homes often at particular points in their lives that signify rites of passage. In the United Kingdom, these predetermined points of separation can include: children being sent to boarding school, sometimes aged as young as five; adolescents being asked to leave home when they are old enough to earn a living; older teenagers leaving home for university; and young adults who leave home to get married.

In her thoughtful paper, Schaverien (2011: 138) describes the trauma of being sent to boarding school, and how this can lead to the development of an encapsulated self, a person for whom intimacy is not permissible: 'Children sent away to school at an early age suffer the sudden and often irrevocable loss of their primary attachments; for many this constitutes a significant trauma. This pattern distorts intimate relationships and may continue into adult life.'

This echoes the work of John Bowlby (1969) on attachment models of development, as described in Chapters 3 and 6. There are clearly many variations in these patterns and life stages, and it appears that they are specific to particular social groups and conventions: traditionally, upper-class and upper-middle-class children were sent to boarding school in the United Kingdom 'for their own good'. The powerful interaction of social and cultural forces in shaping an individual's sense of agency and choice from an early age is evident in this practice; and in the notion of arranged marriages. It could be argued that, while the weight of parental expectations is always a significant pressure on a child, in some instances it is more explicitly articulated and the child has little choice over their response.

Young people leaving home to enter forced marriages

In families whose roots are in certain cultures – including Muslim, Sikh, Orthodox Jewish and Hindu – rituals of leaving home typically involve marriages, often arranged by families rather than being the choice of the young people. For some, these marriages are not simply arranged but 'forced', in that the young person actively opposes them yet has no choice in the matter. They may be coerced psychologically, emotionally or even physically – as some young people are literally kidnapped and taken abroad to marry the partners whom their parents have selected for them. In some cases, they are taken out of school for weeks at a time, or travel during the summer months when most arranged marriages take place. Summer is a popular time for forced marriages, as Homa Khaleeli notes in her article in *The Guardian* in which she interviewed Jasvinder Sanghera, a woman who ran away from home in order to avoid a forced marriage (Khaleeli, 2011).

Exile: Sanghera's story

The underlying forces of dehumanization and brutality that maintain abusive and degrading marriages can be disguised by the mask of 'honour' and duty. Sanghera describes this vividly both in her (2007) autobiography, *Shame*, and a later book, *Daughters of Shame* in which she tells the stories of others, who also suffered from honour-based violence, forced marriages or their threat. In *Shame*, Sanghera describes how she and her sister Robina were both expected to have arranged marriages within their traditional Sikh family. While Jasvinder left home to avoid having to marry at 15 and to have a relationship with a boyfriend of her own choosing, Robina entered a marriage where she was physically, sexually and psychologically abused. Tragically, she eventually committed suicide (although Jasvinder fears she may actually have been murdered by her violent husband). To make her own escape, Jasvinder endured virtual exile from her family.

In her autobiography, Sanghera uses her own experience to reveal the particular oppression and brutality shown to young, South Asian British women who attempt to resist these marriages, and who subsequently lose their sense of home, and their family's love.

Importantly, Sanghera describes how mothers (as well as fathers) in cases of so-called 'honour killings', collude to ensure that the woman who has allegedly brought dishonour on the family is brought to justice, or at least is unable to disgrace the family further.

As a result of her experience, Sanghera established the charity Karma Nirvana in 1993. She has been instrumental in campaigning for the criminalisation of forced marriage. This organisation offers advise, support and education to survivors of forced marriage and so-called 'honour-based' crime, and to professionals involved in cases concerning these issues. It is aimed at South Asian girls and women, but also helps countless others who are affected by these crimes committed in the name of honour, and challenges the conspiracy of silence in which domestic brutality and child marriage are kept secret.

Karma Nirvana also offers help and advice to those worried about the whereabouts of young people who have 'disappeared' for unexplained reasons, as well as supporting direct victims. It is designed to campaign against forced marriage and offer all forms of support for those who find themselves victimized by cultural and religious oppression, of which forced marriage is one manifestation. This courageous and important UK-based organization now has a helpline and offers legal, emotional and practical support to thousands of people each year, offering an alternative body and voice for those whose religion has silenced them.[2]

Whose honour? Whose punishment?

Phyllis Chesler and Nathan Bloom (2012) state: 'Honour killing is the premeditated murder of a relative (usually a young woman) who has allegedly impugned the honour of her family'. Unlike other forms of spousal or child abuse, honour killings invariably are conspiracies involving multiple family members, often including the victim's own siblings, parents and in-laws. As the authors note, the practice:

> tends to predominate in societies where individual rights are circumscribed by communal solidarities, patriarchal authority structures, and intolerant religious and tribal beliefs. Under such conditions, control over marriage and reproduction is critical to the socioeconomic status of kinship groups and the regulation of female behaviour is integral to perceptions of honour, known as *maryada* in many Indian languages and as *ghairat* in Urdu and Pashto.

The cruelty of such murders, and their criminality, appears to be hidden – as indeed are the murders themselves in many cases, where bodies of victims are never found, as the story is spread that the missing women (or men) have been taken abroad. This is a convenient truth, and one that can sometimes go unchallenged when, in fact, the missing have been killed and their bodies disposed of. Authorities may know that a child or adolescent is in danger and feel helpless to intervene, for fear of challenging cultural sensitivities and because of the difficulty in obtaining evidence in a family and/or social system that closes rank and will not allow truthful disclosure of criminal activity.[3]

Child murder and honour-based killing

In 2012, in Bradford in the UK, a couple were convicted of killing their daughter, 17-year-old Shafilea Ahmed, whom they perceived to be bringing shame on the family. During the course of her defence, her mother changed her initial argument, providing evidence against the father as the sole perpetrator of assault on their daughter – but the court found that she too was guilty of murder. The daughter who brought shame on the home was killed, in front of her siblings, to preserve the family's honour and to prevent her from leaving home and further disgracing the family. Tragically, Shafilea had known the danger she faced, and had contacted the police stating that there was violence being planned against her and that she knew she would be forced into an arranged marriage in Pakistan; her lack of consent meant that this would be a forced marriage.

On the second day of the trial, the following details were given in evidence by Shafilea's sister, Alesha, leading to the eventual conviction of both parents, who had denied the murder of their daughter:

> The younger sister of murdered teenager Shafilea Ahmed has described in court how her parents physically abused Shafilea 'nearly every day'.
>
> On the second day of the trial at Chester Crown Court, Alesha Ahmed spoke from behind a curtain so she could not see her mother and father
>
> . . .

> Alesha Ahmed told police she saw her parents suffocate Shafilea, 17, at the family home in Warrington in September 2003.
>
> Shafilea had refused to enter into a forced marriage with her cousin in Pakistan, the court has been told.
>
> Alesha told the jury that her parents' Pakistani culture meant she and her sister were 'restricted in terms of Western culture', which included the clothes they could wear and when they could go out.
>
> Alesha said Shafilea, a British-Pakistani college student, led a 'secret life' because she was doing things she thought her parents would not approve of.
>
> Asked what triggered the physical abuse from their parents, Alesha said it was Shafilea's friends, her use of her phone, and the clothes she was wearing.
>
> (Johnson, 2012: *Sky News*)

Shafilea's use of her phone was considered dangerous in that she was presumed to be contacting men, and conducting herself in an unacceptable fashion, wearing Western clothes and appearing immodest.

Honour-based abuse and crime occur within a wider system, that dictates unquestioning belief in the right of the family to make decisions about how their children will live, dress, marry and procreate, and that the greatest value is the honour of the family. Violence, even murder, is considered to be a justifiable response to shame and humiliation, as nothing is more important than the eyes of the other: the gaze of society, particularly that part of society that is held in highest esteem, those within the same community. This is the driving force for such acts of violence, rather than any individual attachment or ethical concern for the sanctity of life, or the need to protect and cherish one's children.

As Sanghera shows, all too often those outside of the community who witness acts of oppression or even violence will not act or speak – possibly out of fear of being seen to be racist, intolerant or politically incorrect. In some cases, the whereabouts of missing children is not fully investigated. Even those who are tasked with the responsibility for child protection may become paralysed out of a fear of being considered racist or culturally insensitive, or out of ignorance of what a family is capable of doing in order to avoid shame. This is not confined to families from a particular culture, as Websdale (2010) demonstrated in his study of familicide in the United States.

In 2009, in another case, an Afghan father, his second wife and son were found guilty of murdering his three daughters and his first wife, who was living with Mr Shafia in a polygamous marriage arrangement. The family were living in Montreal in Canada. Mohammad Shafia, his wife Tooba, and their eldest son Hamed, were sentenced on 29 January to 25 years in prison without parole. Prosecutors argued that Shafia felt ashamed of the rebellious behaviour of his three teenage daughters – Zainab, Sahar, and Geeti – and arranged for them to die in a staged car accident. The father, wife and son were also convicted of the killing of Rona Amir Mohammad, Shafia's first wife in a polygamous family, for purportedly being too lenient toward the girls.

In this chilling case, the defence lawyer for the accused cast aspersions on the motives and agendas of those he abused. A cultural expert, Mojab, testified on the conception of women within this culture: 'The concept of honour is rooted in a man's need to control [the] female sexuality of a sister, a daughter, a wife.' She went on to quote an Arab adage: 'A man's honour lies between the legs of a woman.'

When convicting the three found guilty of murder, the judge commented on the irony that these killings were justified as defending a family against dishonour. The Ontario Judge, Robert Maranger, made the following statement when summing up:

> It is difficult to conceive of a more heinous, more despicable, more honour-less crime. . . . The apparent reason behind these cold-blooded, shameful murders was that the four completely innocent victims offended your completely twisted concept of honour . . . that has absolutely no place in any civilised society.
>
> (Di Manno, 2012: *Toronto Star*)

Turning away from clear signs of violence and inhumanity is in itself form of prejudice, as if abuse does not 'count' when committed by people from a different culture, or against those with skin that is not white. Perhaps cruelty can be dismissed as 'difference' or be seen as something that people do when they are not fully granted the status of full human beings; that is, that unconscious racism leads to either a lack of concern about cross-cultural (non-white) practices because it 'doesn't matter' what non-white people do to one another, or because it doesn't 'count' as abuse in this other culture. Femicide is homicide, in any culture, and must be treated as such.

The psychodynamics of honour-based violence

Although it is clear that honour-based violence is a societal and cultural problem, we can also understand it in terms of the psychic defences it reveals. In this kind of situation, there is a projection of shameful wishes and desires into another; often the young girl unwilling to participate in a forced marriage, or seeking to express allegiance to another culture, such as a secular Western one. These wishes are repressed in the others, the upholders of the honour code, who express the fury of their underground longings in their vicious attack on the victim. The young woman in search of her own identity, or in touch with her sexual feelings wishes to be free of a restrictive regime and determine her own future. She may take on a symbolic role, representing the repressed sexual and intellectual desires of all in the community, who will not allow these unacceptable wishes to surface.

Ambiguity and ambivalence exist in everyone, and the fervour of the religious leader who insists on certainty and the absence of desire or curiosity can be seen as a reaction-formation: an attack on his own libidinous and aggressive drives. The young person, then, is the embodiment of all desire and freedom that cannot be known, spoken about or acted on, and she becomes highly threatening to those around her. The apparently innocuous crimes of which these young people, usually women, are accused, reveal the symbolic significance of the underlying wishes that all members of the community struggle with. They may appear Western, wear clothes that reveal flesh, use social media sites or fraternize with the opposite sex, apparently flaunting a freedom that is seen to be dangerous. It seems significant, and ironic, that some high-profile cases from some of these same communities reveal that men have been involved in sex-trafficking young girls.

In order to free members of a community from the fears of their own temptations and wishes, such 'badness' and 'danger' is projected into the girls, who are then identified as being non-human, derogated victims of sadism and even murder, as they have lost their status as the future partners of valuable, honourable members of society. The sexism and racism of sex trafficking is not unique to one culture: all girls whose bodies are bought and sold are dehumanized and seen as 'other' – as 'fair game' to be used and abused at will. Tragically, these girls are so often vulnerable and isolated, already outside a family or strong social network and targeted by men who appear to offer sanctity. Their experiences mirror those of the homeless young women described in Chapter 6.

Clinical illustration: A man raging against his arranged marriage and family

In the following illustration, I describe the pressures of an arranged (not forced) marriage on a young man, who retreated into a dangerous fantasy life in order to escape the sense of restriction and tyranny he perceived in his domestic situation. I use this to show how such situations can actually increase the likelihood of violence, as both men and women can feel imprisoned in a situation they have not chosen. As this chapter has focused largely on the experiences of the female victims so far, it is particularly important to also delineate the sense in which men, too, are hurt by these partnerships and how violence risk can escalate. As a forensic psychotherapist and psychologist, I often work with the male perpetrators of violence, and this gives me a rich understanding of the motivations and expressions of their anger and aggression.

Jag was a 27-year-old man working in the post office, who was referred to me for psychotherapy because of recurrent violent fantasies, and behaviour that involved kerb-crawling and sex with an underage girl. He was from a traditional Muslim family and had been told that he would marry a young woman from Bangladesh who was chosen by his parents when he was 21 years old. He married the woman, and lived with her in his parents' home and felt trapped and despairing by the prospect of his future in this restrictive environment, within a largely loveless marriage. He was sometimes violent to his wife, with whom he had almost nothing in common, but mainly diverted his extremely sadistic feelings and impulses onto the young prostitutes he would pick up. His most disturbing fantasy involved.

murdering one of these girls after a particularly brutal rape, including anal penetration. He described how he would become aroused by this fantasy and then go in search of a young female to act it out with but, so far, he had only had sex with one prostitute, and had resisted his desire to brutalize her

He came into treatment with me in order to understand these fantasies, and to find peace from them, as they deeply offended his consciously held beliefs and values. Throughout therapy, he struggled with his wish to enact sexual violence and his recurrent guilt about his vicious assaults on his wife, which had on one occasion brought him into contact with the police. We met weekly for 18 months, during which time he continued to have sexual fantasies about violence, but became able to desist from aggression towards his wife. The breakthrough for him was the realization that his parents, rather than his wife, were the real targets of his rage, as they held such dominance and control over him, and had shaped his sexual and marital choices.

Jag slowly began to realize that his wife was not a perpetrator of this tyranny, though he had been treating her like one, and he decided to move out of the family home with her, hoping to start a family. He was able to express and work through his rage with me for being in what he considered to be a powerful position as his therapist, to whom he felt obligated, and saw me as being a moral agent. In fact, he was tormented by his own super-ego, and felt he partly wanted to commit an actual crime, such as assault against his wife, to be convicted and punished for his guilty secrets: his murderous wishes about his own parents, and their expectations that had imprisoned him. He felt trapped within the confines of clear and rigid cultural expectations and had little sense of how to establish a sense of himself outside of the others' projected images of him as the 'good son' or 'loyal husband'. He had no containment for his violent feelings, other than the therapy with me.

Jag felt he was outcast from the mainstream society in which he found himself, but also in terms of his own community and faith, as his sadistic sexual fantasies left him feeling guilty and sinful. The women Jag targeted, in fantasy and on the streets, were non-Asian women, whom he felt were more 'sacred' and should not be brutalized (failing to see his hypocrisy, as he beat and tormented his own wife, an Asian woman). The 'British girls' he would follow in his car were white, and his wish to hurt, dominate and defile them had rich meaning, revealing his wish to dominate and triumph, particularly over these girls, whom he saw as representing a racist society that put him down. In fact, these girls were themselves vulnerable and outcast. He clearly identified, at an unconscious level, with their 'outsider' status.

On the one hand, his aggression could safely be targeted towards these 'outcast' girls, these prostitutes, some of whom were actually young girls living in local-authority care homes, whose treatment was not closely monitored, and who represented the detritus of society – in Jag's view, the 'slags' and 'whores' whose abuse was not a concern to him. This view was harsh, expressing the brutal dehumanization of these young girls, who were invisible to him and to others, yet were vulnerable children in need of protection. On the other hand, his wish to defile and kill these young girls, sex workers and runaways from care, expressed his clear identification with them as unwanted, uncared for and outcast members of society, who 'deserved' punishment and even death. He was so deeply ashamed of his own 'depraved' wishes that he felt similarly outcast from his own community and from God, as well as having a strong sense that his family had not seen or loved him as he really was, a young man with little interest in the studies they had chosen for him, and a strong desire to travel and see the world. This sense of inner alienation left him feeling violently out of control.

He felt humiliated at home and at work and deeply resentful of his lack of choice in his own marriage partner, lifestyle and future. It was as though Jag's home was a place of artifice and buried rage, and his workplace reflected a similarly false picture of this man; handsome, well dressed and polite to the point of obsequiousness. The unravelling of this facade and 'truth' of his aggressive desires was enacted at night, as he would trawl the city streets, stalking young prostitutes and imagining buying sexual services. As described earlier, he had only once given in to this wish, but was aware that his kerb-crawling was itself risky for him, and could frighten others. At times, he would abandon his car and follow the women, hoping to alarm them. He 'got a buzz' from this, as it affirmed a sense of power and control.

The therapy with him was difficult and challenging as he struggled to articulate his rage at his family, whose strict rules and demands threatened his sense of autonomy and agency. Although the transference was initially one of a kind of false respectfulness towards me, an authority figure, gradually something more genuine, though violent and alarming, emerged. In his mind, I had become his powerful and disapproving father; he lashed out at me in anger during our sessions, telling me he could do what he wanted and I would never find out, and describing my approach as 'weak'. I withstood these verbal assaults and interpreted this as his fear of his own dangerous wishes and worry that neither he, nor I, would be able to stop him acting them out.

He then began to reveal vivid fantasies of sadistic sexual scenarios, occasionally including me, and also revealed that he could, if he chose to, access personal data about me easily through his job. This was a moment of real fear in the consulting room, as his threat to me was clear. I related this to his own sense of powerlessness generally, and interpreted his wish to stalk and rape, to violate those who were not in his immediate family, as a form of revenge on his family. I said he also saw me as a member of this inner gang. This inner mafia kept him bound and gagged, inviting revenge attacks. He agreed with this interpretation and said he had no way of expressing his sense of outrage and fury at the life that constrained him. He acknowledged how even the psychotherapy could feel imprisoning and restrictive. I was free and female, with power and authority relative to him, and this was humiliating.

Through my containment of his rage, and his increasing capacity to reflect on it, and to begin to explore his own complex responses to his sense of captivity, Jag was able to become less aggressive towards his wife, and eventually removed himself from the tyranny of his parents' home. He was also able to undertake a part-time course in geography, a subject of longstanding interest that he had not felt able to pursue, as his parents did not see it as relevant to his future. This development of a sense of interior space and privacy was essential, and allowed him to relinquish the deviant secrecy that had, until therapy, served as its dangerous substitute. He described, too, how he and his wife were now able to spend time together, away from parental figures in their own home, and felt that this gave them the chance to become closer, and more adult in their relations. By the end of therapy, he became more assertive towards his parents, and gentler to his wife; he was less full of rage.

Self-harm and the un-housed body

As described earlier in this chapter, Sanghera's sister Robina committed suicide, perhaps as her only escape from an intolerable situation, imprisoned in a brutal marriage. It is also possible that her violent husband or other family members killed her; a terrible crime that was disguised as suicide, as Sanghera fears. The data indicates that such 'suicides' are not uncommon in 'honour-based' murders.

Rates of self-harm in British Asian women are considerably higher than in other UK groups of women of the same age: 'South Asian women are significantly more likely to self harm between ages 16–24 years than white women' (Husain, Waheed and Husain, 2006). It is possible to speculate that a woman who is threatened with an arranged marriage may mark her own body to brand it as hers, to transform it into a damaged good that cannot be traded in, as well as to make an actual suicide attempt. It can also be an attempt to communicate to others that there is something awful happening, to alert attention to the suffering that is being inflicted. Shafilea, described above, had drunk bleach in what appeared to be a last resort in her attempt to escape from her intended forced marriage in Pakistan, requiring that she be flown back to the UK for treatment. Tragically, she did not find it possible to escape through these means, and perhaps was not able to let the medical professionals who treated her know about the horror of her parents' intentions for her. In turn, they did not see the signs of her distress or the danger of returning her to her captors.

I have worked with women, like Shafilea, who have escaped from the dangers of their own families, but who, in so doing, became virtually exiled from their communities, including their closest family members. They found it hard to tell their stories to anyone, but did eventually find a safe place in therapy. For several of these women, their anger about their own experiences of escaping from plans for forced marriages was not expressed to others, but towards themselves, in the form of self-harm. They had been subjected to violence within the home by parents and siblings acting under parents' instructions, leaving them feeling traumatized and furious, afraid to return home. Although relationships with one or more siblings may be retained, such contact must be maintained in secret, as the rest of the family would not tolerate it. The feelings of betrayal and anger that result from these experiences demand expression.

There are echoes of slavery and its violations in the abuse of these young women's bodies, and in the subjugation of their minds. Branding and inscribing marks on the body can be a form of self-expression and protest, as the woman finds a canvas on her own body. She can inflict secret or visible wounds to communicate her rage, contain her despair or disfigure her own beauty, as an attempt to devalue it in the eyes of other people. When women attack their bodies they are also symbolically assaulting their mothers' bodies, as represented by their own (Motz, 2008, 2009).

The young woman whose own mother has sacrificed her for the sake of honour to a brutal marriage can use her body as a container of her violent feelings. She may also be mocking and attack desire in the onlooker, or the possibility of sexual availability:

> [T]he social expectation that to look upon young women is to gaze at beauty. Femininity, sexual attractiveness and the soft, smooth skin of youth is highly idealized and there is a pressure on young women to give those who gaze at them some satisfaction. For women, and men, who have been sexually abused or otherwise traumatized, the look of the other, and the desire that can be awakened is terrifying. Marking the skin, defacing beauty, can be seen as a way of warding off overtures.
>
> (Motz, 2009)

In her case, the marks were also inscriptions of pain, intended to be read, and responded to.

Scanlon and Adlam (2009: 68) understand some self-harm to be a protest against society as well as an assault on the individual body:

> This, essentially antisocial, attempt to communicate something of this experience through self-harm is a violent one that is simultaneously directed against the inner and outer bodies that can accommodate neither their grief nor their grievance. That is to say, it is directed against the individual's own body, where the pain has come to reside, and is simultaneously an articulation of a complaint to and about the social world from which the individual has become dis-membered. This mutilation or poisoning of their own body is often experienced as bringing relief from this inner torment, born of this sense of

dis-memberment and social exclusion through the relocation of this painful state of mind into the precarious and temporary housing of their pained body.

Women with no place to go

In the cases described here, 'home' is a place in the mind as well as in the body of the community, and it demands conformity to its rules at any price. To be at home in her forced marriage was, for Sanghera's sister, to be in hell, where the brutality had to be hidden away, or borne alone. The price of dissent may be exile, or even death, as it was for her and for many unnamed and un-mourned others. There are, of course, some family members and friends, including siblings, who will mourn the loss of these young people, but this may have to be done in secret, or they too will risk exile and disgrace. The case of Shafilea Ahmed shows that these relatives can sometimes act with great courage and emerge from the shadows.

For Jag, home was prison, but therapy helped him to convert this into a place he could build for himself. Eventually, and fortuitously, he was able to leave the confines of his parental home and find sanctuary in his own freedom and volition. Although it has been argued that men in arranged marriages have a degree of freedom that women do not, it was clear that Jag struggled with a sense of conflict; he had a duty to care for his aged parents, but had a strong desire to live independently. By moving out of a repressive home, Jag reduced the risk not only to his own mental state, but also to others, including his wife, and the potential victims of his fantasized brutal sexual practices. This freedom to leave his childhood home, to become an individual in his own right, and to engage in therapy, offered him and his wife some hope of a different type of existence in which violence was not the only means of self-expression or release of frustration and rage. His desire to stalk women diminished significantly, perhaps revealing that he himself felt less closely tracked, less persecuted by a sense of being watched and judged.

It was evident that one of his aims in following these women and brutalizing them was to give them the experience of close surveillance, humiliation and fear. He would trace their movements, following at a safe distance; his fantasy was to surprise them with his sudden (and aroused) presence, and then force them into unwanted sexual acts. His wish to violate and attack, related directly to his feelings of humiliation and impotence and desire for vengeance, expressed in sexual violence. By reclaiming his own potency in his decision to leave home, Jag had less need to act out violently, feeling far more powerful and free. The addictive force of his sadistic fantasies lessened and he became more able to name and work through his underlying feelings.

While individual psychological dynamics and choices are profoundly important, and Sanghera's courage shows that it is possible to escape abuse, even culturally inscribed oppression and cruelty, it is imperative to have robust legislation that prohibits such cruelty and injustice.

This chapter has described significant developments in relation to outlawing inhumane practices, that include forced marriage, honour-based violence and female genital mutilation. The problem of HBV is complex and often hidden. It is essential to explore the interaction between social forces and the psychodynamics of such culturally sanctioned practices. It is clear that these practices are illegal and violate human rights and that deep-rooted political, societal and legislative change is fundamental.

The dynamics of abuse within forced marriages are beyond those that exist within the couple itself, but are shadows of the wider societal forces that maintain the status quo. In this situation, the tyranny of intimate partner violence is disguised beneath the facade of respectability, and the whole family system is often collusive, either in refusing to speak of what is taking place between the violent man and his wife, or in actively participating in the abuse.

What distinguishes HBV and killing from other types of murder, is the belief that this death (or crime) was committed in order to protect a family or community from being shamed and, in this sense, the death or other violent act was 'deserved' or merited, and that there was little choice on the part of the family or community other than to commit this crime.

There are clear links to previous chapters in this book, not only because honour-based violence is a significant, underground problem in society, but also because it powerfully illustrates implicit views about women, power, consent and the unquestionable sanctity of marriage that can also be seen in toxic couplings in other situations, where the question of honour is not as clear. Within many of the toxic couples described in earlier chapters, there are similar pressures to accept violence, remain in an intolerable situation and keep silent – but these do not generally take as explicit a form, and result from threats by the dominator. In honour-based violence, the wider family and community system are jointly culpable for maintaining the abusive status quo. As described earlier, it is not only men who abuse their family members, but women within the family too, including grandmothers, mothers, sisters and aunts, who ensure that a female does not cause dishonour to the family.

The role of shame

Shame is associated with culturally sanctioned violence, committed to protect the honour of communities. Individual acts of violence are also triggered by the experience of being shamed and humiliated, leading to the wish to retaliate or to affirm a sense of power and status. As Dutton (2007: 192) describes:

> The shame is caused by early family dynamics. . . . The way that shame operates suggests that the psychological precede the social. There is a pool of rage and shame in abusive men that can find no expression – not until, that is, an intimate relationship occurs and with it the emotional vulnerability that threatens their equilibrium.

These feelings of shame are unbearable, and need to be blamed on the woman – the container of his unacceptable sense of humiliation. I suggest that these feelings are actually projected into her so that she becomes the object of shame, vulnerability and humility. Dutton argues that for men across society, a powerful interaction exists between early family experience, a society that prohibits male expressiveness, and shame.

As discussed in earlier chapters, the etiology of intimate partner violence develops over a longer term (Dutton, 2000, 2002) stemming from early family influences such as exposure to violence (Dutton, 2000; Egland, 1993), shaming (Dutton, Starzomski and Ryan, 1996; Dutton, van Ginkel and Starzomski, 1995) and trauma (Dutton and Holtzworth-Munroe, 1997). While discussing primarily individual rather than social forces that create such violence, and arguing that the psychological precedes the social, Dutton and colleagues acknowledge the tremendous power that society has over the way that women are treated and protected.

Although not all violence is the result of patriarchal forces of oppression against women, there are clearly some cultural forces and biases that create mal-treatment and the deprivation of human rights of women and young girls. When these social forces act in conjunction with individual responses to shame, loss and humiliation, the effects can be lethal: honour-based killing is a tragic example of this.

In his important study on familicide in the United States, Websdale (2010) emphasizes the central role of shame and humiliation in men who kill their families and themselves out of a sense of having failed to meet their needs as providers, fathers or partners. This sense of humiliated fury, as he refers to it, can be discharged and honour temporarily restored through acts of fatal violence. This demonstrates how similar motivations for the restoration of honour through murder can be found across cultures, and how the perception of shame, in the eyes of wider society, can lead to irrevocable acts of violence.

8 Xanadu

Addictive states in violent relationships

Kubla Khan, Or, a Vision in a Dream. A Fragment.

In Xanadu did Kubla Khan
A stately pleasure-dome decree:
Where Alph, the sacred river, ran
Through caverns measureless to man
Down to a sunless sea . . .[1]

Samuel Taylor Coleridge, Kubla Khan, 1797

Coleridge's poem cited above was inspired by an interrupted dream he had under the influence of opiates. As well as its evocative images and musicality, it draws attention to the wish for an ideal escape: a 'stately pleasure-dome' where the strains of daily existence vanish. The sense of a drug-addled haze is a compelling one and speaks to a familiar longing in so many violent and despairing couples: the wish to leave this life and enter a blissful state close to oblivion.

In this chapter, I will discuss the addictive nature of acts of violence, both against others and against the self. I look at both the symbolic and physical significance of the marks left by violence within toxic couples, and the self-harm that mirrors this. Such self-harm can also take on the role of an addiction and has the potential to kill.

I discuss how addictive states of mind and body, including self-harm, substance and alcohol abuse, play an important role not only in the creation of violence, but also within destructive partnerships. The metaphors of 'love as a drug' and being 'addicted to love' speak powerfully to romantic conceptions that link destruction and sexual union. Romantic and sentimental notions of passion can be used to justify intimate partner violence. The actual use of substances and alcohol in violent relationships both reflects and exacerbates their toxicity.

The role of alcohol and drug addiction in domestic violence is an important one, and significantly increases danger in the couple, and towards any children involved. The tensions that arise when individuals are dependent on drugs or alcohol are great, and problems of intimacy can be both revealed and intensified through such addictions. It has been well documented that domestic violence is associated with substance and alcohol misuse in perpetrators, increasing the likelihood that they will unleash violent impulses. It also has a raised prevalence in those who are victims of the violence, as they may turn to drugs and alcohol as a result of the abuse.

The association between the ingestion of toxic substances and the rates of violence is a powerful one, for reasons that I begin to explore in this chapter. The interplay of various factors with alcohol and substance abuse is important and requires careful examination. In a study of the rates of alcohol abuse and domestic violence in white, Hispanic and black couples in the US, Caetano *et al.* (2001) found that alcohol use played a significant role in IPV. Their study found that 30 to 40 per cent of the men and 27 to 34 per cent of the women committing violence against their partners were drinking at the time of the event in two of the three ethnic groups who participated in the study:

> Alcohol-related problems were associated with IPV among blacks and whites, but not among Hispanics. Alcohol's role in partner violence may be explained by people's expectations that alcohol will have a disinhibitory effect on behavior or by alcohol's direct physiological disinhibitory effect. It is also possible that people consciously use alcohol as an excuse for their violent behavior or that alcohol appears to be associated with violence because both heavier drinking and violence have common predictors, such as an impulsive personality.
>
> (Caetano *et al.*, 2001: 58)

The impact on children of growing up with one or both parents dependent on alcohol or substances is both physically and psychologically profound. Separation from a drug- or alcohol-dependent parent is difficult and there is an enhanced risk that children exposed to addicted parents will be neglected; physically, sexually and emotionally abused; and also more likely to develop addictions themselves (Bower, 2013). The parent who is addicted is often unavailable or unpredictable, volatile and needy, leaving the child in the position of seeking to nurture, protect or control them. Furthermore, it is often not possible for children with these parents in their early lives to develop a sense either of a reliable containing object, into whom their own toxic feelings can be safely held and processed, or of a creative parental couple. Instead, a notion of a dangerous and unreliable couple develops, not one that can successfully negotiate conflict.

The addicted couple is doubly dangerous, not simply leaving children unprotected and exposed to danger, but also creating the inner couple – the couple in the mind – who cannot come together safely, or manage and contain distress. The child who grows up in this situation has a sense of an unreliable inner object, as a result of his repeated exposure to chaotic, unpredictable and neglectful parents.[2]

There is evidence that parents' addiction to drugs and alcohol increases the risk of child abuse and neglect, and it is known that a large number of children of parents who are addicted to these substances have witnessed violence between them. When combined with mental health difficulties in their parents, these children are exposed to a toxic home environment, and are, in turn, at risk of seeking to escape this through their own use of drugs or alcohol, in an attempt at self-medication or as an emulation of their parent. This may be the child or adolescent's attempt to take in something for herself that the parent has used for sustenance; it is an attempt to care for herself that is, in fact, destructive (Manning *et al.*, 2009).

Violence itself can be an intoxicating force, likened to a drug. It creates a sense of omnipotence, destructiveness and mastery, and protects against the terrors of intimacy. In this way it can be seen as a defence against intimacy, like that found in perversion, a constellation of behaviours and ways of relating that protect the self from vulnerability and dependence. In violent partnerships, dependency and helplessness are cut off and projected into the other person. This is a fantasized attempt at creating a state of invulnerability and absolute control: a physical and psychic enclave. The victim of repeated violent assaults may themself be caught up in a destructive and sadomasochistic pattern of relating to others, with a cruel inner 'other' that demands continual punishment and humiliation. This is a form of addiction to a tyrannical inner force, conceptualized as a harsh superego that demands punishment.

Violence in an intimate relationship takes on an addictive force for both part-ies, an exciting and dramatic experience that obliterates reason, emptiness and depression as it enlivens and destroys in equal measure. The shame and stigma attached to these relationships make it difficult for those who have been either batterers or their victims to acknowledge their active participation in these situations. It is also possible that the passion, excitement and sense of release that the violence affords occurs at an unconscious level, so that the addictive aspect is not one of which the partner is consciously aware. It has been chosen at a level that is not necessarily conscious; exploring and articulating the unconscious forces that lead to these relationships requires both courage and insight.

A polarized notion of an abuser and his or her victim is one that denies the complex, nuanced and unconscious dynamics at play within the couple. This can be seen when the 'abuser' in a violent relationship shows signs of change, becoming less aggressive, and his partner actually resists this change, or finds him less attractive. The homeostasis of a relationship depends on the tacit assignation of particular roles and familiar patterns of behaviour. It is as if an unconscious contract has been made in which one partner carries the burden of violence for the other who, in turn, takes on the role of the vulnerable, weak and frightened one. In this way, unacceptable aspects of the self can be projected into another person and thus disavowed.

I explore the addictive quality of the assaults by intimate partners on one another and how the bruises and marks are a kind of language that has important evidential and symbolic significance. Like other forms of violence, the injuries speak to a psychic wounding that needs to be understood and responded to. It is akin to self-harm in making public private pain, and bringing into the public realm abuse and hatred (including self-loathing) that could have stayed hidden in the private sphere of the home.

Young people who have been treated violently by others will sometimes choose to mark their own body through self-harm, both to release tension and anger onto themselves, but also to stamp their ownership and control onto their flesh. This can be viewed as an act that unconsciously reflects identification with the aggressor, so that part of them has turned on another part of themselves and treats it with rage, as an object to be defiled or written upon. The sense of a euphoric release from depression mirrors an addictive response, and can create a similar sense of momentary elation.

The red mist of violence

The excitement, frenzy and mindlessness of violence is not only experienced by heterosexual men who assault their female partners. Some studies indicate parity in the rates of male and female intimate partner violence (Desmarais *et al.*, 2012a). It is clear that women also abuse children (Motz, 2008) and injure and bruise their male partners; that homosexual men and women are also violent to their same-sex partners; and that parents and siblings can hurt or kill children in the family. The direction of violence does not follow gender-stereotypical patterns in all cases, and mothers are also capable of inflicting severe physical and emotional harm on their offspring and intimate partners.

In their cross-cultural study, Desmarais *et al.* (2012a, 2012b) found roughly equivalent rates of male and female intimate partner violence in terms of perpetration and victimization. Children, too, can be caught up in acts of extreme, sometimes deadly, aggression. Violence can serve a powerful psychic function for women as well as men, and prevents perpetrators from thinking; this disturbing fact requires close exploration. The function of violence is also to defend against unacceptable feelings of shame and vulnerability.

In the moment of assault, there can be an almost euphoric sense of release, as the actors lose all sense of what they are doing. This sense of blanking out and giving in to mindless action has been described as a 'red mist'. It is overwhelming and intense, and stops thought altogether. Those who assault are often in the throes of exciting action that so immerses them that they become oblivious to the suffering of their victim, even when this is someone they love as well as (momentarily) hate; but this awareness does not reach them, in the moment of the violence, in the haze of the 'red mist'. They are caught up in the moment and, when they return to the world, can be horrified by the damage they have inflicted, and also frightened by their potential to do further violence, or even to kill others. It is terrifying to have felt so out of control, so lost to reason and compassion. For some, drug and alcohol consumption will have led to this violence.

Addiction to violence: getting rid of the 'evil eye'

A black eye is a haunting symbol of damage to one of the most vulnerable parts of the face, and evokes fragility, helplessness and pain. It has tremendous symbolic significance, too, as this sense organ is the one that can see and bear witness to the horror of what the violent partner is doing. As in the chilling case of Tina Nash (described in more detail in Chapter 2), whose eyes were gouged out, blinding someone, or damaging their eyes, is also an attack on their role as witness. The sense of shame that so often drives violence, as the forensic psychiatrist James Gilligan (1997) describes, is often located in the gaze of the other. In his interviews of hundreds of men convicted for murder in prisons in the United States, Gilligan discovered that being shamed or disrespected was a central motive. The eye, representing judgement of the other, is unbearable for these men, who feel so humiliated. It seems that this is the externalization of their inner 'witness'; that is, the harsh and critical superego that observes and judges them. Through projective identification, the eye of the victim becomes the external representative of the cruel superego, rejecting and judging. It must be cast out.

The tragic blinding of Tina Nash, described in Chapter 2, was a horrifying example of the wish to destroy another's pleasure in being alive, or the possibility of gazing lovingly at someone else. It seems to be an act of sadistic violence driven by revenge motivations. One of the most under-researched crimes is assaultive enucleation, or blinding through gouging out the eyes of another. This is a brutal, chilling and terrible act of violence that causes, pain, disfigurement and grief for the victim, if they survive the assault.

> 'Lest it see more, prevent it. Out, vile jelly!'
> [Said Cornwall as he plucked out Gloucester's other eye.]
> 'Where is thy luster now?'
> William Shakespeare, *King Lear*, Act 3: Scene 7

According to Bukhanovsky *et al.* (1999): 'A recurrent belief among peoples of various cultures and ages is in the mysterious, puissant ability of the eyes to express evil and cause harm.' It is as if all sense of shame and humiliation has been projected into the eye of the beholder, so that their gaze is felt to be unbearable. A psychotic solution to this situation is to prevent the other from seeing at all.

In their review of typologies of those who enucleate the eyes of others, Bukhanovsky *et al.* (1999: 601) offer the following findings about those perpetrators who were not clearly psychotic at the time of their offence, which was sometimes associated with murder of the victim:

> Five other eye-gouging subjects, representing the psychopathic category, did not suffer from a psychotic disorder or mental retardation. Rather, they showed signs of significant character pathology, sexual paraphilias including sadism, and various degrees of alcohol or drug abuse. Psychopathic personality was suggested by other signs of violent behaviours and preoccupations. Three of the five psychopathic eye-gougers had histories of cruelty to animals, a behaviour that has been associated with deviant aggression and psychopathic or antisocial personality disorder.

The telltale heart: violence and guilt

Tattooing the face is far less common than inking other parts of the body, as the face has a 'sacred' quality. The eyes, arms and heart have particular significance, not only when represented through tattooing ink, but also when damaged or destroyed.

Parts of the body have both symbolic and concrete significance, as is evident in medical as well as romantic discourse. The sound of the human heartbeat both evokes the memory of the baby at his mother's breast, or in her arms, and signifies ongoing life. It can be both a longed-for and a frightening sound. To attack another person is to make violent contact with their body and create intense reactions in their bodies: perhaps the frenetic heartbeat of the frightened victim is reassuring to the perpetrator, as it confirms his power, and distracts him from the sound of his own fear. At other times, the heartbeat can be an unwanted sound, symbolizing guilt.

In his classic gothic tale of 1843 *The Tell Tale Heart*, Edgar Allan Poe describes how the murder of an old man was committed because the killer could not bear to be seen by him:

> It is impossible to say how first the idea entered my brain; but once con-
> ceived, it haunted me day and night. Object there was none. Passion there
> was none. I loved the old man. He had never wronged me. He had never
> given me insult. For his gold I had no desire. I think it was his eye! Yes, it
> was this! He had the eye of a vulture – a pale blue eye, with a film over
> it. Whenever it fell upon me, my blood ran cold; and so by degrees – very
> gradually – I made up my mind to take the life of the old man, and thus
> rid myself of the eye forever. . . . it was not the old man who vexed me, but
> his Evil Eye.

The killer has gone mad with guilt and believes that the heart of the old man still beats, becoming tormented by the imagined sound of his heartbeat. Eventually, the sound of the telltale heart is too much to bear. The first word of the story is 'True!' – an admission of his guilt. One of the driving forces in the opening, and throughout the story, is not the narrator's insistence upon his *innocence* but on his *sanity*. His drive to convince, however, is curious because he fully admits he is guilty of murder. His denial of insanity is based on his systemic actions and precision – a rational explanation for irrational behaviour (murder). He has pro-jected his own cruel superego onto this other man, represented by his eye, and now must destroy it. But as the act of projective identification is a fantasy of getting rid of inner feelings and fears, it is doomed to failure, and his own sense of guilt and self-punishment continue to persecute him, in this case as represented by the omnipresent sound of a beating heart:

> And have I not told you that what you mistake for madness is but over-
> acuteness of the sense? . . . It was the beating of the old man's heart. It
> increased my fury, as the beating of a drum stimulates the soldier into courage.

This heartbeat may even be his own, as his guilt and fear torment him, but again, he externalizes this and imagines it belongs to the dead man. This story can be read as a profound illustration of how violence attempts, and fails, to rid the self of a sense of shame, persecution and guilt, but in fact can only offer temporary relief; as the fantasy of getting rid of these unacceptable feelings recedes, the guilt returns with intensified force.

The violence is a defence against the sense of shameful exposure that drives the individual to assert his power and control through bodily and psychological acts of torture – to subdue, silence and blind the other and obliterate their capacity to judge him. The relief this offers is only transient, and soon violent fantasies return.

Addictive states of mind and the experience of intimate partner violence

The rates of substance and alcohol abuse in violent relationships are high, indicating that such addictions may both enhance the likelihood of engaging in violence, and can be used as a means to escape them, at least temporarily. The direction of causality is unclear, as it could be that individuals with difficulties in early life are both more likely to abuse drugs and alcohol and to find themselves in abusive relationships, so both could be artefacts of adverse early circumstances. Women who have been abused are 15 times more likely to abuse alcohol, and nine times more likely to abuse drugs, than women who have not been abused. Alcoholic women are more likely to report a history of childhood physical and emotional abuse than are non-alcoholic women. There is evidence to suggest that alcohol dependence is an important factor in women remaining in violent relationships. Domestic violence and drug and alcohol addiction frequently occur together, but no evidence suggests a direct causal relationship between substance abuse and intimate partner violence. These factors interact with and exacerbate each other and should be treated simultaneously.

The risk to children is evident. Children of substance-abusing parents are more likely to experience physical, sexual or emotional abuse than children in non-substance-abusing households. A survey of public child-welfare agencies conducted by the National Committee to Prevent Child Abuse found that as many as 80 per cent of child abuse cases are associated with the use of alcohol and other drugs.

The risk of intimate partner violence is increased when either or both partners use alcohol or drugs. This is not an uncommon situation, and is one that can lead to a shared addictive state of mind, in which thinking becomes impossible. The toxicity of this state of mind, and its consequences, are highly significant. The actions committed in the frenzy of addictive violence, often coupled with the use of drugs and alcohol, seem to take the place of thoughts, and symbolize unconscious wishes and fears. The 'red mist' of violence is akin to a drug-addled haze, and offers its own form of 'perverse safe haven', as described below. It keeps intimacy at bay and ensures that the perpetrator is freed from the terrors of perceived abandonment and humiliation.

A 'perverse safe haven'

The following is an illustration of how the use of substances, including skunk cannabis and alcohol, can tip the balance and destroy the apparently 'safe haven' of perverse and violent fantasies – which are then enacted. As long as the fantasies are only real in the mind they serve as a 'haven', but when enacted this sanctuary is destroyed. This expression was coined by Craig, whom I discuss below.

Clinical illustration: Craig and his 'perverse safe haven'

When I first met Craig he was blank, rigid and almost unreachable in his emotionally flattened state, looking ahead as if in a trance and answering in monosyllables. He had been referred for evaluation of his suitability for treatment and psychological assessment of his violent tendencies. His childhood was marked by disruption and absence. His mother had suffered from serious mental health difficulties and would frequently be taken into hospital for treatment, leaving her children with their father, who was a heavy drinker and could not provide consistent care. There were other times when Craig's father was working away and his mother in hospital, so he and his four younger siblings simply had to fend for themselves, living in a state of neglect and uncertainty. All the children were described by neighbours as 'feral'.

Craig was both frightening and frightened in the initial meeting with me, as he related his history to this point, staring at me in a frozen manner. It seemed that there was nothing accessible to him or me that had anything lively or awake that could connect us in this preliminary encounter.

He disclosed that whenever he had refrained from alcohol use, he had replaced it with cannabis, and although he only used a small amount (consuming approximately £20 worth of skunk, a potent variety of cannabis, every month) he felt that he could not survive without the help of either alcohol or cannabis to sustain him and protect him from what appeared to be unbearable internal feelings of emptiness and despair. When questioned about how he felt without any substances, he said 'I feel like I am going to explode'. He went on to describe violent thoughts that included murdering, raping, killing and torturing others, including his neighbours. He then described having had violent fantasises, including the sexual torture and rape of almost everyone who lived in his street.

It was striking that throughout this vivid description of his extremely violent thoughts, Craig did not appear to be emotionally engaged with the content of what he was disclosing to us; his manner appeared disconnected and removed from the highly disturbing images he was describing. He repeatedly said he used drink to 'slaughter myself'. In a somewhat paradoxical fashion he reported that he drank to escape violent fantasises, but was aware that when he drank he became increasingly likely to enact these. In particular, he would enact this violence against his wife. Although he was not physically violent towards his children, he was aware of their presence in the household during times of domestic violence, and the fact that they were exposed to and disturbed by the extent to which he and his wife had arguments. It was unclear if he wanted this 'audience' for his savage acts of violence towards their mother.

Craig did not spontaneously make the connection, but when I asked him about possible links between his own childhood, which he recalled as highly violent, and his own behaviour, he said 'Yes, I have become my father; he was a violent drunk and I am just like him'. Although he was able to recognize that he was subjecting his children to a similar experience to the one he had undergone, he did not appear troubled by this thought, nor had he expressed empathy or concern for his children at any point in the interview. Indeed, his affect when describing the impact of his acts of extreme violence towards his wife was similarly disconnected and 'flat', and he seemed to have little awareness of what I considered to be significant child protection concerns that I raised with him. Although he said 'I love my children', it was difficult for him to feel emotionally connected to them – or, indeed, to anyone. This was clear in his expressionless manner.

At the point where he talked about his well-rehearsed fantasies of rape and murder, his manner changed, and he became animated, seeming to want to convey something to me much more urgently. I suggested that his violence defended him against his underlying sense of emptiness, of deadness, and made him feel excited and alive. He agreed, somewhat surprised, and told me about the violent attacks his father perpetrated on his mother, in frustration at her cut-off, withdrawn state, and how terrifying this had been for him as a little boy – he had thought he would kill her. I said he would rather put himself in the place of the powerful, violent man who beats a helpless woman than recall the fear and helplessness that both he and his mother experienced. This was his solution to feeling so frozen by fear: to take control and create a life through threatening others, feeling then that he was the master of the situation, not its hostage. He agreed, seeming both slightly more connected emotionally, but also thoughtful, and decided he wanted to engage in treatment. We subsequently met for over two years, during which time he often retreated to his 'perverse safe haven'.

He said he had grown up 'wild and stray' but did not blame either parent for their clear neglect (or actual abuse) of him and his four siblings. He accepted his lot, but felt ashamed of his past, still shuddering as he recalled the sense of being unwanted and poor. He described how he and his siblings were treated as 'charity cases' in their street, occasionally being taken in by neighbours when his mother was admitted to a psychiatric hospital, as she so frequently was. From an early age, he had prepared his own food and drink; his only memory of being fed something his mother had made was of drinking black tea and sugar from a baby bottle. This was his mother's version of nurturing him and left him with an addiction to black tea and coffee, with excessive sugar, drunk throughout the day and night, up to thirty cups a day. This was, to me, a symbol of his hunger and thirst for real succour that he could not meet, as he had never learned how to, and yet he clung to this familiar, destructive and addictive drink. This need to take in something, however unfulfilling, was also mirrored in his alcohol and drug addiction – which would, eventually, cost him his life.

As a young man, he was socially isolated, though he had a few friends in early adolescence with whom he would thieve and vandalize property. He joined the Navy at 17 to escape from home, wanting to belong to a community of men. This served him well, seeming to contain his violent feelings, until he seriously injured his leg in an accident and received medical discharge at 20. Following his release from the containing and secure environment of the Navy, his underlying anger was unleashed during violent episodes directed at his first serious girlfriend, who left him shortly afterwards, further fuelling his sense of failure and rage.

Craig had eventually married Beth. She was warm and loving, and often shared a drink with him. He felt they were opposites as she was so gregarious and he was trapped inside himself; she gave him a home and sense of being cared for. He found this a shameful situation as she had a family who supported her and by whom he felt alienated; his own background was one of deprivation and gross abuse, leaving him feeling he was not good enough for her. Any sense of dependency tormented him. Whenever he felt abandoned, criticized or rejected, he would react violently, saying he hated knowing how much he relied on her, and how much he would mind if she left him. She eventually gave birth to a physically disabled daughter, and then to a healthy baby boy.

There was a strong suspicion that his daughter's disability was the product of her mother's alcohol use in pregnancy, but it was also possible that Craig had injured his wife during her pregnancy, indirectly harming the unborn baby. He felt that he connected most to his daughter, and showed her tremendous care and affection. I wondered if his special care towards this child reflected his guilt, as well as his disavowal of his own disability and vulnerability, that he could project into her and then care for her. He regularly inflicted brutal and sadistic violence on his wife, and the animals in the household were weapons in his abuse. He would then have periods of repentance followed by more brutality, which developed into a familiar cycle.

Clinical illustration: progress of therapy

Craig had a long history of being unable to engage in therapy, due to his terror of intimacy. Despite his horror of what his father had done to his mother through his violent beatings, he also identified with his violent, distant father (known as 'identification with the aggressor'). Despite these obstacles to intimacy, he was an articulate and, at times, poetic man, who appeared to be able to trust me, at least with an admission of his fears. It became clear that the cost of engagement was the threat to his entrenched psychic defences. It was likely that as his defensive armour was deconstructed, his underlying depression would overwhelm him. His violence could be understood as a perverse life force, keeping his deadly sense of depression at bay. I felt that at some level he understood the link between his violence and his underlying terrifying mental state – that it served to enliven him and defend him against both depression and psychosis. Because he had acted on violent fantasies before, it was very hard for him to feel that they were 'safe', as he sometimes lost the ability to distinguish between fact and fantasy. He did not trust himself to know the difference.

Eventually he was able to articulate and acknowledge these primitive, vulnerable feelings, and realized, with horror, that he had become both his abusive and neglectful father and his withdrawn, cut-off mother, alternating between the two while his children bore witness. He saw that he was treating his wife exactly as his father had treated his mother, subjecting her to assaults and explosive rages, in the presence of the children.

When he started to make these links between past and present, and become really curious about them, the therapeutic work seemed to become properly alive, with a real sense of emotional connection between us. He explored his graphic and disturbing fantasies, which had given him false liveliness and fuelled his rages with new understanding, and wanted to forsake them, seeing them as psychic refuges, ultimately doomed to failure. He said of his retreat into this zone: 'It is my perverse safe haven – familiar in a dark way.' He was able to leave these havens and engage in the less predictable world outside his own violent fantasies, and to begin to allow his feelings to find expression in words and in behaviour other than violence and drinking. He also started to communicate with his wife, and to predict and deflect violent impulses towards her; he began to see that these rages were manifestations of his fears of being found wanting, and abandoned. Rather than displace these feelings into anger alone, he was able to address his underlying sense of shame, vulnerability and fear.

Clinical illustration: 'She saw into my soul and found it wanting'

Eventually, despite his increased insight and reduced level of violence, his marriage began to break down. Craig found that he was more able to see the triggers for his rage and that drinking was a huge problem for him: this estranged him further from his family and he also became more depressed, more in touch with his underlying sadness. Beth took on part-time work and became more independent, finding a renewed sense of freedom as their children were now older, requiring less intensive care. Beth insisted that her brother, who had recently separated from his wife, came to live with the family, despite a long history of conflict between him and Craig. The two men lived together in disharmony for some nine months, and Craig became increasingly moody and withdrawn, terrified of being on his own but feeling unable to stay. He tried to tell her how he felt, but this led to arguments, and she eventually asked him to leave the family home. He had confessed that he hated her brother and wanted to kill him; he came to me the following week and said: 'She saw into my soul and found it wanting.'

Craig believed that his inner inadequacy and dark desires were the reasons why Beth wanted him to leave, and it confirmed his fears about his lack of self-worth and inability to tame his savage impulses. He felt unloved and unlovable, fundamentally lacking and hopeless, which led him to a darker place of self-pity and self-loathing. He was unable to understand that it was his periodic substance abuse, binge drinking and the violence this unleashed that had become intolerable, and that she would not enter the 'perverse safe haven' to which he all too often retreated.

I met Beth, too, who described Craig as a Jekyll and Hyde character and was worried that he was mentally ill. She had not consciously invited her brother to live with her to oust Craig, but I thought it was possible that Beth had unconsciously set this up, as she had no other way of escaping from what was a high-risk situation. Even when Craig had left, he would often return and the couple, deeply enmeshed, simply could not separate. Like me, she felt unduly responsible for his welfare. Only caring for her brother, and protecting him from future violence, allowed Beth to feel she had the right to set a boundary in relation to Craig. It was possible that she also felt protected now that he was there, as a part of her was very worried about the harm that Craig could do to her and to himself were she to leave him and live on her own with the children.

After leaving home, Craig felt adrift in a world that had no place for him, often describing his sense of profound alienation from the world. He had the constant experience of feeling he was an actor on a stage, being watched by a distant audience; he felt he was both the actor and the faraway spectator, and that neither were authentic aspects of a substantial self. He had a sense of not belonging, and never having properly belonged. It was as if only through violence could he assert his existence, and feel embodied and real. It seemed to be a proof of his existence, and also a strong protection against psychotic disintegration, which he feared. The experience of his own mother's mental instability and profound fragmentation left him desperate to create a coherent sense of himself, which he could only find through the false empowerment of violence and the sense of grandiosity induced through alcohol and drug abuse.

Clinical illustration: outcome

Tragically, our work was cut short as Craig started to take more hard drugs after his wife's brother moved into the family home. He had moved out to a shared flat, and struggled with his sense of rejection. He became obsessed with thoughts of killing his brother-in-law, and was arrested and charged after attacking him with a weapon. Although he did not receive a custodial sentence for this offence he was lost to therapeutic work, as I had to turn him away from sessions; he had arrived drunk and stoned. This seemed to reflect his desperation and terrible fear of becoming dependent on and rejected by me; he pre-empted our ending. It was possible that I had precipitated this by refusing to see him when he was clearly intoxicated. Although this was an essential boundary in the work, he felt humiliated, abandoned and angry with himself when I turned him away.

The dilemma Craig presented to me was either to allow him to abuse the therapy, and me, by coming intoxicated, unable to work, or to abandon him. It was a choice between abandoning Craig or corrupting the work. Every time he felt he could turn away from his own inner death instinct he would feel terrified, and so return to the destructive activity – abandoning others, including his wife, children, and ultimately me. In the countertransference, as well as in my actual set of choices in relation to continuing the work with him, I was forced to contend with this terrible dilemma. If I turned a blind eye to his flagrant flouting of our rules and boundaries, and his disregard for his own safety, I would be an accomplice to his own self-destructiveness.

He would interpret 'forgiveness' as a hollow triumph in its acceptance of behaviour he knew was wrong, but felt that the imposition of consequences, and my withdrawal, was cruel, and confirmed that he had never been wanted in the first place. In facing this dilemma, I felt torn apart by my conflicting feelings and wishes. In identifying with his wife, there was a strong part of me that wanted to overlook his total disregard of the rules and show him love. He was so attuned to the slightest sign of disregard and potential abandonment that he unconsciously set up traps and tests of commitment, which demanded that one accept his transgressions and attacks. At the same time, there was a part of him that longed for a strong parental figure who could stand firm on the lines of right and wrong, and would not succumb to his intimidation.

Although, intellectually, he understood the need to come to therapy without having used drugs or being intoxicated, he said he was furious with himself about his continued use of substances, and felt that he had let me down. He expressed his commitment to attend the remaining sessions we had contracted, on the condition that he attend a detoxification course with a view to ending sessions with me and learning mindfulness skills.

The offer of then returning to the sessions after he was able to commit himself to abstinence was one he welcomed. He was not able to maintain his abstinence, however, and returned to drinking most days. After a crisis point where he was actively suicidal and homicidal, he attended four more times, and then withdrew entirely, making it impossible to work through the ending of the therapy. He left me fearful for his future and with a strong sense of having failed him.

He ultimately abandoned our work, as he had himself been abandoned, and it seemed that he could not bear to have a good object in his life, unless its permanence could be ensured. The fact that I had imposed conditions earned his respect, but was also intolerable. His inability to work towards the ending of therapy also revealed how unbearable he found separations and his profound difficulty in mourning. I later learned he had died in an apparent accident, while under the influence of Class-A drugs.

Clinical illustration: discussion

Craig's inability to allow his own vulnerability a voice, or to engage with help, revealed how he was in thrall to a pathological inner organization, designed to protect him from pain, but actually blocking psychic change or growth. He was reliant on alcohol and on the excitement and illusory omnipotence of his 'perverse safe haven' to act as blocks to feelings of dependency on another. He had learned early on that there was no one reliable or containing in his external world and that any attachments to others would only lead to disappointment. He could only count on alcohol and violence to re-establish his sense of power and control, and expel feelings of helplessness and need. In this way, his addictions served as idealized bad objects, whose consumption he could control. It was as if he had an inner criminal gang who kept him protected, but at a great cost.

Rosenfeld (1971) describes a pathological defence organization that denies the experience of need and is hostile to the needy part of the self and parental figures. Within the internal world, omnipotent and destructive aspects of the self offer protection and freedom from psychological pain to other more vulnerable parts of the self. Rosenfeld calls this the 'Mafia' (Bower, 2013). The metaphor of the inner Mafia is apt, as it highlights the rigidity and violence of these pathological defences.

The role of Craig's wife Beth is also important to consider. Even though she was able, at times, to leave the relationship and to receive support from others, her feelings for him, including a sense of being responsible for his survival, seem to have repeatedly led her back into the relationship. Her sense of protectiveness in relation to him and her understanding of the roots of his disturbed behaviour and feelings of aggression and despair made her feel sympathetic towards him and to tolerate extreme violence towards her and his threats of violence towards others. What is also striking is that, at times, she herself engaged in violence towards him and displayed somewhat unpredictable and impulsive behaviour in relation to him.

It is clear that this relationship was highly compelling for both individuals, and that both tolerated frequent arguments and threats. Both of their children had been exposed to their violence since their early childhoods and, at one point, social services had become involved when their daughter was injured in the 'crossfire' as she caught a blow by Craig that was intended for the mother. The relationship was obviously destructive, with both parties engaging in violence despite the proximity of their young son and highly vulnerable daughter.

It appeared that the mother both disavowed her own aggressive impulses into her partner, and also believed that she deserved no better than this form of treatment. Through this abusive relationship, she was able to split off her own violent impulses and locate them in her partner. Her description of her own family relationships revealed a high level of volatility, conflict and discord between family members in her early life, resulting in one sister moving out and a strong sense of betrayal and anger between them.

The roles in Craig and Beth's relationship were not simply those of abuser and victim but indicated a powerful attraction between two disturbed and unhappy people with an 'unconscious fit' between them. They became highly enmeshed in one another and committed to maintaining a relationship with one another. Beth was also overwhelmed by intense feelings and felt deeply attracted to Craig. Although she was intellectually aware of domestic violence and its occurrence during the relationship, she tended to minimize the impact this had on the children and also acknowledged that she had grown used to the violence, which made her feel that it was in some ways acceptable. Indeed, Beth said that, at times, she had covered up her bruises and had lied to members of her family about what had caused them. Clearly her self-esteem had been eroded by Craig's emotionally abusive statements and physical violence towards her, and the longer she remained in this violent relationship, the less likely she would be to retain a sense of self-esteem or self-efficacy. However, her decision to remain in this relationship (despite available sources of escape and help) indicated her entrenched attraction to him, and her enmeshment in this partnership. In the end, she too became intoxicated by the intensity, drama and passion of their relationship, and it was only when she introduced another man, her brother, into her home that she could finally be free of this addictive and destructive love. She was unwilling to enter couples therapy with Craig, believing that the problem was his, not theirs, and also anxious about being 'on [social services'] radar' in relation to her own drinking, and exposing their children to violence. Craig would not engage consistently in alcohol and drug misuse programmes, indicating his entrenchment in his escapist, destructive 'safe haven'.

The last stanza of Coleridge's *Kubla Khan* describes the narrator's fantasized re-creation of the Abyssinian maid's music, and the dreadful awe and fear this will inspire in others. Like the opiate of Craig's fantasies, his drug- and alcohol-fuelled violent binges, the hope seems to be that, through being feared, the man becomes a force to be reckoned with: that touching the sublime (drinking the milk of Paradise) leaves others in a state of wonder and fear: 'Beware! Beware! His flashing eyes, his floating hair!' The omnipotent fantasy is clear in the line 'and close your eyes with holy dread', as this creature has tasted of Paradise and has the power to build domes in the air. He can build both icy caves and sunny domes, that do not touch the ground. This is the depiction of the omnipotent fantasy of those in their perverse 'safe havens', where they create their own universe, and feed on their own imaginings. For Craig, as for so many others, this offers a seductive alternative to the perceived dangers of intimacy.

> Could I revive within me
> Her symphony and song,
> To such a deep delight 'twould win me
> That with music loud and long
>
> I would build that dome in air,
> That sunny dome! those caves of ice!
> And all who heard should see them there,
> And all should cry, Beware! Beware!
> His flashing eyes, his floating hair!
> Weave a circle round him thrice,
> And close your eyes with holy dread,
> For he on honey-dew hath fed
> And drunk the milk of Paradise.
>
> Samuel Taylor Coleridge,
> *Kubla Khan*, 1797

9   Conclusion

Out of the shadows

Whereas recognition of the inherent dignity and of the equal and inalienable rights of all members of the human family is the foundation of freedom, justice and peace in the world,

. . .

Everyone has the right to life, liberty and security of person.

> (From 'Preamble' and 'Article 3' of the
> International Declaration of Human Rights)

In previous chapters, I have drawn attention to the development of violence and aggression within couples and the mental states that accompany it, describing the particular roles played by each partner. The notion of unconscious choices is central, as people often find themselves repeating destructive and unwanted patterns of relationships, apparently without conscious awareness of how they created them. One of the aims of psychotherapeutic work with perpetrators and victims of intimate partner violence, including those who are both abused and abuser, is to bring these unconscious compulsions to awareness, so that these patterns can finally be recognized and modified.

In this concluding chapter, I address how these cycles of destructive relationships can be altered, and how participants and witnesses to domestic violence can be helped. I explore how early identification, advocacy, treatment and preventative measures can be taken to reduce the risk of intimate partner violence reoccurrence, and how social, psychological and criminal justice responses can support those who have been harmed by domestic abuse.

I have argued throughout, and demonstrated through clinical illustrations and empirical data, that domestic violence needs to be understood as a hugely destructive phenomenon, affecting all individuals within the family, including children, and that its roots are developmental, as well as societal. It is not simply an expression of patriarchal forces, although the subjection of women, and children, plays a role in the abuse of these family members. Men, and of course male children, are also victims of domestic violence.

While it is undeniable that the most extreme forms of domestic violence, namely homicides and intimate terrorism, frequently involve men as perpetrators and women as victims, it is also clear that such violence is relational, revealing entrenched and destructive dynamics between the partners, and that women also inflict physical and emotional abuse on their partners. Much violence appears to be enacted in response to perceived threat or loss, sometimes in the context of substance misuse. This view is not expressed to exonerate or excuse the perpetrators, but in order to understand their motivations, both conscious and unconscious, with the aim of bringing them to consciousness, challenging and modifying them. The ultimate aim of therapy is the reduction of violence and its damaging consequences.

Relational issues in domestic violence

Any violent relationship is made up of two parties, and the relational component is essential. At no point do I wish to exonerate the perpetrator of violence, or make any suggestion that those who suffer abuse are responsible for, or deserve it. All perpetrators of violence and abuse are responsible for their actions and must take steps to modify their behaviour, and should face prosecution if required. However, I believe that prosecution and conviction alone will not change the fundamental behavioural and emotional disturbances that create and maintain violence and the societal forces within which these flourish. Furthermore, the power of unconscious attractions and the repetition compulsion is significant, and both partners, whether male or female, are subject to this 'unconscious fit' with the other person. This attraction unites the couple and requires careful understanding.

It is clear that the phenomenon of domestic violence is a highly complex one, attacking human rights and psychological integrity. Furthermore, there are a variety of factors that contribute to its development and maintenance, including cultural, societal and individual differences. It is not simply the result of patriarchal forces, attachment experiences or unconscious masochism in the abused partners. None of those explanatory paradigms does justice to the complexity of individual factors that create a toxic partnership, although the contribution of social, psychological and developmental factors should be considered carefully in each case. Nonetheless, whatever the form of aggression between partners, there is overwhelming evidence that children who are exposed to domestic violence are harmed over both the long and short term, across a wide range of domains.

Ultimately, there is no one explanation for the complex, multifaceted problem of domestic abuse, and it is clear that women – as well as men – are capable of violence triggered by anger, threat of loss and abandonment, feelings of shame, humiliation, despair or the wish for revenge.

Creating conditions for change

As well as exploring the known psychological and physical consequences of domestic violence on its victims, and the cost to the National Health Service and other agencies of this major public health problem, I have focused on the intra-psychic damage caused, which is intense and complex. Not only are victims of domestic violence harmed, often in ways that persist for a lifetime, but those who witness it – the children – are deeply affected, and can find themselves unconsciously replicating these patterns of destructive relating.

Hiding in the shadows

As difficult as it has been for the public to acknowledge the scale of this major social and psychological problem, there are some groups for whom domestic violence has been particularly hidden, though no less prevalent than in 'mainstream families'. It is evident that intimate partner violence transcends class and race and can occur in same-sex couples, in relationships where partners are vulnerable (for example, where one partner suffers from a physical or intellectual disability or severe mental health difficulties) and where social forces are also instrumental in victimizing individuals (such as forced marriage, the neglect of vulnerable young people in care, the lack of provision for treatment of homeless young people with substance and alcohol problems, and the failure of services to screen for domestic violence routinely within a range of health and social agencies).

People with learning disabilities are vulnerable to sexual, physical and emotional abuse and exploitation, including financial manipulation. The hidden nature of domestic abuse can be even more difficult to detect in this group, particularly if it is not easy to speak about or communicate, or if professionals don't routinely enquire about the dynamics of intimate relationships. Curen and Sinason (2010) describe the particular vulnerability of this group and the societal difficulty in acknowledging the risk they face of domestic abuse.

There are other social groups that are at risk of domestic violence, including spouses of military personnel, and women and men who are refugees, perhaps living without legal status in a country and so even less able to seek help or involve criminal justice agencies when they are abused. Their plight is resonant of those who are homeless, and arguably, even more difficult. Likewise, there is a body of research that identifies the problems of domestic abuse in the elderly, and in those with long-term health difficulties. Another important issue is the financial exploitation of vulnerable groups. Although it has not been possible to address these important areas here, I believe that some of the dynamics I have outlined also apply to them, in terms of the motivations of perpetrators and the silence of those they abuse. In these circumstances, too, I would suggest that violence occurs within a relationship and is often triggered by shame, fury and a failure to view the other as a fully subjective and separate individual. It continues because it serves particular functions for the perpetrator, and because destructive dynamics are entrenched within toxic relationships, often reinforced by social and cultural pressures. As I have described in Chapter 3, there is a danger that children who grow up in households where violence and abuse are the norm, grow up accepting this, and recreate these patterns in adulthood against their conscious wishes.

Same-sex relationships

The situation in same-sex relationships clearly requires further exploration, and cannot simply be understood in terms of male-on-female violence. Violence occurs within lesbian and homosexual relationships and may be under-reported, as is often the case within minority groups, who are unsure of the likely response of the police or other criminal justice agencies.

It is suggested that aggression in same-sex relationships also follows gendered patterns of relating. Speaking on a podcast on the subject of gender crime, Mackinnon (2011) argues that in cases of male rape, the rapist is taking on the male gender while he forces his victim to take on the female role. She has developed the notion of 'gender crime'. The evidence for the rates of violence within same-sex relationships is equivocal, but some studies have indicated that rates of intimate partner abuse occur at similar or higher rates to those identified in heterosexual couples.

Recent reports suggest that the rates of victimization in same-sex relationships are higher than in heterosexual relationships as a result of intimidation and threats to 'out' one of the partners. It is difficult to assess levels of abuse in same-sex relationships accurately for multiple reasons. It may be that few health professionals screen for violence in same-sex relationships, or it may be under-reported because of reluctance to disclose the abuse, out of a fear of not being believed, having fewer advocacy or support services to turn to, or out of a sense of loyalty to a socially marginalized group. This can also be seen in some cases of aggression in ethnic minority communities, where reporting violence could be seen as disloyal, or as tantamount to fuelling prejudice. The shame and stigma of being part of an abusive relationship is found across the various groups in which it takes place, and keeps the existence of interpersonal violence in the shadows.

There are some similarities between same-sex violence and heterosexual intimate partner violence, including the following:

* psychological abuse is most common;
* physical and sexual abuse co-occur;
* violence that is ongoing becomes more frequent and more severe;
* physical violence can lead to a range of injuries, including bruises, cuts and broken bones;
* it more commonly occurs among younger persons (under 40 years of age);
* no race, ethnicity, class or socioeconomic status is immune.

However, there are also important differences:

* The percentage of women who experience IPV in their lifetime appears to be higher for lesbian women than for heterosexual women.
* However, this is because lesbians (as opposed to heterosexual women) are more likely to have experienced IPV at the hands of female *and* male partners. Many lesbians have intimate relationships with men prior to coming out as

lesbians. One study on same-sex IPV found that about half of the 79 women in the sample had also had relationships with men as well as with women. Their findings indicate that male partners may pose a greater risk for IPV than female partners: of the total sample, about 39.2 per cent reported being raped and/or physically abused by a partner in their lifetime (30.4 per cent by male partner and 11.4 per cent by a female partner).

- Rates of physical partner violence/victimization appear to be higher among gay men than heterosexual men.
- Due to societal homophobia, gay men and lesbian victims of IPV may experience situations that are not experienced by heterosexual victims of IPV. As mentioned above, an abusive partner may threaten to 'out' his or her partner's sexuality to their family, friends or employees.

Young people in care

The vulnerability of young people in care is a social problem, raising difficult questions about the quality of protection and care that is offered in lieu of abusive parental homes. These young people, even when known to be engaging in risky behaviour, may not be offered requisite levels of supervision and support and can be repeatedly targeted by predatory adults. The recent cases of sex gangs in the United Kingdom, who preyed on adolescent girls, many of whom were in local-authority care, drew attention to systemic problems in addressing abuse in adolescents; these young people were then caught up in a cycle of sexual exploitation, drug and alcohol addiction and physical abuse.

Several recent highly publicized cases of sex trafficking of young girls in care brought the scale of this criminal activity into the open. One such case took place in Oxford in the UK in 2013, when seven men were found guilty of sexual and violent offences against young girls, the majority of whom were in local-authority care. One vulnerable girl's accidental pregnancy at the age of 12 provoked rage in her abuser, who not only beat her, but then forced her to undergo a dangerous back-street abortion. Beating and raping her was not uncommon and, on occasion, he used weapons in sexually sadistic and depraved acts. Her fear and desperation in the relationship kept her under his strict control, further enhanced by her dependence on the drugs he fed her, even forcing them on her when she tried to refuse.

This child was subjected to the kind of brutality and psychological manipulation that characterizes 'intimate terrorism' and included beatings, sexual abuse and threats. Her abusive partner told her that if she loved him she needed to do what he asked to prove this love; through a combination of fear, intimidation and emotional abuse he eventually exerted total control over her. In exchange, he gave her small gifts and showed her the affection of which she had been deprived in her short life; eventually he wholly abused her attachment and loyalty to him, prostituting her out to other men, threatening to kill her and her family, and using drugs and alcohol to secure her compliance with his sexual demands.

The tragedy of this case, like so many others that take place on a daily basis, is that children's very deprivation and vulnerability – in this case, young girls – is targeted by predators who then subject these young people, who are desperate for affection, to severe forms of sexual, physical and emotional abuse, from which they see no escape. In this case, they were also introduced to addictive substances including alcohol, crack cocaine and heroin, and then further exploited (see Chapter 6). It is thought that the handful of successful prosecutions represents the tip of the iceberg of the actual number of perpetrators involved in the sexual exploitation of, and violence towards, vulnerable young people. The systemic collusion in this case of abuse was truly shocking and is revealed in the following description of how another resident in the hotel where this took place made an official complaint:

> Once – just once – a fellow guest overheard the expressions of pain and suffering, and rang 999. But the police investigation fizzled away, as others had done, deflected and defeated all too easily when the vulnerable child involved withdrew her complaint that she had been raped.
>
> (Laville and Topping, *The Guardian*, 14 May 2013)

This kind of insidious, underground activity took place with some of the most vulnerable young people in society. It is alleged that the police and the local authority had been made aware of these relationships, though both agencies were reportedly unaware of the scale of the abuse, or what appears to be organized sexual exploitation of young girls. If society, and the prime agencies responsible for the safety and welfare of the most vulnerable children, is powerless to stop this abuse, it becomes effectively socially sanctioned. It is as if the reality of their exploitation is too painful to bear and so the fact of the abuse is not recognized, and that vital pieces of information are not communicated between the agencies involved: the emotional pain of the knowledge is too much to bear (Cooper and Lousada, 2005). Cohen's seminal work (2001) on the power of denial is relevant here, as it is alleged that, rather than face up to the facts of gross exploitation and abuse, in the cold light of day, several agencies – including, at times, those charged with parental responsibility – either turned a blind eye to the association between adult men and vulnerable adolescent girls, or became powerless to prevent it.

Prevalence and scale of domestic violence

As I have emphasized throughout this book, intimate partner violence is a very common problem, despite the shame and stigma associated with it. Its victims are not found only in shelters, hiding, but are found in the children at school who seem unsettled, clingy and regressed, in ordinary women and men who appear to have a good relationship with others, in patients attending antenatal clinics, general practice surgeries and psychology outpatient clinics.

The perpetrators are the 'ordinary' men and women who may appear to be calm, caring and wholly in control in public, but who nonetheless act out violently against their intimate partners in private. Domestic violence cuts across lines of class, race, privilege and education, although there are some factors that increase the risk:

> In a large, diverse, community-based population of primary care patients, 1 of every 20 women had experienced domestic violence in the previous year; 1 of every 5 had experienced violence in their adult life; and 1 of every 3 had experienced violence as either a child or an adult. Current domestic violence is associated with single or separated status, socioeconomic status, substance abuse, specific psychological symptoms, specific physical symptoms, and the total number of physical symptoms.
>
> (McCauley et al., 1995)

Domestic violence is not a working-class problem or an ethnic-minority problem: it is everyone's problem, requiring victims and perpetrators to come out of the shadows to speak openly about it, alongside policy makers, criminal-justice agents, clinicians, medical professionals and human-rights activists. It is a social, political and psychological problem of profound consequence and it is incumbent on us all to understand, address and prevent it.

Taking domestic violence out of the shadows

Domestic violence between celebrities is newsworthy: from Ike and Tina Turner, to Madonna and Sean Penn and, more recently, the highly publicized cases of Nigella Lawson and Charles Saatchi, and pop stars Chris Brown and Rihanna. In February 2009, Brown assaulted Rihanna in his car, punching and biting her in the face and limbs, for which she required stitches. Brown later pleaded guilty to the assault and was sentenced to one year's probation. A photograph of Rihanna's bruised face was leaked to the press. In an interview with *Glamour* magazine in 2009, she described her feelings of humiliation about the photograph, and her wish to make public the shameful phenomenon of domestic violence. Rihanna expressed her hope that people would learn from her situation about the fact of domestic violence, and take heart from her recovery:

> Domestic violence is a big secret. No kid goes around and lets people know their parents fight. Teenage girls can't tell their parents that their boyfriend beat them up. . . . My story was broadcast all over the world for people to see, and they have followed every step of my recovery.

Rihanna and Chris Brown split up after the assault. A sensational outcry followed singer Chris Brown's new neck tattoo, ostensibly showing the bruised face of his ex-girlfriend Rihanna. Although the tattoo created outrage, if indeed it had been intended to depict Rihanna, its meaning is nonetheless ambiguous. Brown, who pleaded guilty of assault, may wish never to forget what he did to his then girlfriend. As well as being an expression of his violence, it was an attack on her beauty, as his fists defaced her. The idealized image of this beautiful singer was temporarily shattered and her vulnerability, her humanity, was revealed. At the moment of rage, she was presumably not seen as a subjective creature, suffering, but an object, in whom to pour his anger and sense of frustration. At a later point, he, like so many violent partners, might find it impossible to reconcile this behaviour with his usual desire to treat her with respect and care. Inscribing this striking image on to his flesh may serve to remind him of the shame of his misdeed. In fact, he has denied that this is an image of Rihanna at all, insisting that it depicts a Mexican sugar skull related to the Day of the Dead. The image remains open to interpretation.

Kira Cochrane (2012) wrote in *The Guardian*:

> Chris Brown's new tattoo is sickening. The singer's body art may or may not be intended to look like Rihanna, but it does look like a battered woman, which recalls the biggest scandal of his career, and sends a terrible message.

The censorship implicit in the condemnation of his choice of tattoo seems disproportionate to the crime, as the real misdemeanour was the act of violence in the first place, to which he pleaded guilty.

Rihanna herself was reported to have thought Chris Brown committed the act of violence on her in an attempt to get help. It is reported that she is now reconciled with him. If her hypothesis is correct, one might understand the tattoo as an act not of bravado, but one of possible penitence.

Breaking the cycle

There are three main ways that change can be achieved:

1. Early identification of the existence of domestic violence.
2. Intervention on the basis of this identification, to offer effective help to those affected, including the perpetrators themselves. This will include treatment programmes for perpetrators and victims of domestic violence, including children, and must involve multiple agencies, including schools, health providers, psychological services, social services where required, and specialist psychological and psychotherapeutic bodies. The police, probation and other representatives of the criminal justice system may need to be involved to ensure there is adequate response and integration across the services.
3. Social and legislative changes that ensure the problem is properly addressed and that legal sanctions are applied to outlaw the crime of domestic violence.

1: Improve risk assessments and identification

There are many ways to improve identification of domestic violence, and perhaps the most important is to bring awareness of it to as many members of the public as possible. Those with particular responsibility for the welfare and protection of children and adults also need specialist training in its identification and assessments. Below, I describe one such programme that has been established in Bristol.

The Identification and Referral to Improve Safety (IRIS) programme is a general practice based domestic violence and abuse (DVA) training support and referral programme that has been evaluated in a randomized controlled trial. Core areas are training and education, clinical enquiry, care pathways and an enhanced referral pathway to specialist domestic violence services. The target patient population is women who are experiencing DVA by a current partner, ex-partner or adult family member. IRIS also provides information for male victims and for perpetrators.

IRIS is targeted at primary-care clinicians and administrative staff to improve referrals to specialist domestic violence agencies and to identify women experiencing domestic violence. The findings of the randomized control trial demonstrated the benefit of training and support interventions in primary-care settings for domestic violence, and show that screening of women patients for domestic violence is not a necessary condition for improved identification and referral to advocacy services (Feder *et al.*, 2011). The women were referred to specialist agencies after domestic violence was accurately identified in the 24 practices in the experimental group; this was significantly different from the control group of 24 GP practices that did not have this programme to enable identification of cases of domestic violence.

Domestic violence advocacy includes the provision of legal, housing, financial and safety planning advice, facilitating access to community resources, such as refuges or shelters, emergency housing and psychological support.

Advocacy for women with recent experience of domestic violence can reduce the risk of further physical violence, and improve quality of life and mental-health outcomes (Ramsay *et al.*, 2009; Casteel and Sadowski, 2010; Feder *et al.*, 2009).

Risk assessments and standardized screening for domestic violence

As well as the identification-training programme described above, there are a variety of ways in which all who come into contact with family members can be educated to look for signs of domestic violence. General practitioners and dentists, along with other health professionals, are in a privileged position in relation to the physical wellbeing of their patients, and can be on the frontline when it comes to identifying suspected violence, particularly in relation to head, neck and facial injuries. Other professionals with a key role to play include midwives and practice nurses involved in antenatal care, who can identify the most at-risk groups of clients, as well as protecting their unborn babies from exposure to domestic violence or direct harm. Apart from those individuals generally involved in child protection, such as social workers, these professionals include health visitors, antenatal clinic staff, child health providers, educators and nursery nurses, as well as school nurses.

The pathways that lead to identifying domestic violence are many, and injury to children can signify not only that they are at direct risk, of suffering further harm, both physical and emotional, but that their parents or carers may be engaged in intimate partner violence. In order for victims of domestic violence to be identified and supported, and the perpetrators held responsible – and, where possible, treated and helped, or prosecuted and convicted – it is essential that agencies work together, across society and across the lifespan, to recognize, enquire about and protect against domestic violence.

Risk factors for lethality

When assessing the severity of domestic violence, professionals conducting the evaluation should pay particular attention to certain features of the violence, including some aspects identified below in a study by Heru (2007), specifically focusing on the risk of fatal violence. Clearly, the risk of fatality is a crucial consideration for any worker who is coming into contact with either perpetrators or victims of domestic violence. While it is never possible to predict with full accuracy whether or not a violent relationship will lead to death, the presence of the following would point to increased risk and should raise the level of concern, vigilance and potential need for intervention:

- the victim's fear of serious injury from their partner;
- the victim's experience of severe violence that has required medical attention;
- the perpetrator's uncontrolled continuous use of alcohol or drugs;

Other features of the perpetrator that increase risk are as follows:

- conviction for a violent crime or violation of a restraining order;
- prior use of a weapon against the partner, prior threat to kill the partner;
- stalking or other partner-focused obsessive behaviour;
- bizarre forms of violence such as sadistic violence.

The following guidelines are also suggested for healthcare professionals who are assessing women and men for routine complaints:

> *Ask patients about relationship violence.* Some patients may prefer to discuss 'aggression' in their relationships, because of the stigma associated with the words 'violence' or 'domestic violence' and the fear that either they or their partner will be reported to the police. They may prefer to differentiate between psychological, sexual and physical aggression. Patients are more likely to report violence on a questionnaire than during direct questioning.
>
> (Heru, 2007)

Campbell *et al.* (2007) also emphasize that when women are identified as abused in medical settings, it is important to assess perpetrators' access to guns and to warn the abused partners of the significant risk that guns present. This is especially true in the case of women who have been threatened with a gun or another weapon and in conditions of estrangement.

Guidelines for assessing intimate partner violence

Although this book is not intended as a guide for practitioners to conduct risk assessments, I hope that the following can help shape an interview with a couple where violence has taken place:

- Ask about the relationship in general, with particular emphasis on sources of tension and conflict. Stressors such as financial pressures and physical health problems are areas to explore.
- Try to ascertain the level, frequency and any history of violence in the relationship. Consider the use of questionnaires such as the Conflicts Tactics Scale (Strauss, 1979; Strauss and Gelles, 1990).
- The use of language is important, as many perpetrators will not consider pushing and shoving to be violence and so it may be necessary to spell this out.
- It is important to ask about forms of control, intimidation, verbal abuse, strict financial control and sexual jealousy in the relationship, as these are all indicators of domestic abuse.
- Strangulation attempts, violence in pregnancy, threats to kill, stalking during previous separation periods, use of weapons, alongside a diagnosis of personality disorder in the violent partner, are clear indicators of elevated risk and suggest that there is a risk of lethal violence. The assessor is building up a picture of the nature of the violence, and these are signs of 'intimate terrorism' rather than the mutual, situational violence that is far less likely to lead to fatal consequences.
- If present, determine severity and ask about fear of partner in the abused partner. The violent partner himself may well be frightened of what they are capable of and it is worthwhile to explore this with them.
- If possible, both partners may be asked specific questions relating to threats to kill, previous occasions of physical aggression, use of weapons, harm to others, presence of weapons in the house and use of alcohol and/or substances. Information about these issues is crucial in an assessment.
- Identify risk factors for a potentially lethal relationship including access to weapons, previous attempts to kill and any specific plans for homicide or suicide by perpetrator.
- If alcohol or substance misuse present, consider the motivation for detoxification treatment. Campbell and Mills (cited in Kantor and Jasinski, 1998) state: 'Aggression does not inevitably follow from alcohol intoxication, but alcohol is the drug most consistently related to intimate assaults. Alcohol facilitates aggression in many ways, including pharmacological effects that interfere with reasoning, perceptions, calculations of the consequences of behaviour and perceptions of threat.'

- A qualified mental health professional should screen abused partners for common co-morbidities including depressive disorder and post-traumatic stress disorder (Heru, 2007). Children should also be assessed to see if there is evidence of post-traumatic stress or other psychological disturbance.

2: Interventions: psychological treatment and psycho-education for violent perpetrators

The evidence base for treatment efficacy remains limited at the present time, although some programmes report encouraging results in terms of violence reduction for victims and other family members. Heru (2007) summarizes the results of treatment for violence perpetration as follows:

> Most studies have involved female victims who have come to the attention of the authorities or male perpetrators mandated to treatment by the courts. In community studies, couples must be highly motivated to enter treatment for a condition that is socially stigmatised. . . . Rigorous studies using control groups have shown that male perpetrators do not respond to the traditional gender-specific Duluth model. . . . Multi-couple group therapy has been shown to be effective in select studies involving court-referred perpetrators. Aggressors who are mandated into treatment will require programmes that are sanctioned by the court. Both male and female perpetrators of violence who seek help voluntarily are likely to be more motivated and treatment more successful.
>
> (Heru, 2007: 380)

Treatment models for perpetrators of domestic violence have been greatly influenced by the Duluth model, that locates issues of male oppression of women at the very core of the problem. According to this model, which was developed in the early 1980s in Duluth Minnesota, men who abuse women do so by abusing power and control. In order to help battered women understand why and how their abusers were able to maintain power and control in all spheres of domestic life, the programme leaders developed the concept of the 'Power and Control Wheel', which also depicts the cyclical nature of battering, contrition and re-abuse. Although the Duluth model of intimate partner violence considers domestic abuse to be a problem related to power and control within a patriarchy, the evidence indicates that women are also capable of extreme cruelty and aggression and that this model is reductive and ultimately unhelpful (Dutton and Corvo, 2007; Dutton, 2008).

The Strength to Change programme

The Strength to Change programme is an innovative, multi-agency and successful intervention, designed to engage male perpetrators of violence. It was developed in Hull under the leadership of Mark Coulter. This unique and effective programme has made use of social marketing campaigning to draw attention to the major problem of domestic violence in the community and its impact on families, as well as on the perpetrators themselves. It also offers support to partners of violent men, and works closely with the police and other members of the criminal justice system.

In the initial evaluation of the efficacy of the programme, after 18 months, the following findings were reported:

> Evidence that the Strength to Change (STC) programme has achieved a positive impact on behaviour and attitudes was provided by a range of sources. Both domestic violence incidents and other offences reduced while men were on the programme in comparison to the period of two years prior to joining the programme.
>
> (Stanley *et al.*, 2011)

This is just one example of an effective psycho-educational intervention that does not demonize violent men, but offers them the opportunity to change their violent behaviour and confront underlying difficulties. Clearly, there is a need for a wide range of interventions including those tailored to particular groups, such as people living in exile and members of ethnic minority groups. Where possible, interpreters should be employed as the most vulnerable members of families may not be able to communicate effectively in English. The new National Institute for Health and Care Guidance (NICE) Guidelines on Domestic Violence will be published in the UK later in 2014 and will outline recommended treatments that have an evidence base.

There is a powerful association between domestic violence and alcohol and substance misuse (see Chapter 8). Indeed, one of the recommendations in the Centre for Criminal Justice's report is that programmes for perpetrators are embedded in work that addresses the wider issues of substance and alcohol misuse. Such work can include behavioural assignments that help the couple to reduce reliance on these addictive substances and improve communication.

Successful treatment of alcoholism can significantly reduce intimate partner violence (Stuart *et al.*, 2006). O'Farrell *et al.* (2004) enrolled 303 male, married alcoholics into couples treatment. Greater treatment involvement was related to greater reduction in violence. The treatment consisted of behavioural assignments, a sobriety contract to abstain from alcohol use, and relapse prevention. The behavioural assignments were aimed at increasing positive feelings, shared activities and constructive criticism. At the end of treatment, each couple completed a continued recovery plan to be reviewed quarterly for two years. The reduction in violence was mediated by reduced problem drinking and enhanced relationship functioning.

Systemic approaches for violence victims and perpetrators

In 1997, Jan Cooper and Arlene Vetere (2005) founded the Reading Safer Families project in Berkshire in the UK, based on a systemic approach to domestic violence in which all parts of the family system are considered. The model underpinning this is attachment-based, in which the bonds between children and parents, and parents and one another, receive central consideration. Problems are viewed within the context of the whole system of human relationships, and the violent couple are seen together with the presence of a 'safe third' party, such as a friend or family member who can offer a third perspective – that of observer – and can offer the safety of this position. This also prevents the possibility of the therapist colluding with the violent couple and enables the whole family system to be represented in the work.

The success of this treatment approach led to the establishment of Safer Families projects in other areas in the United Kingdom, including Barnet and Gateshead. The main aim of this project is early intervention. Piloted in 2010, the Barnet Safer Families project funds a dedicated project manager and three domestic violence workers to support families where abuse or low-level violence is a regular feature of family life.

Cooper and Vetere (2005: xiii) describe their thinking in relation to the inclusion of men in their treatment programme and the way that they work with violence while holding issues of responsibility in mind:

> In our view services for men should also focus on safety and should be part of a range of community-wide responses. We should be able to engage with and try to understand both men's and women's choices, whether or not we are in agreement: to stay, to leave, to come and go, to seek safety, to seek danger, to deal with fear, to take responsibility for their own and others' safety, to connect with their children safely as mothers and fathers, and all the rest of the messy complexity of working with violence in family life.

Family therapies

Goldner (2004) at the Ackerman Institute for Family Therapy in New York, offers work to couples similar to that described above. She states that 'conjoint abuse work can create a transitional space between public and private – a space in which these couples can tell these horrible stories and retell and rework them from multiple perspectives' (2004: 371). The role of the therapist is to 'help clients develop a rich psychological understanding of the abuse' (349) without blame or shame and without letting the perpetrators avoid responsibility for their actions. Goldner uses attachment theory and feminist theory (especially the work of Jessica Benjamin) and views the work of the family therapist as inserting a moral perspective.

There are numerous organizations in the United Kingdom that aim to protect victims of domestic violence and offer treatment programmes to those affected. Below are a few that I have selected as examples of innovative practice.

Mankind Initiative

This organization is based on the proposition that domestic abuse affects people from all walks of life regardless of gender, sexual orientation or race. The Mankind Initiative is a national charity that provides help and support for male victims of domestic abuse and domestic violence. Their mission is 'to directly, and indirectly, help others to support male victims of domestic abuse and domestic violence across the UK and within their local communities'. It aims to help men who, it argues, often suffer because of the lack of recognition and awareness by society and the lack of local services available to support them.

The Freedom Programme

The Freedom Programme offers support and psycho-educational groups to women and children who have been subjected to male violence. These groups are found nationally and women attend the psycho-educational sessions for at least 12 weeks. Founded by Pat Craven, these groups are designed to help women from all parts of society and with varying levels of education, and have attracted a large following.

In the United Kingdom, Refuge, Karma Nirvana and Southall Black Sisters are all inspirational examples of other agencies that offer support to women and children who are subjected to domestic violence or are at risk of this abuse. Refuge also offers housing for women leaving these relationships who otherwise would have nowhere to turn.

Couples counselling

The Tavistock Centre for Couple Relationships and RELATE are two UK-based organizations that provide specialist help for couples whose relationship is in difficulty. RELATE will not necessarily accept referrals until the violent perpetrator has sought and completed specialist help for their aggression, and will work to find the appropriate programme through RESPECT if necessary.[1] There is an implicit premise that most violence in relationships is not mutual, but is perpetrated by one partner primarily. Other couples counselling and family therapy organizations also offer help, but not all will accept referrals from partners where violence has already taken place.

3: Social and legislative changes

There are a variety of responses to violence that require more than intra-psychic change in perpetrators (and victims) of domestic violence, and these require societal responses including legislative and policy responses, funding for women and men's refuges, criminal justice responses that take this major problem seriously and recognize it as an unacceptable form of interpersonal behaviour. It is essential that, like rape in marriage, it is not conceptualized as a predictable and acceptable mode of relating between two individuals in their private realm of the home and is not dismissed as 'a domestic'. The use of the term 'domestic violence' has been criticized for this very reason in its connotation of a particular type of abuse that happens only in the home.

Domestic violence is the abuse of one or more members of a family that can happen anywhere within or outside of the home, and is illegal, just as sexual abuse is. For perpetrators to recognize the unacceptability of their aggression committed 'in private' towards those they may consider aspects of their property or home, it is essential that all agencies involved in regulation of law and order respond with appropriate urgency and condemnation. At times, it may be necessary to remove the perpetrators from the household and apply a variety of orders that prohibit further contact, including a restraining order. The point of separation from a violent partner is often the most risky time, and for this reason the full support of the criminal justice system is required to help those seeking to end these relationships to feel safe enough to do so. Mental health services may also be required in order to offer those affected by this violence help to recover from its traumatic consequences.

Legislative and policy responses

Recent research in the United Kingdom has indicated that multi-agency work is required in order to ensure not only that perpetrators are brought to justice and violence is criminalized, but also to offer requisite interventions for all affected. The sense in which perpetrators can be helped to overcome their violence is also embedded in a document entitled 'Beyond Violence: Breaking the Cycles of Domestic Abuse' (Farmer and Callen, 2012) which incorporates legislative policy recommendations alongside treatment recommendations. The integration of psychological intervention and social and legislative change is clearly essential if individuals are to be supported, encouraged, or even mandated to modify dangerous behaviour. The report highlighted the complexity of domestic abuse and the consequent challenges. It also examined the lifelong impact on children of exposure to domestic abuse and argued that their needs should drive developments in policy and practice. It identified the need to de-stigmatize support for victims to help them overcome the trauma of abuse and address vulnerabilities to revictimization, and it argued that for perpetrator programmes to bring about lasting change they must be driven by principles of effective (as well as ethical) therapeutic practice.

This document, published by the Centre for Social Justice, made specific recommendations in relation to legislation that I fully support, as they reconcile individual responsibility with the opportunity for perpetrators to participate in programmes to modify their behaviour.

Their recommendations included the pilot perpetrator projects, that substance misuse providers work with couples, and consideration of a new serious criminal offence whereby a prosecution could be brought in relation to a 'course of conduct' in which someone acts to deliberately control, isolate, degrade and intimidate their victims.

Since the report was published in 2012, the UK government has changed the definition of domestic violence to make it more inclusive and encompass coercive and controlling patterns of behaviour.

Legislative changes: Clare's Law

In July 2011, in the United Kingdom, the Home Secretary was asked to consider the proposal of Clare's Law, a proposal designed by Michael Brown, father of Clare Wood who was murdered by her violent ex-partner George Appleton in February 2009. In September 2012, a one-year Home Office experiment entitled the Domestic Violence Disclosure Scheme was rolled out in Greater Manchester, Wiltshire, Nottingham and Gwent in response to the campaign by Ms Wood's family. This scheme enables individuals who are entering into a relationship with someone of whom they feel frightened to contact the police to request details of their partner's pasts to learn if they have prior criminal convictions for violence. This would, Michael Brown believes, have saved his daughter's life. Ms Wood had repeatedly called the police following Appleton's threats to her and sexual violence against her. The National Disclosure Scheme is designed to protect people from unwittingly subjecting themselves to dangerous partners.

It is assumed that the individuals in need of protection don't already know about the risks of being with their new partners. A criticism of this scheme is that once people learn about their partners' violent pasts they may still be at risk, depending on available resources and police response. It has been controversial, and some charities devoted to the care of women who are escaping violent relationships are sceptical on the grounds that by the time women contact the police, they are already aware of the risk they face and it is therefore not necessarily helpful or protective to learn the details of their record at that point.

Sandra Horley, Chief Executive of Refuge, has made the point that what most helps women is appropriate legislative and social responses. Karen Ingala Smith, chief executive of NIA, a London charity that has supported victims of domestic abuse for more than 40 years, was reported in *The Guardian* as saying that although she generally supported Clare's Law, it would not help women to know that a relationship could be abusive without then offering support to leave it. She noted the cuts to funding for domestic violence services in recent years and raised a serious question:

> What if a woman finds out that she is with a man with a history of violence, but funding cuts mean she can't access help to leave him? She then has to stay in the relationship knowing that she is with a person who has the capacity to harm her.
>
> (Boggan, 2013, *The Guardian*)

Opponents include Lucy Reed who, writing in *The Guardian*, pointed out that the police record may not indicate the scale of the danger, as Appleton's history of violence was actually quite unremarkable, including one conviction for assault and two for harassment. Many perpetrators of domestic violence will have similarly unremarkable criminal records or none at all, partly because victims are reluctant to prosecute out of fear, intimidation or even a sense of loyalty. Other cases are heard in family rather than criminal courts and victims of domestic violence seek civil injunctions for protection; these will not result in criminal convictions for the perpetrators. The Disclosure scheme, she argues, would allow information about partners to be shared but would not substantially reduce the capacity of an aggressor to continue to form violent relationships one after the other. Furthermore, the wish of the new partner to excuse past violence, or their belief that she can change this aggressive man, may be a powerful force:

> it is easy to imagine a potential victim still in the romantic haze of a new relationship being persuaded that it was just malicious gossip, a misunderstanding, perhaps mistaken identity or, as is often the defence in such cases, that their lover was defending themselves against a violent ex-partner.
>
> (Reed, 2011, *The Guardian*)

This Disclosure Scheme has now been piloted and its efficacy will be evaluated in due course. It was recently reported that at least some individuals have used it to discover risk factors in their partner's histories and to end these relationships (Boggan, 2013).

However, as this book has argued, the forces involved in creating and maintaining violent relationships are complex; some are unconscious, while others are explicit. The assumption that people are forming dangerous relationships out of ignorance of their new partner's past makes multiple inaccurate assumptions, including that they have a desire to know about it or could use this information to protect themselves. This is in contrast to my clinical experience, which commonly demonstrates a desperate wish *not* to know on a conscious level anything about risk, history or new partners' pasts. There is also an assumption that what is known can be intellectually processed and put to practical effect. This ignores the power of denial, which operates to protect individuals from unwanted knowledge, so that even if facts about a person's past are made explicit, the new partner (assumed to be the female) will make an informed risk assessment and conclude that she too may be in danger. It is far more likely that she will consider herself to be in an altogether new position in relation to the man, and may even accept his version of events unconditionally, even if she does feel worried, curious or able to ask him about them.

Additionally, the force of unconscious factors in the choice of a partner is completely ignored. Paradoxically, for many individuals (both male and female) there is clearly an unconscious pull towards people who carry the same risks as previous partners, or parents and carers who have been abusive; this familiar scenario is extremely compelling and seductive. So the question of *knowing* is not necessarily a simple, conscious and uncomplicated one in which the provision of information is the solution to the complex and destructive problem of violent relationships. Sometimes, too, what is known is impossible to bear in mind and to keep alive as an active worry, or as the basis for taking pre-emptive protective action. The dynamics that keep people in situations of risk and harm are entrenched and compulsive for conscious and unconscious reasons.

It is clear that without social, economic and practical support to help women and men leave situations of domestic violence, it will not be possible for them to survive. Recent responses to the UK government's initiatives have been criti-cized for their lack of efficacy (including Clare's Law) in the context of cutting benefits for those most at risk. This may force some individuals to return to their violent partners in order to survive financially. The need for appropriate police responses to people reporting domestic violence, and exit routes for those leaving these relationships, is urgent. Focus needs to remain on ensuring funding for refuges and other programmes of support for those who have experienced domestic violence.

Specific treatment interventions can include post-traumatic stress disorder (PTSD) services, as well as intensive or supportive psychotherapy to enable people to recognize patterns of relationships and break the familiar cycle. Self-help support groups for survivors of violent relationships can also play an important role.

As described above, couples work, family therapy, individual and group psy-chological and educational programmes, and engagement with practical sources of social support are all important components of making and maintaining change. Working with couples to improve their relationships and ensure that violence ceases will be one of the most important interventions on offer to enable toxic couples to become healthy ones, where possible. This can have a tremendous impact on the whole family.

Conclusion: working with perpetrators and victims of violence

Working with people with long histories of violence (as perpetrators and as victims) can be highly disturbing for therapists and other workers, and can feel like a physical and psychic assault. The premise of forensic psychotherapy is that victim and perpetrator co-exist in the same individual in many cases, and through understanding and containing dangerous and depressed feelings it will be possible for clinicians to work with these clients and enable them to address the pain that underlies so much violence and perverse acting-out. To do this, however, requires skill, courage and sensitivity in the worker, as well as close supervision and support. It is as though these men and women directly communicate their pain so that and the experiences they have lived take root in those who work with them. Sometimes, the task of bearing witness and attempting to work with these clients is painful, frightening and distressing.[2]

Bearing witness can involve careful attention to understanding the level of risk. As Websdale (2012) argues, good risk assessment of intimate partner violence requires emotional availability, sensitivity and attunement on the part of the assessor; clinicians must be able to 'bear the unbearable' in order to listen, hear and respond to situations of serious and escalating violence. This capacity to think the unthinkable may make the difference between life and death for victims. A longitudinal assessment that can detect change over time is essential.

The goal of treatment, using the therapist as a 'safe base' and as a transference figure, will be to bring about change in the traumatic bonds of attachment to the abusive partner, and freedom from the compulsive need to repeat trauma. As van der Kolk (1989) writes, in his description of the need to escape from the tyranny of the repetition compulsion:

> Compulsive repetition of the trauma usually is an unconscious process that, although it may provide a temporary sense of mastery or even pleasure, ultimately perpetuates chronic feelings of helplessness and a subjective sense of being bad and out of control. Gaining control over one's current life, rather than repeating trauma in action, mood, or somatic states, is the goal of treatment.

> (van der Kolk, 1989)

It is essential that, in trying to understand and overcome the rage of the perpetrators, we do not ignore the lasting damage of exposure to violence of their children and family members, and we must also offer them robust treatment and support packages at the earliest possible point of intervention. This may prevent these victims from becoming perpetrators themselves. Those individuals who are let down by the services that failed to protect them must not be betrayed a second time when they seek help for the harm they have suffered; the needs of injured and traumatized family members have to be a central concern of those clinicians and workers in the field of domestic violence.

Where workers *can* make a difference is by retaining neutrality, an empathic and supportive stance, but absolute clarity about the boundaries of their work and the total unacceptability of violence. Clear boundaries about the limits of confidentiality are essential, and the most effective agencies of change have transparent contracts with the clients about inter-agency working and communication of risk.

As a clinical psychologist and psychotherapist working with staff and patients in secure settings, I am often struck by how denial and dissociation operate to enable staff to view serious offenders as though they are without any kind of risk or perverse impulse. While this may be protective at one level, it actually exposes the workers to greater dangers, as they split off awareness of risk in the attempt to get alongside and befriend these patients. This is a defence against facing the unbearable anxiety of working with highly dangerous people and addresses the conflict between the tasks of offering care for them and judging them for their actions. It is also an unconscious identification with the victims of violence who, like the partners of aggressive individuals, rely on defences such as denial, dissociation and repression to be able to carry on in frightening situations. In an important sense, thinking is shut down in order to preserve action and to be able to bear intolerable feelings and danger. It is essential, then, to find a way to process the experience and not simply banish it from conscious awareness.

This presents the thoughtful clinician – from all disciplines – with a paradox. How is it possible to recognize and know about dangerous behaviour and murderous thoughts without responding either collusively or with fear, as if a victim of this violence? It can seem that there is nowhere for clinicians to go, no safe place in which to position themselves. However, accepting that they will play discordant and various roles in the transference and undergo powerful countertransference experiences, allows therapists to face the destructiveness of their violent patient, or their victim, head on. Seeing, and not turning away, is crucial in this work.

Sometimes, clinicians are forced to bear almost unbearable states of mind and can feel that their own bodies and mind are under siege. Containing this disturbance is part of the work, difficult as it is. Effective work with violent perpetrators requires that their dangerous impulses be brought into the realm of thought, talked and known about, expressed verbally and detoxified: therapists and other workers need to have the psychic equipment and confidence to engage in this process. It is essential that we as members of society – as well as professionals, victims or perpetrators – face the facts, open our eyes and ears to the reality of intimate partner violence and address its origins; this offers us the best chance of modifying or preventing it, and protecting vulnerable children and adults from serious harm or even death.

Through combined legislative, social and psychological interventions, real progress can be made in reducing the scale of this destructive phenomenon, with its terrible impact on the bodies and minds of its victims, and on the perpetrators themselves. The cost to society is huge and its legacy is imprinted on impressionable young minds; these children are then at heightened risk of re-enacting abusive patterns of relating.

As James Gilligan (1997) beautifully outlines in his conceptualization of violence as a response to shame and the wish to restore a sense of honour, both men and women are constrained by the equation of violence with the expression of power and strength. Those who were treated as objects and 'poison containers' in their early lives, either through direct abuse or through exposure to violence, will feel humiliated, empty and dead inside. Violence is a means to feeling alive and to demanding recognition. While not confined to men, this form of self-assertion and means of communication in those who feel shamed and humiliated, has the capacity to destroy the lives of those it touches.

In his penetrating and humane analysis of the underlying sense of shame, humiliation and dependency of men who kill their partners, families, and often themselves, Websdale (2012) describes the tremendous need in these men for a sense of emotional connection. Their partners have offered this, but when they leave them, the men feel they have nothing and perceive no other choice but to kill in order to restore some sense of potency and honor. Other men feel so ashamed of their inability to provide that they kill their family and themselves, and had, until that moment, no history of violence or abusiveness. Both Websdale and Gilligan have illuminated the horror of shame and its dangers. There is an urgent need for clinicians to engage with both perpetrators and victims of intimate partner violence and to begin to understand what motivates this murderousness at the deepest level.

Although it has not been possible to discuss this in depth in this book, social stresses – including poverty, unemployment, religious and ethnic discrimination – are, of course, highly significant factors in creating the conditions for despair and humiliation leading to a rise in aggression – both domestic and political. The roots of violence in society can be found in states of injustice, deprivation and oppression, as well as in individual suffering.

Ultimately, the destruction caused by violence can only be prevented through thoughtful, humane and comprehensive responses not only to actual violence, but even before it begins, through social and psychological interventions at the earliest stages. This support should continue throughout the lifespan of those most at risk of perpetrating and experiencing violence, including those particularly vulnerable groups described above, and should be readily available to any member of society who finds themselves in a situation of domestic abuse. We need to start with infancy and use our knowledge about the causes and effects of domestic violence to promote and protect loving attachments that create a lifelong sense of security, trust and wellbeing.

Notes

1 Introduction

1 Munir Hussain is a British businessman and community leader who was jailed for 30 months in 2009 following an attack on a burglar who had broken into his High Wycombe home and threatened him and his family. There was a public outcry, because the law was seen as being biased in favour of the perpetrator instead of the victim.
2 Here, Segal emphasized the difference between the symbol as representative and the earlier stage of symbol as equivalent: 'Only when separation and separateness are accepted does the symbol become the representative of the object rather than being equated with the object.'

2 Russian roulette

1 After adjusting for demographics, the authors found the risk of becoming an attempted or completed homicide victim was three times higher for women abused versus non-abused during pregnancy (OR = 3.08; 95% CI = 1.86–5.10).
2 Some statistics cite that 30 per cent of violence starts in pregnancy.
3 Bion (1962) describes the importance of the therapist being able to process their own countertransference feelings and to engage with the patient in a free state, able to contain their projections and communications without prejudice based on their own wishes or expectations.

3 Action replay

1 While cerebral palsy is a blanket term commonly referred to as 'CP' and described by loss or impairment of motor function, cerebral palsy is actually caused by brain damage. The brain damage is caused by brain injury or abnormal development of the brain that occurs while a child's brain is still developing – before birth, during birth, or immediately after birth. Cerebral palsy affects body movement, muscle control, muscle coordination, muscle tone, reflex, posture and balance. It can also impact fine motor skills, gross motor skills and oral motor functioning, and in some cases, result in a learning disability. In Vanessa's case it appeared to affect her ambulation but there was no intellectual impairment and she had good use of her arms and hands. In this clinical vignette I by no means wish to convey the sense that Vanessa's cerebral palsy was responsible for her unhappy choices with her partners, or the impoverished quality of her own childhood experiences, but to highlight that it was an additional vulnerability factor in a constellation of difficulties. Furthermore, in a nurturing childhood home, difficulties related to her prematurity and subsequent brain damage would not necessarily lead to significant emotional and social consequences (Weiner, P, 2014, personal communication).

2 K. Harris (personal communication, 1990) argues that there are 'unconscious plans in unplanned pregnancies'.

3 Dutton describes these two choices of defence in socio-biological terms: to either attempt to escape from an uncontrollable event through avoidance and escape (dissociation) or to actively fight against it, through violence, viewing it as a controllable event that may be altered through action.

4 Beauty and the beast

1 Id, ego and super-ego are the three parts of the psychic apparatus defined in Sigmund Freud's structural model of the psyche (1920, *Beyond the Pleasure Principle*); they are the three theoretical constructs in terms of whose activity and interaction mental life is described. According to this model of the psyche, the id is the set of uncoordinated instinctual trends; the super-ego plays the critical and moralizing role; and the ego is the organized, realistic part that mediates between the desires of the id and the super-ego.

5 Murder in the family

1 The term 'homicide' in the United Kingdom, covers the offences of murder, manslaughter and infanticide. Murder and manslaughter are common law offences that have never been defined by statute, although they have been modified by statute. The offence of infanticide was created by the Infanticide Act 1922 and refined by the Infanticide Act 1938 (s1).

2 The findings were based on the national *Confidential Enquiry into Stillbirths and Death in Infancy 1993–1996*, a study of the outcome of half a million births.

3 Intimate Partner Violence Risk Assessment Validation Study NIJ 2000WTVX0011. Final Report: March 28, 2005.

4 The data on homicide/suicide incidents collected in the first two years of the National Violent Death Reporting System (NVDRS), as cited here, was consistent with patterns observed in earlier studies of populations in smaller geographic areas. Specifically, the findings that most homicide victims in homicide/suicide incidents are female and most homicide perpetrators are male, that over half (58 per cent) of the victims are current or former intimate partners of the perpetrator, that less than 5 per cent of homicide/suicide incidents occur between strangers, that most homicide/suicide incidents (82.3 per cent) occur in a residence, and that most deaths (81.6 per cent) result from a gunshot wound, are all consistent with past research on homicide/suicide.

5 Filicidal mothers showed mental distress and often had psychosocial stressors of marital discord and lack of support. They often killed for altruistic reasons, and then committed suicide. Maternal perpetrators also dominated in filicide cases in which death was caused by a single episode or recurrent episodes of battering. Psychosis and psychotic depression were diagnosed in 51 per cent of maternal perpetrators, and 76 per cent of mothers were deemed not to be responsible for their actions by reason of insanity. Paternal perpetrators, on the other hand, were jealous of their mates, had a personality disorder (67 per cent), abused alcohol (45 per cent), or were violent toward their mates. In 18 per cent of cases, they were not held responsible for their actions by reason of insanity. During childhood, most of the perpetrators had endured emotional abuse from their parents or guardians, some of whom had also engaged in alcohol abuse and domestic violence.

6 Shelter from the storm

1 According to Bick, 'In its most primitive form, the parts of the personality are felt to have no binding force amongst themselves and must therefore be held together in

a way that is experienced by them passively, by the skin functioning as a boundary. The stage of primal splitting ... can now be seen to rest on this earlier process of containment of self and object by their respective skins' (1968: 484).

7 Without honour

1 According to Allen (2008: 4): 'On average, to the best of our knowledge, 12 people are murdered every year for transgressing someone else's perverted notions of honour. We do not know how many commit suicide as an alternative or an escape. We know that around 500 men and women report to us every year their fear of being forced into marriage, or their experience of rape, assault, false imprisonment and much more as the consequence of being in a marriage without their consent.' ACPO Honour Based Violence Strategy.

2 Karma Nirvana describes itself thus: 'We are your listening ear in confidence and many of us have the experience of forced marriage and issues related to honour-based abuse. We are here for you when you are at home or when you leave, and will talk over the phone wherever you are. One of our key principles is that we never talk to or engage with your family. Our commitment and loyalty is to you, as we understand the fears when family members become involved.'

3 While there are no easy answers in this tragic case, alarm bells had been ringing for *more than a year* about potential violence in the home before Mohammad Shafia, his second wife and son conspired to murder half the family. A parade of police, school officials and teachers, social workers and a child-protection worker had contact with the family in 2008 and 2009, and heard tales of emotional and physical abuse. They had ample reason to worry that the daughters were at risk.

   Just months before the deaths, Zainab fled the home, sought refuge in a women's shelter and married a boy she hardly knew, hoping to escape. For a year, Sahar had been telling teachers and others that she was frozen out by her parents, that she feared her father would beat her, that she had tried to kill herself, and her brother had attacked her. Geeti, who was doing miserably at school, complained of violence and begged to be put in foster care.

8 Xanadu

1 Opium was the avenging daemon or *alastor* of Coleridge's life, his dark or fallen angel, similar to Milton's Satan. Opium was for him what wandering and moral tale-telling became for the Mariner – the personal shape of repetition compulsion. The lust for paradise in 'Kubla Khan', Geraldine's lust for Christabel – these are manifestations of Coleridge's revisionary demonization of Milton.

2 See Chapter 3 for further discussion of the impact of traumatic early parenting on children's psychological development and secure attachment relations.

9 Conclusion

1 RELATE offer the following guidelines for couples where violence has been an issue. When a couple tell us there has been some abusive or violent act and ask us to help them, we make a careful assessment in order to check whether we can offer them a service or not. The assessment looks at the following areas, which will help us and them decide whether we are the right agency to support them:

   • Does the perpetrator fully accept the responsibility for their action?
   • Are they motivated to change?
   • Does their partner really want to accompany them in this work?
   • Is it viable to make a realistic safety plan to allow us to work with the couple?

- When there are two people, are we able to offer a service to both partners, or just one person?
- Each person is assessed on an individual basis.

The outcome of some assessments will show that we cannot offer a service yet but may be able to in the future when the person concerned has had more specialist support. The counsellor will make recommendations about where specialist support will be sought.

2 Doctor and Kirtchuk (2009) offer a rich analysis of the impact of such work in their edited volume *Psychic Assaults and Frightened Clinicians*.

Further reading

Out of the many books and papers cited throughout this book, there are some that I consider outstanding in their clarity, sensitivity and insight. I have therefore recommended them here.

Bateman, A. and Fonagy, P. (2008) Comorbid antisocial and borderline personality disorders: Mentalization based treatment. *Journal of Clinical Psychology*, 64: 1–14.

Campbell, J. C., Koziol-McLain, J., Webster, D., *et al.* (2004) *Research results from a national study of intimate partner homicide: The danger assessment instrument.* Available at: www.ncjrs.gov/pdffiles1/nij/199710.pdf.

Clulow, C. (Ed.) (2001) *Adult Attachment and Couple Psychotherapy: The Secure Base in Practice and Research.* London: Routledge.

Clulow, C. (Ed.) (2009) *Sex, Attachment and Couple Therapy: Psychoanalytic Perspectives.* Library of Couple and Family Psychoanalysis. London: Karnac.

Cooper, J. and Vetere, A. (2005) *Domestic Violence and Family Safety: A Systematic Approach to Working with Violence in Families.* London: Whurr Publishers.

Craven, P. (2008) *Living with the Dominator.* London: Freedom Publishing.

Dutton, D. G. (2007) *The Abusive Personality: Violence and Control in Intimate Relationships.* New York: Guilford Press.

Fonagy, P. (2003) Towards a developmental understanding of violence. *The British Journal of Psychiatry,* 183: 190–192.

Gerhardt, S. (2004) *Why Love Matters: How Affection Shapes a Baby's Brain.* London: Routledge.

Gilligan, J. (1997) *Violence: Reflections on a National Epidemic.* New York: Vintage.

Goldner, V., Penn, P., Sheinberg, M. and Walker, G. (1990) Love and violence: Gender paradoxes in volatile attachments. *Family Process*, 29(4): 343–364.

Harris-Hendriks, J., Black, D. and Kaplan, T. (2000) *When Father Kills Mother: Guiding Children Through Trauma and Grief.* London: Routledge.

Hudson-Allez, G. (2011) *Infant Losses; Adult Searches: A Neural and Developmental Perspective on Psychopathology and Sexual Offending, Second Edition.* London: Karnac.

Jasinski, J. L., Wesely, J. K., Wright, J. D. and Mustaine, E. E. (2010) *Hard Lives, Mean Streets: Violence in the Lives of Homeless Women.* Boston, MA: Northeastern University Press.

Johnson, M. P. (2008) *A Typology of Domestic Violence: Intimate Terrorism, Violent Resistance, and Situational Couple Violence.* Boston, MA: Northeastern University Press.

Mills, L. G. (2008) *Violent Partners: A Breakthrough Plan for Ending the Cycle of Abuse*. Philadelphia: Basic Books.

Music, G. (2011) *Nurturing Natures: Attachment and Children's Emotional, Sociocultural and Brain Development*. Hove: Psychology Press.

Nash, T. (2012) *Out of the Darkness*. London: Simon and Shuster.

Sanghera, J. (2007) *Shame*. London: Hodder Books.

Sanghera, J. (Ed.) (2009) *Daughters of Shame*. London: Hodder Books.

Websdale, N. (2010) *Familicidal Hearts: The Emotional Styles of 211 Killers*. New York: Oxford University Press.

Welchman, L. and Hossain, S. (Eds.) (2005) *Honour: Crimes, Paradigms and Violence against Women*. London: Zed Books.

Welldon, E. V. (1988) *Mother Madonna Whore: The Idealisation and Denigration of Motherhood*. London: Free Association Books.

Yakeley, J. (2010) *Working with Violence: A Contemporary Psychoanalytic Approach*. Basingstoke: Palgrave Macmillan.

Additional recommended websites for further information on all aspects of domestic violence

http://cdc.gov/ViolencePrevention/intimatepartnerviolence/index.html

http://refuge.org.uk/

http://www.karmanirvana.org.uk/

http://www.mankind.org.uk/

http://www.nice.org.uk/
In particular on this website: *Domestic violence and abuse – how services can respond effectively*. (February 2014)

http://www.nspcc.org.uk/

http://www.nspcc.org.uk/Inform/publications/domesticviolence_wda56390.html

http://www.respect.uk.net/

http://www.who.int/violence_injusry_prevention/violence/global_campaign/en/chap4.pdf

http://www.womensaid.org.uk/

References

Adlam, J. and Scanlon, C. (2005) Personality disorder and homelessness: Membership and 'unhoused minds' in forensic settings. *Group Analysis,* 38(3): 452–466 (Special Issue – Group Analysis in Forensic Settings).

Allen, S. (Foreword) (2008) *Honour Based Violence Strategy.* Association of Chief Police Officers of England Wales and Northern Ireland.

American Psychiatric Association (2012) *Diagnostic and Statistical Manual of Mental Disorders* (DSM-IV-TR). Arlington: VA: American Psychiatric Publishing.

Ascione, F. R., Kaufmann, M. E. and Brooks, S. M. (2000) Animal abuse and developmental psychopathology: Recent research, programmatic, and therapeutic issues and challenges for the future. In A. Fine (Ed.) *Handbook on Animal-Assisted Therapy: Theoretical Foundations and Guidelines for Practice.* New York: Academic Press, pp. 325–354.

Bailey, B. (2010) Partner violence during pregnancy: Prevalence, effects, screening, and management. *International Journal of Women's Health,* 2: 183–197.

Bateman, A. and Fonagy, P. (2001) Treatment of borderline personality disorder with psychoanalytically oriented partial hospitalization: An 18-month follow-up. *American Journal of Psychiatry,* 158: 36–42.

Bateman, A. and Fonagy, P. (2004) Mentalization-based treatment of BPD. *Journal of Personality Disorders,* 18: 36–51.

Bateman, A. and Fonagy, P. (2010) Mentalization based treatment for borderline personality disorder. *World Psychiatry,* 9(1): 11–15.

Bateman, A. and Fonagy, P. (2012) Antisocial personality disorder. In A. Bateman and P. Fonagy (Eds.) *Mentalizing in Mental Health Practice.* Washington: APPI, pp. 357–378.

Bateman, A., Bolton, R. and Fonagy, P. (2013) Antisocial personality disorder: A mentalizing framework. *Focus: Journal of Lifelong Learning in Psychiatry,* XI: 1–9.

Bartholomew, K., Henderson, A. and Dutton, D. (2001) Insecure attachment and abusive intimate relationships. In C. Clulow (Ed.) *Adult Attachment and Couple Psychotherapy.* London: Routledge, pp. 105–118.

Beck, L. F., Johnson, C. H., Morrow, B., Lipscomb, L. E., Gaffield, M. E., Colley Gilbert, B., Rogers, M. and Whitehead, N. (2003) PRAMS 1999 Surveillance Report. Atlanta, GA: Division of Reproductive Health, National Center for Chronic Disease Prevention and Health Promotion, Centers for Disease Control and Prevention.

Bentley and Dolan (2013) Mick Philpott convicted of attempted murder of Kim Hill, 17, in 1978. *Daily Mail,* 2 April 2013.

Bick, E. (1968) The experience of the skin in early object relations. *International Journal of Psycho-Analysis,* 49: 484–486.

Bion, W. R. (1962) *Learning from Experience*. London: Heinemann.

Black, M. C., Basile, K. C., Breiding, M. J., Smith, S. G., Walters, M. L., Merrick, M. T., Chen, J. and Stevens, M. R. (2011) The National Intimate Partner and Sexual Violence Survey (NISVS): 2010 Summary Report. Atlanta, GA: National Center for Injury Prevention and Control, Centers for Disease Control and Prevention.

Boggan, S. (2013) A history of violence: Is Clare's Law working? *The Guardian,* 21 April 2013.

Bossarte, R. M., Simon, T. R. and Barker, L. (2006) Characteristics of homicide followed by suicide incidents in multiple states, 2003–04. *Injury Prevent,* 12: ii33–ii38. doi:10.1136/ip.200

Bower, M. (2013) Won't they just grow out of it? Binge drinking and the addictive process. In M. Bower, R. Hale and H. Wood (Eds.) *Addictive States of Mind.* Tavistock Clinic Series. London: Karnac.

Bowlby, J. (1969) *Attachment and Loss: Volume 1: Attachment.* London: The Hogarth Press and the Institute of Psycho-Analysis.

Bowlby, J. (1973) *Attachment and Loss: Volume 2: Separation.* New York: Basic Books.

Bowlby, J. (1977) The making and breaking of affectional bonds. I. Aetiology and psychopathology in the light of attachment theory. An expanded version of the Fiftieth Maudsley Lecture, delivered before the Royal College of Psychiatrists, 19 November 1976. *The British Journal of Psychiatry,* 130(3): 201–210.

Bowlby, J. (1980) *Attachment and Loss: Volume 3: Loss, Sadness and Depression.* New York: Basic Books.

Brownbridge, D. A., Tallieu, T. L., Tyler, K. A., Tiwari, A., Chan, K. L. and Santos, S. C. (2011) Pregnancy and intimate partner violence: Risk factors, severity, and health effects. *Violence Against Women,* 17(7): 858–881.

Browne, A. (1987) *When Battered Women Kill.* New York: Simon and Schuster.

Browne, A. (2000) When battered women kill. Presentation given at International Association for Forensic Psychotherapy, Boston: USA.

Bukhanovsky, A. O., Hempel, A., Ahmed, W., Meloy, J. R., Brantley, A. C., Cuneo, D., *et al.* (1999) Assaultive eye injury and enucleation. *Journal of the American Academy of Psychiatry and the Law,* 27(4): 590–602.

Caetano, R., Schafer, J. and Cunradi, C. B. (2001) Alcohol-related intimate partner violence among white, black, and Hispanic couples in the United States. *Alcohol Research and Health,* 25(1): 58–65.

Callen, S. and Farmer, E. (2012) *Beyond Violence: Breaking the Cycle Centre for Social Justice.* London: The Centre for Social Justice.

Campbell, J. C. (2002) Health consequences of intimate partner violence. *Lancet,* 359: 1331–1336.

Campbell, J. C. (2006) Homelessness and containment: A psychotherapy project with homeless people and workers in the homeless field. *Psychoanalytic Psychotherapy,* 20(3): 157–174.

Campbell, J. C., Sharps, P. and Glass, N. (2000) Risk assessment for intimate partner violence. In G. F. Pinard and L. Pagani (Eds.) *Clinical Assessment of Dangerousness: Empirical Contributions.* New York: Cambridge University Press, pp. 136–157.

Campbell, J. C., Webster, D., Koziol-McLain, J., Block, C. R., Campbell, D. W., Curry, M. *et al.* (2003a) Risk factors for femicide in abusive relationships: Results from a multisite case control study. *American Journal of Public Health,* 93(7): 1089–1097.

Campbell, J. C., Webster, D., Koziol-McLain, J., Block, C. R., Campbell, D. W., Curry, M., *et al.* (2003b) Assessing risk factors for intimate partner homicide. *National Institute of Justice Journal*, 250: 14–19.

Campbell, J. C., Glass, N., Sharps P. W., Laughon, K. and Bloom, T. (2007) Intimate partner homicide: Review and implications of research and policy. *Trauma Violence Abuse*, 8(3): 246–269.

Casteel, C. and Sadowski, L. (2010) Intimate partner violence towards women. *Clinical Evidence (Online)*, p. ii: 1013. 24 February 2010.

Chang, J., Berg, C. J., Saltzman, L. E., and Herndon, J. (2005) Homicide: A leading cause of injury deaths among pregnant and postpartum women in the United States, 1991–1999. *American Journal of Public Health*, 95(3): 471–477.

Chesler, C. (2009) Are honor killings simply domestic violence? *Middle East Quarterly*, Spring, pp. 61–69.

Chesler, P. and Bloom, N. (2012) Hindu vs Muslim honor killings, *Middle East Quarterly*, 19: 343–352.

Chugani, H. T., Behen, M. E., Muzik, O., Juhász, C., Nagy, F. and Chugani, D. C. (2001) Local brain functional activity following early deprivation: A study of postinstitutionalized Romanian orphans. *NeuroImage*, 14: 1290–1301.

Clulow, C. (2001) Attachment, narcissism and the violent couple. In C. Clulow (Ed.) *Adult Attachment and Couple Psychotherapy: The Secure Base in Practice and Research*. London: Routledge, pp. 105–118.

Clulow, C. (2009) *Sex, Attachment and Couple Therapy: Psychoanalytic Perspectives*. Library of Couple and Family Psychoanalysis, London: Routledge.

Cochrane, K. (2012) 'Chris Brown's new tattoo is sickening'. *The Guardian* 11 September 2012.

Coleridge, S. T. (1816) Kubla Khan. In Arthur Quiller-Couch (Ed.) *The Oxford Book of English Verse: 1250–1900*. Oxford: Oxford University Press.

Cohen, S. (2001) *States of Denial: Knowing about Atrocities and Suffering*. Cambridge: Polity Press.

Coid, J., Petruckevitch, A., Feder, G., Chung,W., Richardson, J. and Moorey, S. (2001) Relation between childhood sexual and physical abuse and risk of revictimisation in women: A cross-sectional survey. *The Lancet*, 358: 450–454.

Coid, J., Petruckevitch, A., Chung, W., Richardson, J., Moorey, S. and Feder, G. (2003) Abusive experiences and psychiatric morbidity in women primary care attenders. *British Journal of Psychiatry*, 183(4): 332–339.

Coker, A. L., Davis, K. E., Arias, I., Desai, S., Sanderson, M., Brandt, H. M., *et al.* (2002) Physical and mental health effects of intimate partner violence for men and women. *American Journal of Preventative Medicine*, 23(4): 260–268.

Cooper, A. and Lousada, J. (2005) *Borderline Welfare: Feeling and the Fear of Feeling in Modern Welfare*. (Tavistock Clinic) Karnac: London.

Cooper, J. and Vetere, A. (2005) *Domestic Violence and Family Safety: A Systemic Approach to Working with Violence in Families*. London: Whurr Publishers.

Couldrey, C. (2010) Violence within the lives of homeless people. University of Southampton, School of Psychology, Doctoral Thesis: p. 155.

Craven, P. (2008) *Living with the Dominator*. London: Freedom Publishing.

Curen, R. and Sinason, V. (2010) Learning-disabled adults and children. In C. Itkin, A. Taket and S. Barter-Godfrey (Eds.) *Domestic and Sexual Violence and Abuse: Tackling the Health and Mental Health Effects*. Abingdon: Routledge, pp. 132–138.

Currie, C. (2006) Animal cruelty by children exposed to domestic violence. *Child Abuse & Neglect,* 30: 425–435.

Desmarais, S. L., Reeves, K. A., Nicholls, T. L., Telford, R. P. and Fiebert, M. S. (2012a) Prevalence of physical violence in intimate relationships, Part 1: Rates of male and female victimization. *Partner Abuse,* 3(2): 140–169.

Desmarais, S. L., Reeves, K. A., Nicholls, T. L., Telford, R. P. and Fiebert, M. S. (2012b) Prevalence of physical violence in intimate relationships, Part 2: Rates of male and female perpetration. *Partner Abuse,* 3(2): 170–198.

Department of Finance and Personnel (April 2012) The right to choose: Multi-agency statutory guidance for dealing with forced marriage.

Di Manno, R. (2012) Shafia family members guilty of first-degree murder. *Toronto Star,* 30 January 2012.

Doctor, R. (2013) Murder. Paper given in Konstanz at 22nd Annual Meeting of the International Association for Forensic Psychotherapy, 21–23 March 2013.

Doctor, R. and Kirtchuk, G. (2009) *Psychic Assaults and Frightened Clinicians.* London: Karnac.

Dube, S. R., Anda, R. F., Felitti, V. J, Edwards, V. J. and Williamson, D. F. (2002) Exposure to abuse, neglect, and household dysfunction among adults who witnessed intimate partner violence as children: Implications for health and social services. *Violence and Victims,* 17(1): 3–17.

Dutton, D. G. (2000) Witnessing parental violence as a traumatic experience shaping the abusive personality. *Journal of Aggression, Maltreatment and Trauma,* 3(1): 59–67.

Dutton, D. G. (2006) *Rethinking Domestic Violence.* Vancouver: University of British Columbia Press.

Dutton, D. G. (2007) *The Abusive Personality: Violence and Control in Intimate Relationships (2nd Edition).* New York: Guilford Press.

Dutton, D. G. (2008) My back pages: Reflections on thirty years of domestic violence research. *Trauma Violence Abuse,* 9: 131.

Dutton, D. G. and Corvo, K. (2007) The Duluth model: A data-impervious paradigm and a failed strategy. *Aggression and Violent Behavior,* 12: 658–667.

Dutton, D. G. and Holtzworth-Munroe, A. (1997) The role of early trauma in males who assault their wives. In D. Cicceti and R. Toth (Eds.) *The Rochester Symposium on Development.* Rochester.

Dutton, D. G. and Nicholls, T. L. (2005) The gender paradigm in domestic violence research and theory: Part 1 – The conflict of theory and data. *Aggression and Violent Behavior,* 10(6): 680–671.

Dutton, D. G., van Ginkel, C. and Starzomski, A. (1995) The role of shame and guilt in the intergenerational transmission of abusiveness. *Violence and Victims,* 10: 121–131.

Dutton, D. G., Starzomski, A. J. and Ryan, L. (1996) Antecedents of borderline personality organization in wife assaulters. *Journal of Family Violence,* 11(2): 113–132.

Dutton, D. G., Nicholls, T. and Spidel, A. (2005) Female perpetrators of intimate violence. In F. Buttell and M. Carney (Eds.) *Journal of Offender Rehabilitation (Special Issue),* 41(4): 1–32.

Egland, B. (1993) A history of abuse is a major risk factor for abusing in the next generation. In R. J. Gelles and D. L. Loseke (Eds.) *Current Controversies on Family Violence.* Newbury Park: Sage, pp. 197–208.

Eliot, T. S. (1922) *The Wasteland.* London: W.W. Norton & Co.

Ewing, C. P. (1991) *Fatal Families: The Dynamics of Intrafamilial Homicide.* California: Sage.

Farmer, E. and Callen, S. (2012) *Beyond Violence: Breaking the Cycles of Domestic Abuse*. London: Centre for Social Justice.

Feder, G., Ramsay, J., Dunne, D., *et al.* (2009) How far does screening women for domestic (partner) violence in different health-care settings meet criteria for a screening programme? Systematic reviews of nine UK National Screening Committee criteria. *Health Technol Assess*, 13: 47–58.

Feder, G., Agnew Davies, R., Baird, K., Dunne, D., Eldridge, S., Griffiths, C., Gregory, A., Howell, A., Johnson, M., Ramsay, J. and Rutterford, C. (2011) Identification and Referral to Improve Safety (IRIS) of women experiencing domestic violence with a primary care training and support programme: A cluster randomised controlled trial. *The Lancet*, 378(9805): 1788–1795.

Felthous, A. R. and Yudowitz, B. (1977) Approaching a comparative typology of assaultive female offenders. *Psychiatry*, 40(3): 270–276.

Fish-Murray, C. C., Koby, E. V. and Van Der Kolk, B. A. (1987) Evolving ideas: The effect of abuse on children's thought. In B. A. van der Kolk (Ed.) *Psychological Trauma*. Washington, D.C.: American Psychiatric Press, pp. 89–110.

Fleming, P. J., Blair, P. S., Sidebotham, P. D. and Hayler, T. (2004) Investigating sudden unexpected deaths in infancy and childhood and caring for bereaved families: An integrated multiagency approach. *British Medical Journal*, 328(7435): 331–334.

Foreign and Commonwealth Office Forced Marriage Unit (FMU) (2012) Statistics on forced marriage for 2012. Foreign and Commonwealth Office: UK. Available online at https://www.gov.uk/forced-marriage

Foster, A. (2013) The deprivation of female drug addicts: A case for specialist treatment. In M. Bower, R. Hale and H. Wood (Eds.) *Addictive States of Mind*. Tavistock Clinic Series. London: Karnac.

Foundation for the Study of Infant Deaths (2004) Sudden unexpected deaths in infancy: A suggested approach for police and coroner's officers. London: Foundation for the Study of Infant Deaths.

Freud, A. (1936) *The Ego and the Mechanisms of Defence*. Reprinted Karnac: London (1993).

Freud, S. (1914) Remembering, repeating and working-through (Further recommendations on the technique of psycho-analysis ii). *The Standard Edition of the Complete Psychological Works of Sigmund Freud, Volume XII (1911–1913)*. London: Hogarth Press.

Freud, S. (1916) *Introductory Lectures on Psycho-analysis*. SE16: London: Hogarth Press, p. 209.

Freud, S. (1920) *Beyond the Pleasure Principle*. SE18: pp. 1–64. London: Hogarth Press.

Freud, S. (1921) *Group analysis and the Analysis of the Ego*. SE18. London: Hogarth Press.

Gazmararian, J. A., Adams, M. M., Saltzman, L. E., Johnson, C. H., Bruce, F. C., Marks, J. S. and Zahniser, S. C. (1995) The relationship between pregnancy intendedness and physical violence in mothers of newborns. The PRAMS Working Group. *Obstetrics & Gynecology*, 85(6): 1031–1038.

Gazmararian, J. A., Lazorick, S., Spitz, A. M., Ballard, T. J., Saltzman, L. E. and Marks, J. S. (1996) Prevalence of violence against pregnant women. *Journal of the American Medical Association*, 275(24): 1915–1920.

General Accounting Office (2002) Violence against women: Data on pregnant victims and effectiveness of prevention strategies are limited. Report to the Honorable Eleanor Holmes Norton, House of Representatives. GAO-02-530. Washington, DC: GAO.

Gerhardt, S. (2004) *Why Love Matters: How Affection Shapes a Baby's Brain.* London: Routledge.

Gilligan, J. (1997) *Violence: Reflections on a National Epidemic.* New York: Vintage.

Girardi, A. and Pozzulo, J. D. (2012) The significance of animal cruelty in child protection investigations. *Social Work Research*, 36: 53–60.

Glaser, D. (2001) Child abuse and neglect and the brain – A review. *Journal of Child Psychology and Psychiatry and Allied Disciplines*, 41(1): 97–116.

Glasser, M. (1979) Some aspects of the role of aggression in the perversions. In I. Rosen (Ed.) *Sexual Deviation (2nd Edn).* Oxford: Oxford University Press, pp. 278–305.

Goodall, E. and Lumley, T. (2007) *'Not Seen and not Heard' – Child Abuse: A Guide for Donors and Funders.* London: New Philanthropies Capital.

Golding, J. (1999) Intimate partner violence as a risk factor for mental disorders: A meta-analysis. *Journal of Family Violence*, 14(2): 99–132.

Goldner, V. (2004) When love hurts: Treating abusive relationships. *Psychoanalytic Inquiry*, 24: 346–372.

Grossman, W. (1991) Pain, aggression, fantasy, and concepts of sadomasochism. *Psychoanalytic Quarterly*, 60: 22–51.

Grosz, S. (2013) *The Examined Life: How We Lose and Find Ourselves.* London: Chatto and Windus.

Harris-Hendriks, J., Black, D. and Kaplan, T. (2000) *When Father Kills Mother: Guiding Children Through Trauma and Grief, 2nd Revised Edition.* London: Routledge.

Hatters Friedman, S., McCue Horwitz, S. and Resnick, P. J. (2005) Child murder by mothers: A critical analysis of the current state of knowledge and a research agenda. *American Journal of Psychiatry*, 162: 1578–1587.

Hatters Friedman, S., Cavney, J. and Resnick, P. J. (2012) Behavioural sciences and the law, 'Mothers who kill: Evolutionary underpinnings and infanticide law. *Special Issue: Violent and Aggressive Behaviors in Women: Part II*, 30(5): 585–597.

Heffer, S. (2010) Edlington attack: We don't have to breed such savages: Parents such as those who bred the Edlington savages should be in prison, not the likes of Munir Hussain. *The Telegraph.* Available online at http://www.telegraph.co.uk/comment/columnists/simonheffer/7055648/Edlington-attack-we-dont-have-to-breed-such-savages.html.

Heru, A. M. (2007) Intimate partner violence: Treating abuser and abused. *Advances in Psychiatric Treatment*, 13: 376–383.

Hornor, G. (2008) Reactive attachment disorder. *Journal of Pediatric Health Care*, 22(4): 234–239.

House of Commons Home Affairs Committee (2008) Domestic violence, forced marriage and 'honour'-based violence. Report, together with formal minutes v. 1: Sixth report of session 2007–08. London: Stationery Office.

Hudson-Allez, G. (2011) *Infant Losses; Adult Searches: A Neural and Developmental Perspective on Psychopathology and Sexual Offending: Second Edition.* London: Karnac.

Husain, M., Waheed, W. and Husain, N. (2006) Self-harm in British South Asian women: Psychosocial correlates and strategies for prevention. *Annals of General Psychiatry*, 5: 7.

Hyatt Williams, A. (1998) *Cruelty, Violence and Murder.* London: Karnac.

Jaffe, P., Lemon, N and Poisson, S. (2003) *Child Custody and Domestic Violence: A Call for Safety.* London: Sage.

Jaffe, P. G., Wolfe, D. A. and Wilson, S. K. (1990) *Children of Battered Women.* Newbury Park CA: Sage.

Janssen, P. A., Holt, V. L., Sugg, N. K., Emanuel, I., Critchlow, C. M. and Henderson, A. D. (2003) Intimate partner violence and adverse pregnancy outcomes: A population-based study. *American Journal of Obstetrics and Gynecology*, 188: 1341–1347.

Jasinski, J. L. (2004) Pregnancy and domestic violence: A review of the literature. *Trauma Violence and Abuse*, 5(1): 47–64.

Jasinski, J. L., Wesely, K., Mustaine, E. and Wright, J. D. (2005) *The Experience of Violence in the Lives of Homeless Women: A Research Report.* US Department of Justice.

Johnson, B. (2012) Parents starved and threatened killed teen. Sky News, 22 May 2012. Available online at http://news.sky.com/story/20582/parents-starved-and-threatened-killed-teen

Johnson, M. P. (1995) Patriarchal terrorism and common couple violence: Two forms of violence against women. *Journal of Marriage and the Family*, 57(2): 283–294.

Johnson, M. P. (2006) Conflict and control: Gender symmetry and asymmetry in domestic violence. *Violence Against Women,* 12(11): 1003–1018.

Johnson, M. P. (2008) *A Typology of Domestic Violence: Intimate Terrorism, Violent Resistance, and Situational Couple Violence* (Northeastern Series on Gender, Crime, and Law). New Hampshire: Northeastern University Press.

Kahr, B. (2007) *Sex and the Psyche: The Secret World of Sexual Fantasy.* London: Penguin.

Kantor, G. K. and Jasinski, J. L. (1998) Dynamics and risk factors in partner violence: Chapter summary. In J. L. Jasinski and Linda M. Williams (Eds.) *A Comprehensive Review of 20 Years of Research.* New York: Sage.

Kaufman, M. (2012) Violence against women is an issue for men too. *The Guardian*, 26 March 2012.

Kauppi, A., Kumpulainen, K., Karkola, K., Vanamo, T. and Merikanto, J. (2010) Maternal and paternal filicides: A retrospective review of filicides in Finland. *Journal of the American Academy of Psychiatry and Law*, 38(2): 229–238.

Khaleeli, H. (2011) Summer is a dangerous time for those at risk of forced marriage. *The Guardian*, 4 August 2011.

Klein, M. (1946) Notes on some schizoid mechanisms. *International Journal of Psycho-Analysis*, 27: 99–110. In *The writings of Melanie Klein, Volume 3.* London: Hogarth Press, pp. 1–24.

Krug, E. G., Dahlberg, L. L., Mercy, J. A., Zwi, A. B. and Lozano, R. (Eds.) (2002) *Statistical Annex: World Report on Violence and Health.* Geneva: World Health Organisation Publications.

Kuijpers, K. F., van der Knaap, L. M. and Winkel, F. W. (2012) Risk of revictimization of intimate partner violence: The role of attachment, anger and violent behavior of the victim. *Journal of Family Violence*, 27(1): 33–44.

Laming, H. (2003) The Victoria Climbié inquiry: Report of an inquiry by Lord Laming. London: The Stationery Office.

Laville, S. and Topping, A. (2013) Oxford gang skillfully groomed young victims then sold them for £600 a time. *The Guardian,* 14 May 2013.

Lazenbatt, A. (2010) The impact of abuse and neglect on the health and mental health of children and young people. London: NSPCC Briefing Paper.

Mackinnon, C. (1987) *Feminism Unmodified: Discourses on Life and Law.* Cambridge: Harvard University Press.

Mackinnon, C. (2011) *Philosophy Bites.* Audio podcast. Available online at http://philosophybites.com/2011/03/catherine-mackinnon-on-gender-crime.html 25 March 2011.

Manning, V., Best, D. W., Faulkner, N. and Titherington, E. (2009) New estimates of the number of children living with substance misusing parents: Results from UK national household surveys. *BMC Public Health*, 9: 377.

deMause, L. (1990) The history of child assault. *The Journal of Psychohistory*, 18(1): 1–29.

McCauley, J. (1995) The 'battering syndrome': Prevalence and clinical characteristics of domestic violence in primary care internal medicine practices. *Annals of Internal Medicine*, 123(10): 737–746.

McCauley, J., Kern, D. E., Kolodner, K. L., Dill, L., Schroeder, A. F., DeChant, H. K., et al. (1995) The "battering syndrome": Prevalence and clinical characteristics of domestic violence in primary care internal medicine practices. *Annals of Internal Medicine*, 123(10): 737–746.

McEwan, I. (1978) *The Cement Garden.* London: Jonathan Cape.

McVeigh, C., Hughes, K., Bellis, M., Reed, E., Ashton, J. and Syed, Q. (2005) *Violent Britain. People, Prevention and Public Health.* Liverpool: John Moores University.

Merez-Perez, L., Heide, K. M. and Silverman, I. J. (2001) Childhood cruelty to animals and subsequent violence against humans. *International Journal of Offender Therapy and Comparative Criminology*, 45(5): 556–573.

Metropolitan Police *Honour Based Violence* (2008) leaflet. Available online at www.londonscb.gov.uk/files/honourbasedviolence.doc

Mill, J. S. (1869) The Subjection of Women. London: Longmans, Green, Reader & Dye.

Miller, A. (1981) *Prisoners of Childhood: The Drama of the Gifted Child and The Search for the True Self.* New York: Basic Books.

Mills, L. G. (2008) *Violent Partners: A Breakthrough Plan for Ending the Cycle of Abuse.* Philadelphia: Basic Books.

Mirrlees-Black, C. (1999) Domestic violence: Findings from a new British Crime Survey self-completion questionnaire. Home Office Research Study No. 191. London: Home Office.

Morse, B. J. (1995) Beyond the conflict tactics scale: Assessing gender differences in partner violence. *Violence and Victims*, 10(4): 251–272.

Motz, A. (2001/2008) *The Psychology of Female Violence: Crimes Against the Body, Second Edition.* Hove: Brunner Routledge.

Motz, A. (2009) Self harm as a sign of hope. In A. Motz (Ed.) *Managing Self Harm: Psychological Perspectives.* Hove: Routledge.

Music, G. (2011) *Nurturing Natures: Attachment and Children's Emotional, Sociocultural and Brain Development.* Hove: Psychology Press.

Nash, T. (2012) *Out of the Darkness.* London: Simon and Shuster.

O'Connor, T. G. and Zeanah, C. H. (2003) Attachment disorders: Assessment strategies and treatment approaches. *Attachment and Human Development*, 5(3): 223–244.

O'Farrell, T. J., Fals Stewart, W., Murphy, C. M., et al. (2004) Partner violence before and after couple based alcoholism treatment for male alcoholic patients: The role of treatment involvement and abstinence. *Journal of Counseling and Clinical Psychology*, 72: 202–217.

Perry, B. D (2000) *Maltreated Children: Experience, Brain Development, and the Next Generation.* New York: W.W. Norton.

Pines, D. (1993) *A Woman's Unconscious Use of Her Body.* London: Virago.

Poe, E. A. (1843) *The Tell Tale Heart.*

Putkonen, H., Amon, S., Almiron, M. P., Cederwall, J. Y., Eronen, M., Claudia Klier, C. et al. (2009) Filicide in Austria and Finland: A register-based study on all filicide cases in Austria and Finland 1995–2005. *BMC Psychiatry*, 9: 74.

Putkonen, H., Amon, S., Almiron, M. P., Cederwall, J. Y., Eronen, M., *et al.* (2011) Gender differences in filicide offense characteristics: A comprehensive register-based study of child murder in two European countries. *Child Abuse and Neglect*, 35(5): 319–328.

Radford, L. (2008) The paediatrician's role in safeguarding children and young people exposed to domestic violence. *Paediatrics and Child Health*, 18(12): 535–541.

Ramsay, J., Carter, Y., Davidson, L., Dunne, D., Eldridge, S., Feder, G., *et al.* (2009) Advocacy interventions to reduce or eliminate violence and promote the physical and psychosocial well-being of women who experience intimate partner abuse. *Cochrane Database Syst Rev*, 3: CD005043.

Reed, L. (2011) Why Clare's law won't prevent domestic violence. *The Guardian*, 22 July 2011.

Rew, M., Gangoli, G., and Gill, A. K. (2013) Violence between female in-laws in India. *Journal of International Women's Studies*, 14(1): 147–160.

Rey, H. (1994) Universals of psychoanalysis. In J. Magagna (Ed.) *Treatment of Psychotic and Borderline States*. London: Free Association Books.

Roehl, J., O'Sullivan, C., Webster, D. and Campbell, J. (2005) *Intimate Partner Violence Risk Assessment Validation Study, Final Report*. Unpublished research report submitted to US Department of Justice.

Rosenfeld, H. R. (1987) *Impasse and Interpretation: The Influence of Narcissism on the Analyst's Task*. London: Tavistock Publications Ltd. The New Library of Psychoanalysis.

Sanghera, J. (2007) *Shame*. London: Hodder Books.

Sanghera, J. (Ed.) (2009) *Daughters of Shame*. London: Hodder Books.

Scanlon, C. and Adlam, J. (2009) Why do you treat me this way?: Reciprocal violence and the mythology of deliberate self harm. In A. Motz (Ed.) *Managing Self Harm: Psychological Perspectives*. Hove: Routledge.

Schaverien, J. (2011) Boarding school syndrome: Broken attachments a hidden trauma. *British Journal of Psychotherapy*, 27(2): 138–144.

Segal, H. (1957) Notes on symbol formation. *International Journal of Psycho-Analysis*, 38: 391–397.

Shadigan, E. M. and Bauer, T. (2005) Pregnancy-associated death: A qualitative systematic review of homicide and suicide. *Obstetrical & Gynecological Survey*, 60(3): 183–190.

Sharps, P. W., Campbell, J., Campbell, D., Gary, F. and Webster, D. (2001) The role of alcohol use in intimate partner femicide. *The American Journal on Addictions*, 10(2): 122–135.

Shengold, L. (2000) *Soul Murder Revisited: Thoughts About Therapy, Hate, Love, and Memory*. New Haven, CT: Yale University Press.

Sinason, V. (1986) Secondary mental handicap and its relationship to trauma. *Psychoanalytic Psychotherapy*, 2(2): 131–154.

Slavkin, M. L. (2001) Enuresis, firesetting, and cruelty to animals: Does the ego triad show predictive validity? *Adolescence*, 36(143): 461–466.

Sonkin, D. (2005) Attachment theory and psychotherapy. *The California Therapist*, 17(1): 68–77.

Stanley, N., Borthwick, R., Graham-Kevan, N. and Chamberlain, R. (2011) *An Evaluation of a New Initiative for Male Perpetrators of Domestic Violence*. Preston: University of Central Lancashire.

Steiner, J. (1993) *Psychic Retreats*. London: Routledge.

Stoller, R. (1975) *Perversion: The Erotic Form of Hatred*. London: Maresfield Press.

Stuart, G. L., Meehan, J. C., Moore, T. M., Morean, M., Hellmuth, J. and Follansbee, K. (2006) Examining a conceptual framework of intimate partner violence in men and women arrested for domestic violence. *Journal of Studies on Alcohol and Drugs*, 67(1): 102–112.

Strauss, M. A. (1979) Measuring intrafamily conflict and violence: The Conflict Tactics (CT) Scales. *Journal of Marriage and Family*, 41(1): 75–88.

Strauss, M. A., and Gelles, R. J. (1990) *Physical Violence in American Families: Risk Factors and Adaptations to Violence in 8,145 Families*. New Brunswick, NJ: Transaction Publications.

Swinburne, M. (2000) Home is where the hate is. *Psychoanalytic Psychotherapy*, 14(3): 223–238.

Tjaden, P. and Thoennes, N. (2000) *Extent, Nature and Consequences of Intimate Partner Violence*. NCJ Publication No. 181867. Washington DC: US Department of Justice.

van der Kolk, B. (1989) The compulsion to repeat the trauma: Re-enactment, re-victimisation and masochism. *Psychiatric Clinics of North America*, 12(2): 389–411.

Verlinden, S. (1999) Risk factors in school shootings. Unpublished doctoral dissertation. Pacific University, Forest Grove, Oregon.

Walby, S. and Myhill, A. (2001) Assessing and managing the risk of domestic violence. In J. Taylor-Browne (Ed.) *What Works in Reducing Domestic Violence?* London: Whiting and Birch.

Walby, S. and Allen, J. (2004) Home Office Research Study 276: *Domestic violence, sexual assault and stalking: Findings from the British Crime Survey*. London: Home Office Research, Development and Statistics Directorate.

Walker, P. (2010) 'Toxic family life' of Edlington brothers. *The Guardian*, 22 January 2010.

Watson, D. and Parsons, S. (2005) *Domestic Abuse of Women and Men in Ireland: Report on the National Study of Domestic Abuse, NCC/ESRI*. Dublin: Stationery Office.

Websdale, N. (2010) *Familicidal Hearts: The Emotional Styles of 211 Killers*. New York: Oxford University Press.

Websdale, N. (2012) Exploring the Risk of Intimate Partner Homicide. The 2012 Arizona Domestic Violence and Risk Conference. Tucson, Arizona April 3, 2012.

Welchman, L. and Hossain, S. (Eds.) (2005) *Honour: Crimes, Paradigms and Violence against Women*. London: Zed Books.

Welldon, E. V. (1988) *Mother Madonna Whore: The Idealisation and Denigration of Motherhood*. London: Free Association Books.

Welldon, E. V. (2002) *Ideas in Psychoanalysis: Sadomasochism*. London: Icon Books.

Welldon, E. V. (2008) Dancing with death. Paper given at conference to celebrate 20 years since publication of *Mother Madonna Whore*. London: Tavistock Clinic. Reprinted in *Playing with Dynamite* (2011). Karnac: London.

Welldon, E. V. (2012) The malignant bonding. In Adlam *et al.* (Eds.) *Therapeutic Milieu Under Fire*. London: Jessica Kingsley Press.

Whitaker, D. J., Haileyesus, T. and Saltzman, L. (2007) Differences in frequency of violence and reported injury between relationships with reciprocal and nonreciprocal intimate partner violence. *American Journal of Public Health*, 97(5): 941–947.

Wind-Cowie, M., Cheetham, P. and Gregory, T. (2012) *Ending Forced Marriage*. DEMOS: London.

Winnicott, D. W. (1960) The theory of the infant–parent relationship. *International Journal of Psycho-Analysis*, 41: 585–595.

Winnicott, D. W. (1965) *The Maturational Processes and the Facilitating Environment*. New York: International Universities Press.

Winnicott, D. W. (1967) Mirror-role of the mother and family in child development. In P. Lomas (Ed.) *The Predicament of the Family: A Psycho-Analytical Symposium.* London: Hogarth, pp. 26–33.

Wolfe, D. A., Jaffe, P., Wilson, S. and Zak, L. (1985) Children of battered women: The relation of child behaviour to family violence and maternal stress. *Journal of Consulting and Clinical Psychology*, 53(5): 657–665.

Women's Aid Federation of England (2000) Unpublished Census.

Wood, H. (2013) The nature of the addiction in 'sex addiction' and paraphilias. In M. Bower, R. Hale and H. Wood (Eds.) *Addictive States of Mind.* Tavistock Clinic Series. London: Karnac.

Wykes, M. and Welsh, K. (2009) *Violence, Gender and Justice.* London: Sage.

Yakeley, J. (2010) *Working with Violence: A Contemporary Psychoanalytic Approach.* Basingstoke: Palgrave Macmillan.

Yakeley, J. (2012) Treating the untreatable: The evolution of a psychoanalytically informed service for antisocial personality disorder. In Lemma, Alessandra (Ed.) *Contemporary Developments in Adult and Young Adult Therapy. The Work of the Tavistock and Portman Clinics, Volume 1.* Tavistock Clinic Series. London: Karnac.

Yarwood, D. J. (2004) *Child Homicides: Review of Statistics and Studies.* Dewar Research.

Youell, B. (2013) Parental addiction and the impact on children. In M. Bower, R. Hale and H. Wood (Eds.) *Addictive States of Mind.* The Tavistock Clinic Series, London: Karnac.

Zeanah, C. H. and Gleason, M. M. (2010) *Reactive Attachment Disorder: A Review for DSM 5.* American Psychiatric Association.

Index

murder of children, rehearsed in fantasy
before enacted in reality 107
Muslim advocacy organizations, argument
relating to HBV 142
mutilation *see* self-harming
mutual consent *see* consent
mutual couple violence 7, 8
mythologies of domestic violence, critique
of the accepted 12–23

Nash, Tina 28–30, 160
National Committee to Prevent Child
Abuse 162
National Institute for Health and Care
Excellence (NICE), Guidelines on
Domestic Violence 184
National Society for the Prevention of
Cruelty to Children (NSPCC), on the
impact of domestic abuse on children 44
National Violence Against Women Survey
131–2; data indicating physical
consequences 5
National Violent Death Reporting System
(NVDRS) 99
neglect: as adverse childhood experience
ix; increased likelihood for children
exposed to IPV 9, 44; adverse effect on
Romanian orphans 64; consequences
and implications of future harm 55;
suffered by Lori and her sister 123, 127;
and uncertainty, Craig living in a state of
163, 164–5
neonaticide 95, 96
neurological development, critical age for
60; damaged by abuse, neglect and
exposure to violence in infancy 64
neutrality, retaining in field of domestic
violence 191
NIA, London charity supporting victims of
domestic abuse 188
NICE *see* National Institute for Health and
Care Excellence
Nicholls, T. x, 7, 25, 202
Noah, clinical illustration 109
non-accidental injuries, scars and evidence 27
No-one Escapes, film 108
NSPCC *see* National Society for the
Prevention of Cruelty to Children
numeric extent, of violence against
women/men 7
nurses, identification-training for domestic
violence 180–1
NVDRS *see* National Violent Death
Reporting System

objectification: female body as property
27, 30, 119, 157; in perversion, 73, 75
Oedipal wishes, not to be enacted in order
for healthy development to take place 83
offspring *see* children
outcast from mainstream society, Jag
identifying with outcast girls 149
outsiders together, Sinead and Quentin a
couple in search of home 133
Owen 53–4, 57
'owned', by father in incest case 87
ownership: assault as an assertion of
129–30; Lori as part of Troy's property
127
ownership and marking, links with slavery
10, 25–6
Oxford, sexual exploitation of young girls
119, 176

paedophilic activity, in the household 85
pain, and marking as evidence of 25, 28
Pakistani culture, Shafilea and Alesha
restricted 145
paranoid-schizoid state of mind (primitive
defence of) 130–1
parentage, revelation of biological 53
parental distress, and the impact on
children 44
parental incest, and damaged offspring
82–3
parental separation, filicides occurring
following 97
parenting assessment 23
parents, Craig's father's violent attacks on
his mother 164
parents' experiences, repetition of in later
life 51–3, 54–5
partner murder *see* intimate partner homicide
partnerships *see* destructive partnerships
perceived threat or loss, violence enacted
in response 173; association with
disturbed attachment 10, 14, 33, 35
perpetrators: important to assess access to
guns 181–2; interventions for violent
183–6; multiple, in honour-based
killings 138; multiple, parallels in
homelessness and HBV 142; women as
21, 105–7
personality disorders: antisocial
personality disorder (ASPD) 39–40;
borderline personality disorder (BPD)
69; risk factor in insecure relationships
35, 49 *see also* conduct disorder,
post-traumatic stress disorder

toxic partnerships, power and complexity
of factors that create 3–6, 173
toxic substances: impact on children of
dependent parents 157–8; role of in IPV
156–7 *see also* substance abuse
trafficking, of vulnerable young people 119
transference, and countertransferance
44–7
trauma: alternative responses to 64;
internalised 58; mastering, projecting
unbearable feelings onto others 107 *see
also* childhood trauma; post-traumatic
stress disorder (PTSD)
traumatic bond, Jay's 113
traumatic bonding 62–3 *see also* malignant
bonding
traumatic 'shutdown' 43
traumatization, too overwhelming to
process 86
traumatized family members, needs must
be a concern 191
treatment issues: working with mothers
who have killed/harmed children 105–7
see also forensic psychotherapy;
psychotherapy; therapy
treatment for violent perpetrators,
summary of results 183
Troy, Lori's violent ex-partner 126
trust, abuse of in incestuous relationships
83; therapist's sense of loss of in when
working with women returning to
violent partnerships 44–5; not clear that
Jay could trust herself 112

UN *see* United Nations
unconscious choices, notion of 25, 172 *see
also* repetition compulsion
unconscious contracts, within a violent
couple 18; in perverse and
sadomasochistic relationships 94
unconscious dynamics within a violent
relationship 18–19 *see also* projective
identification
unconscious fantasies, and fears of men in
relation to pregnancy 34
unconscious guilt, in Craig 50; in children
who identify with abused parents 61
under age, forced marriage 141–2
underground activity, with vulnerable
young girls 177
under-reporting: of child homicide 96; of
domestic violence 5; victims of violence
in pregnancy 31; of violence in
same-sex relationships 175

United Kingdom: child homicide victims
95; Forced Marriage (Civil Protection)
Act 2007 142; reporting of domestic
violence 5–6; scale of HBV in 141–2
United Kingdom government, core
definition of domestic violence 4
United Kingdom law, and honour-based
violence 139–41
United Nations (UN), Declaration of
the Elimination of Violence against
Women 5
United States: child homicide victims 95;
homicides of women by their
partners or former partners 97; study of
rates of alcohol abuse and domestic
violence 157

van der Kolk, B. 191
Vanessa: clinical illustration of sexual
abuse and exploitation of a vulnerable
woman 65–9; vulnerability to
exploitation 82
Vetere, Arlene 184, 185
victim: becoming aggressor 20; and
perpetrator, Quentin as 134–5; children
as hidden victims in IPV 49
victimization: in the lives of homeless
people 131–2; in same-sex relationships
175
victims: child witnesses of domestic
violence 41; complexity of brutalized
woman's response 19; of homicide
followed by suicide 98–9; raised
prevalence of substance and alcohol
misuse 157; risk factors for both
females and males in intimate partner
homicides 8
violence: an intoxicating force 158–9;
antisocial personality disorder (ASPD)
and the alien self 39–40; as re-enactment
of childhood trauma 11–12, 46; as
response to perceived abandonment, in
illustration of Shane 12–17, Quentin
134–6; related to insecure attachment
47; conceptualization 192; Craig's false
empowerment 166, 167, 169; during
pregnancy 30–4, 129–30; of intimate
partner, as gratifying 18; Jay tacitly
accepting it as the norm 113; as seen as
a justifiable response to shame in
honour-based crimes 146; in the lives
of homeless people 131–2; Lori's
tolerance of extreme levels of 126;
perverse life force keeping Craig's